This book is cause for celebration! Many of us have long ha
and principles of permaculture to be translated to serve a
Looby Macnamara has been worth waiting for: she fills the bil
lean eloquence and an exquisite knowledge of systems. He
'Thinking like an Ecosystem' should be required reading in ...., ... from
third grade through graduate school. Equally rewarding are her applications of permaculture
to health, communication and the life of the mind. It's part of the genius of the book
that all this, once you see it, can seem as natural as breathing.
— Joanna Macy, author of *Coming Back to Life, World as Lover, World as Self*
and co-author, *Active Hope: How to Face the Mess We're in without Going Crazy*

The application of permaculture principles and thinking to peoplecare has long been
a vexed issue for permaculture activists, designers and teachers. In this book Looby
Macnamara uses her solid grounding in permaculture to show that its principles and
thinking can help us all be effective and hopeful in an age of change and challenge.
In the process she draws in kindred ideas and influences from the field of peoplecare,
making a significant contribution in the ongoing evolution of permaculture as a concept
and a movement creating a better world.
— David Holmgren, co-originator of the Permaculture concept

Looby Macnamara's inspiring and groundbreaking book is a rich celebration of the
interconnectivity of all life and is filled to the brim with the potential of our future
growth and happiness. It is the very best of guidebooks: entertaining, instructive,
nurturing and profound. It will become a constant companion and is one of those books
you will want to give to everyone you know!
— Glennie Kindred, author of several books on Earth wisdom,
our native trees and plants, and celebrating the Earth's cycles

We all have our dark moments of the soul, when we go deep into our individual beings
and ask hard questions and sometimes get unwelcome answers. Are humans a plague
on the planet? Can one person, when that one person is me, really make a difference?
Can the juggernaut of consumer society be turned? Why should we single out our
fellow humans for a special degree of care over, say, salmon, or whales? The answer is
in this book. We take care of people because people matter, and because that is our
nature as creatures who care. What we care about matters to the fate of the world, now
as never before. If permaculture as a design tool is about making connections, this book
is about how we reconnect ourselves – to each other, to our inner selves, to our highest
aspirations and, finally, to the cycles of life, of which we are just a small, but incredibly
important, part.
— Albert Bates, author and educator, The Farm Ecovillage Training Center,
Tennessee USA

Thanks to Looby Macnamara for bringing us a heart-warming book which invites us
to step from our comfortable sofa into a world of adventures, explorations and connections – and blesses us to return for a good rest and some quiet when we need it. She
offers us the world as our playground – not something we have to set straight, but something we have the honour of engaging with. A roadmap for the joyful expression of our
love for each other and this wild, beautiful planet we call our home.
— Kosha Anja Joubert, president of the Global Ecovillage Network

People & Permaculture is a book of practical wisdom that can improve our lives, our relationships and our ability to act for our world.

— Chris Johnstone, author of *Find Your Power*
and co-author of *Active Hope: How to Face the Mess We're in without Going Crazy*

Land design is complex, but trees don't answer back! In my experience the most challenging aspect of any design is not which plants or elements to include, but how to work with my fellow humans, and create situations where each person feels valued and able to make their best contribution. Looby has done the permaculture community a great service with this book. It has helped me explore my own potential and think in new ways. I've gained insight into how I can work more effectively with others and, in turn, move towards a more harmonious and abundant relationship with our amazing Earth. Looby's book is an important step towards our goal of personal, social and ecological well-being, and I urge you to read it.

— Andy Goldring, CEO, The Permaculture Association (Britain)

Living in today's global climate can be fraught with fear, overwhelm and despair. Looby Macnamara effortlessly eases you out of that predicament and on to an upwardly-spiralling path of practical exercises, solutions and earth-based wisdom. *People & Permaculture* offers a pragmatic and holistic approach to transforming our relationships, not only with each other, but with nature as a whole. Its timing couldn't be more fortuitous; this book holds enough insight and inspiration to help us thrive throughout these changing times and create a brighter future for all. Essential reading for anyone who wishes to reclaim their most intimate connection to people, place and planet.

— Natalie Fee, author of *The Everyday Alchemist's Happiness Handbook*
and *The Everyday Alchemist's Book of Poems*. www.nataliefee.com

Peoplecare is as important to permaculture as earthcare – unless we learn to live in harmony with each other, we'll never get anything done. Looby's book fills a gap that has long been there in permaculture literature. I heartily congratulate her.

— Patrick Whitefield, permaculture teacher and author

I do believe that we all love this Earth, everyone of us. Yet finding the way to express the joy of this life has become so complicated, our very actions in celebrating often causing the destruction we so desperately don't need. Permaculture offers a glimpse to a kinder future, where our expression meets the right actions. This book is a manual in how to get there – grounded, practical and brimming with joy for the good stuff. What I like most about this book, is that we are not banished from nature, but centred in it, which I believe is our rightful place.

— Alys Fowler, gardener, writer and presenter (who deeply loves soil)

This is a work of significant courage – for years now considerations of the peoplecare aspect of permaculture have been so conflicting that no-one has dared publish a volume like this. Bravo to Looby for breaking through the wall of silence and producing this book. I found it to be of startling breadth, timely relevance and it contains a handsome blend of insights drawn from Looby's own experience integrated with the wisdom of others. The agile extension of the design approach that is, along with the principles, at the core of permaculture into the field of humans relations is particularly useful to me. I recommend this encyclopedic book to you.

— Andrew Langford, co-president, Gaia University, www.gaiauniversity.org

Looby Macnamara presents an exciting and inspiring vision for humanity in *People & Permaculture*. Most importantly she also equips readers with the tools and techniques needed to make this vision a reality. An enlightening handbook for those who want to change the world.
— Melissa Corkhill, editor of *The Green Parent* magazine, www.thegreenparent.co.uk

I'm inspired by the scope and depth of *People & Permaculture* – it captures the current trend focusing on how permaculture really is an emerging culture – and how it can inform our lives and community, helping us navigate through the maze of building a sustainable future.
— Stefan Geyer, chair-person of the Permaculture Association (Britain)

All too often, promising environmental projects are thwarted by burnout or conflict. *People & Permaculture* sounds a clarion of hope, empowering us with practical solutions that make people central to permaculture design. This book is a treasure trove of wise observations and a manual for how to put the peoplecare ethic into practice.
— Rebecca Laughton, author of *Surviving & Thriving On The Land*

In *People & Permaculture* Looby Macnamara displays an uncanny knack for laying a safe path of stepping stones into new territories of personal abundance. This handbook is so full of golden keys: explanations, illustrations, adventurous exercises and powerful quotations, each unlocking a forgotten limiting belief, freeing more love to come out and play. Looby is a masterful hand-holder, redesigning our inner landscape with raw distinctions and organic intelligence. With so many new options to choose from it is easy to change the ways we live on Earth. If the universe is made of consciousness, and we are in fact the Earth talking to herself, what a shame it would be to continue living isolated confusing lives when a book such as *People & Permaculture* can so thoroughly weave a thrilling resonance between ourselves, each other, and the Earth herself. This is a book of learning – learning from other cultures, from ancestors, from nature, learning from our own pain. Looby helps us remember that out of deep rich compost grows the best fruits, herbs, flowers and vegetables.
— Clinton Callahan, originator of Possibility Management and author of *Conscious Feelings*, www.nextculture.org

What a great idea – to explore how permaculture principles can be applied to designing healthy human culture at all levels of scale, from individual, to group, to global. This book is rich with ideas, real life examples and tried and tested tools for creating happy, effective and resilient people and projects.
— Sophy Banks, Transition Town Totnes and Transition Network

The first half of the book was invaluable to me and transformed my view of perma-culture. As a former leadership development person and independent consultant, I am familiar with many of the processes later in the book. But that does not diminish its value for readers – particularly those in our Berkhamsted Transition Town and others trying to facilitate change and personal development. The text is not only in the form of the written word but also beautifully drawn pictures and models. It is all excellent.
— Bruce Nixon, author of *A Better World is Possible*, www.brucenixon.com

This is a wonderful book, both wise and pragmatic, as imaginative as it is intelligent.
— Jay Griffiths, author of *Wild: An Elemental Journey*

The future of culture and agriculture is in permaculture. This book is perhaps the first to give readers the big picture and a comprehensive understanding of permaculture and how it can underpin our ecological, social and spiritual paradigm. The book is an outstanding contribution to an ever evolving vision which is creative, imaginative, sustainable and joyful.

— Satish Kumar, editor of *Resurgence*

This is a very timely and important book. Our world is calling for people to stand together in heart-centred, creative and powerful ways for a healthy future, a future where humans naturally love and care about our beautiful Planet Earth, all creatures and also themselves. Permaculture principles provide common sense design strategies, not only for redesigning our physical environments for a sustainable world, but also for creating supportive, dynamic, caring and restorative systems that care for people. This is a must read book for all who care for themselves and our world.

— Robin Clayfield, author of *The Manual For Teaching Permaculture Creatively* and *You Can Have Your Permaculture and Eat It Too*

A lovely, refreshing way to look at permaculture. Full of common sense for a world where common sense is so often lacking. Well structured, full of enthusiasm, bringing simplicity into a complex theme with appeal well beyond permaculture – put down the remote control, pour yourself a homebrew and enjoy!

— Max O Lindegger, permaculture pioneer, peasant farmer and beekeeper

Drawing upon experiences of people around the world, this is a book full of wisdom. Looby pulls together the principles of permaculture in an inspiring and personal way to help us improve our own lives and the lives of others.

— Naomi Saville, International community development specialist and researcher

Reading this book is like taking a shower under a fresh flowing waterfall: stimulating and revitalising. It contains not only passion and vision but a compendium of tools and ideas to turn our collective fear of scarcity into trust in abundance. Looby places personal and interpersonal work within the context of world-work and earthcare, no idle navel-gazing but a revolution in understanding which is as critical to our survival as a species as the tools to regenerate land. The writing is clear and engaging, and the book includes quotations, images and activities to keep the reader involved, reflecting Looby's experience as a skilled teacher. *People & Permaculture* is a pioneering book, opening the way for much more thinking in this area. I am excited to think of what riches may flow from it.

— Jackie Singer, celebrant and author of *Birthrites*

This long-overdue book allows the peoplecare and fair share ethics of permaculture to find their place in the sun. To sustain ourselves, and all life on Planet Earth, we need to redesign the way we do things. Not all of us manage land, but all of us have responsibility for what we consume each day and how we relate to others. By taking small steps we can achieve great things. This book is packed with practical suggestions as well as underlying concepts to help us live in harmony with each other and with the Earth.

— Ian Lillington, permaculture teacher and author of *The Holistic Life*

People & Permaculture

caring and designing for ourselves,
each other and the planet

LOOBY MACNAMARA

ILLUSTRATED BY REBECCA STORCH

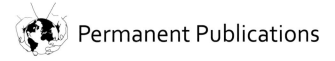 Permanent Publications

Published by
Permanent Publications
Hyden House Ltd
The Sustainability Centre
East Meon
Hampshire GU32 1HR
England
Tel: 01730 823 311
Fax: 01730 823 322
Overseas: (international code +44 - 1730)
Email: enquiries@permaculture.co.uk
Web: www.permanentpublication.co.uk

Distributed in the USA by:
Chelsea Green Publishing Company
PO Box 428, White River Junction, VT 05001 Web: www.chelseagreen.com

First published 2012, reprinted 2014

Designed by Two Plus George Limited, www.TwoPlusGeorge.co.uk

Cover design by John Adams

Front cover image by Red rockerz Design Studio/Shutterstock

Back cover 'people star' image by Jenny Solomon/Shutterstock

Printed in the UK by Cambrian Printers, Aberystwyth

All paper from FSC certified mixed sources

The Forest Stewardship Council (FSC) is a non-profit international
organisation established to promote the responsible management of the
world's forests. Products carrying the FSC label are independently certified
to assure consumers that they come from forests that are managed to meet
the social, economic and ecological needs of present and future generations.

British Library Cataloguing-in-Publication Data
A catalogue record for this book is available from the British Library

ISBN 978 1 85623 087 2

Contents

---

* The activities relate to different stages of the design web process as outlined on pages 45–49

The Author

Looby has been teaching permaculture since 2002, and is partner of a leading teaching and consultancy partnership, Designed Visions. She runs full permaculture design courses as well as teacher training, advanced permaculture design and peoplecare courses. She has a passion for creative teaching methods and likes inventing participatory activities and games to enhance learning. Her degree in Human Sciences provides a wealth of perspectives to bring into her teaching and writing.

Looby travels to Nepal to support the Himalayan Permaculture Centre and has founded a Fair Trade business, Spirals of Abundance, importing organic cotton clothes and other Nepalese handicrafts (www.spiralsofabundance.com).

She has supported the development and growth of permaculture nationally through her input as trustee of the Permaculture Association (Britain) for 5 years (2001–2006) and was the Chairperson for two of these. She is still an an active member of the permaculture community and is engaged with the education working group and is a diploma tutor.

She lives in Herefordshire with her partner Chris Evans and two daughters, Shanti and Teya. She enjoys singing, yoga, gardening and making all sorts of things from cakes to wine, and clothes to blankets.

Acknowledgements

I have always wondered at the long list of acknowledgements often found at the beginning of books, and now I have first hand experience of the multitude of support that arrives while immersed in a project like this. Without any one of these people the threads of this book might have started to unravel, revealing the web of co-operation that has woven this written tapestry. My gratitude is deeply felt.

Thanks to Maddy and Tim Harland who had faith in this venture from the start, and for their warm friendship and professional guidance.

Thanks to Rebecca Storch for her creativity and dedication to providing the beautiful illustrations which help bring my words to life.

Thanks to Nicola Willmot for interpreting my work so well in designing the book, and for being such a pleasure to work with.

I am deeply grateful to Jules Heavens for many things – her friendship, amazing voice workshops, co-facilitating the first two peoplecare and permaculture courses, and insightful coaching which moved this book from something I wanted to do in the future to something I could do now.

Thanks to Chris Dixon, Holly Creighton-Hird, Debbie Terry, Jed Picksley and Marion McCartney for spending time reading the manuscript at various stages and providing invaluable feedback and offering ideas with non-attachment to inclusion.

Thank you to Bill Mollison, David Holmgren, Joanna Macy and Rob Hopkins for coining the terms 'Permaculture', 'The Work That Reconnects' and 'Transition Initiatives', that have provided new frameworks to bring about a positive future and that are key inspirations for this book.

Thanks to all the fellow permaculturists I have met along my permaculture pathway. From John-Paul Frazier who first introduced me to permaculture with his wondrous garden and Bryn Thomas and Pippa Johns my first teachers for facilitating one of my best learning experiences, to my current teaching partners Chris Evans, Aranya and Hannah Thorogood. And thanks to all my other permaculture friends for their optimism, dedication, inspiration, fun and friendship. Thanks also to all the course participants for the two-way exchange of ideas and information, and sharing of many edges.

Thanks to all my teachers past, present and future. In particular to those whose workshops I attended which expanded my edges while writing this; thanks to Sue Weaver, Alan Bellamy and Rosie Bell for the Council of All Beings; Penny Spawforth and Gayano Shaw for a heartfelt NVC course, Andrea Brown for a down-to-earth NLP course, and Starhawk for an informative workshop on groups.

Thanks to everyone I interviewed, for their insights which strengthened the book and made it much richer than I could have managed alone. Maddy and Tim

Harland, Rod Everett, Zoe Scott, Martin Powdrill, Suzi High, Caroline Molloy, Andy Goldring, Graham Burnett, Pippa Johns, Marion and Richard Price, Tomas Remiarz, Nigel Mclean, Joe Atkinson, Jodie Tellam, Suzy Erskine, Mike Pattinson, Chris Evans, Gemma Suggit, Steve Hack, Kari Lucas, Sarah Robens, Alex Balerdi, Inez Aponte, Silvia Roche, Sam Collins, Theo Wildcroft , Angela Smythe, Jean Clack, Jules Heavens, Nick Osbourne, Jo Barker, Klaudia Van Gool, Lusi and Danny Alderslowe, Linda McDermott, Thereza and Tom Macnamara, Nick Gunton, Mari Shackell, Sophy Banks, Chris Dixon, Tara Joy, Genevieve Ellison, Isabel Calabria, Annike Kubler, Surya and Saraswati Atakaria, Naomi Saville, Maria Svennbeck, Nicole Freris, Rod Cunningham, Gary Finch, Helen and Jim Morris-Ridout and Aranya.

I am appreciative of the time Suzi High, the staff at the Permaculture Association, Ed Tyler and Hom Maya Gurung spent on the design case studies.

Thanks to all my friends for their kindness, sharing, support, laughter and companionship. Extra special appreciation for Linda and Mike, Isabelle and Ben, and Caz and Mike for helping so much with Shanti and Teya while I've been writing. Thank you to my friends in Nepal for their hospitality and for showing me a different way of life is not only possible but enjoyable.

I am indebted to Debbie and Dave Terry for providing their summerhouse as a sanctuary to write in, without which it would undoubtedly have taken much longer. And to Louise Chodecka for holding the fort with my business and freeing up my time.

Thanks to my Mum, Dad and brother for the immeasurable support over my life, and in particular while I was writing for their technical support and help with my children.

Thank you to Margaret and Ted for all of their kindness over the years and showing so much peoplecare in action. May Margaret rest in peace.

And the biggest appreciation to my partner, Chris, and daughters, Shanti and Teya, for their love, friendship and for sharing my life with me. Thank you to Chris for his patience with countless late night conversations, sharing all of his permaculture expertise, and contributing so much to the content of this book. I am thankful for his commitment and for freeing up so much of my time to allow me to write.

And thanks to Shanti and Teya for being such beams of light in my life, and being such powerful reasons for me to believe in the Great Turning and giving my energy to helping it happen.

Foreword

by Polly Higgins

Picking up this book for the first time is to hold a route map to the future in the palm of your hand. Use what you learn from it and – be warned – your life will change forever. You will become a co-creator of a beautiful new world.

Are you ready to take the step into the world of abundance, beauty and harmony? It may be a rocky journey at the beginning and full of challenges along the way, but I urge you to take the first step. That is the hardest bit. After this you will find life opens its doors to you and all you need do is walk through. Keep a sense of humour and when things don't quite work out as you thought, take it as a step in the learning curve. Give it a year and see how you feel when your world becomes increasingly more connected.

Permaculture has so much to teach us about life itself; by applying the principles of permaculture to our lives we can begin to transform each problem into a solution. Look to the margins, where the greatest ideas are to be found. It is the same in life too – seek out the edge as this is where the greatest innovation grows. Where two ecosystems meet is the home of the most creative activity – neither lives in isolation – both become a soup of many ingredients that would not otherwise meet. When they do, new life flourishes. So too in our lives, or when we meet with some form of living that runs counter to our own – that is a moment when we can either reject or engage the two different lives – so that something more can come into being. The two can become co-creators of a new world. When that happens the unlikely alliance bears fruit.

We are creating a new world, where people and planet come first. Do this, and the Earth becomes all of our business and we humans all become one big co-operation. Imagine that our Earth is our pot of gold. Each time we co-create with others we are adding to our pot and when we do this the pot fills up with all that we grow, both from our land and within our souls. The remarkable thing is that our pot continues to grow too; the more we put into the pot, the larger it becomes, the more we have to share with others. Permaculture is in the widest sense the biggest job creation scheme in the world. By creating abundance we are giving into the lives of those all around us, as well as gifting a legacy for those who have yet to come. Each seed we plant will grow and give to us for many generations to come. What could be better?

I have applied permaculture principles to my life and to my work – and believe me they work! When I remind myself to look to the problem and see how to make it the solution, inevitably I find the way forward. I am a lawyer, a lawyer who loves the Earth. My journey started when I decided the Earth was in need of a good lawyer and that we can create a legal duty of care. Now I am bringing into being a whole new body of law called Earth Law where people and planet are put first. I am changing the rules of the game – after all, that is all law is – the rules of the game of life. The Earth has a right to life and we can all help nourish the life of the land beneath our feet. When we change our thinking about our lives, we come to the point of understanding that we are all inter-related and when we know that it is then just a small step to the thought that we are all interconnected. I woke up to that thought some years ago and it changed my understanding forever.

As a child I feared being stung by a bee; now I love them! They are the carriers of life itself. We can be like bees, seeding and pollinating literally and metaphorically. When we do that, new life and new ways of thinking can evolve very quickly. Take time to just be with the Earth and you will find there is so much to learn by looking to nature for our wisdom; if anyone knows the rules of the game of life it is the Earth. By just spending time with nature we will become more attuned to her rhythms and her song of love. I marvel when I hear the sounds of nature; not one of them is out of tune. When we attune ourselves to nature so too do we begin to thrum with the very vibration of life itself. It's a very different tune to the ones we have previously known; this one creates perfect harmony and with harmony comes happiness.

I have a vision of a Garden of Eden where each and every one of us is enjoying our new world. My vision is filled with great love for all living beings. I can see a world full of abundance for all, a world where people and planet are loved and given freedom to be. This is a world where the health and well-being of us all comes first. When this happens, we all become one – a living, breathing organism that is thrumming with love. I can almost hear the sound now.

People and Permaculture is a pathway to this new world. It will indeed change your life if you absorb its wisdom and apply its tools and techniques. It will enhance your personal and professional relationships and help you to design better projects. It is a big step forward in permaculture thinking and a valuable addition to any library. May it bring you balance and fulfilment and enable you to become an even more effective advocate for the Earth.

POLLY HIGGINS
Barrister, author of *Eradicating Ecocide* and lawyer for the Earth

Introduction

There is a vision for humanity, a way of being with each other and ourselves that doesn't harm or pollute; that empowers and allows us to be the best we can. Mostly this vision is obscured by our lack of energy and motivation, petty everyday quarrels and the horrors of the daily news. At other times the vision is shining before us and within us, drawing us closer.

This book shines a light on how we can use permaculture thinking and design in our interactions with ourselves and other people to create harmony. We will explore how to see things differently, find new ways of approaching our lives, care for ourselves, act compassionately with other people and move towards our hope for humanity.

To live a life of abundance – to have what we need, to be thriving, to have enough to be generous – is magical. True abundant living permeates all levels of our lives; abundance in our well-being, in the quality of our relationships, in our communities and into the world.

Using permaculture can benefit us on a personal level; we can feel more empowered, healthy, grounded and able to make appropriate decisions. On a social level permaculture connects people and enables synergistic and co-operative relationships. Globally it can help alleviate poverty and improve quality and access to food, water and shelter, so we can meet our needs in non-polluting and non-damaging ways. For the environment, permaculture can restore and protect ecosystems, increase biodiversity, and preserve and regenerate our fundamental resources of life; soil, water and trees.

This book has arisen out of the need to focus on us as people, how we can interrelate, motivate, inspire, act co-operatively and effectively to bring about positive benefits for the planet and people to secure our future.

With a rising population we must move quickly to ways of connecting and supporting, giving and receiving, nurturing and growing. We must break down existing paradigms of fear, greed and competition that are pulling apart the seams of our life-support systems on the planet. We need to turn our attention to how we interact with each other if there is any hope for our species' survival. It is we as humans that we need to save – by saving ourselves we will save the planet through the realisation that this is one and the same thing. We can only live in harmony with the planet if we can live in harmony with ourselves.

It is an aspirational goal that we can work towards in small steps. This book is intended both to share this bigger vision and stimulate you to make improvements in your own lives. Permaculture gives us the opportunity and tools to actively create peace and understanding, to weave our own webs of abundance.

Structure of the book

The book expands out from the self into relationships and groups, then into society and beyond into a global context. On either side we have edges of permaculture thinking. There is a glossary at the end for reference to unfamiliar terms; it can also be used as a review.

Part 1: Thinking like an ecosystem

We begin with opening up our thinking, to imagining how ecosystems hold the abundance that they do. We gain familiarity with permaculture concepts.

Part 2: Looking deep into the centre

From this we focus on our own self-care, improving our well-being and how we can expand into the true potential of ourselves.

Part 3: Hearing each other

We explore how we can truly listen to each other to improve our relationships, families and groups. We look at how we can provide support, give and receive feedback, make decisions, and prevent and resolve conflict.

Part 4: Living in society

Here we expand our vision to examine what is happening in our communities and how, with shifts of thinking, we can create abundant systems of peoplecare.

Part 5: Feeling connected globally

Taking this out as far as we can, we expand our consciousness to feel connected to everyone in the world and to the planet.

Part 6: Sensing our futures

With the final part we return to permaculture design as an approach for making sense of our futures and manifesting change. The book concludes with many voices sharing their vision for humanity.

Author's note

This book is intended as a springboard for further research, discussion and application. It gives us tools to further develop peoplecare in our own lives. It is not intended as a definitive guide or encyclopaedic volume.

What I have selected here are only some of the perspectives, theories, tools and concepts that are useful for permaculture; there are many more. We are learning and evolving all the time; inevitably new information will come in and new perspectives arise.

Given here is a wide enough viewpoint to see the whole picture and show the variety of possible applications; any part of this could be zoomed in on further and further to see more detail and complexity.

Activities

Throughout there are activities to help deepen your learning. Doing the activities will turn this from someone else's ideas and words on a page into your own first hand experience. You will be actively creating knowledge personal to you rather than just passively absorbing it. The learning will move from just words in your mind into your muscles and body.

During permaculture courses it is often remarked that it is all common sense – it is, but common sense isn't all that common these days. Recognising this shows that the new information is resonating with your innate wisdom. You are invited not to put your old brain aside to learn these new concepts, but to integrate them with your lifetime of experience and observation.

There are questions, self-enquiries to probe deeper into your true feelings, to reflect upon experiences and access your self-knowledge. Each of us has our own answers, when asked the right questions. These exercises will support you in the process of connecting with your own sense of being. By enhancing understanding of ourselves we improve our understanding of other people.

The activities are starting points for design, and can be part of the design process, which we will look at in closer detail as we go. They can be translated to other chapters. For example, a visioning exercise for ourselves could also be used for our families.

All of us have our own ways of engaging with books, and so too with the activities. Some of them will filter through and you might find yourself doing it in a different way. Others you might come back to in a couple of months' time, when you arrive in a new situation in your life. Other activities you might have a strong rapport with and begin to do every day. Find a way that suits you; there is no right or wrong way, and you don't need to feel guilty to be moving past activities without doing them. They are intended to be fun and engaging, not guilt inducing.

Discussions with friends can help assimilate your thoughts. A word of caution here; being too enthusiastic about the ideas and using lots of new words with your family and friends can be off-putting for them. There's been many a person who has rushed home after a course espousing permaculture this and permaculture that and their husband/wife/housemate has got to the point where they don't want to hear anything about it any more. It can be a question of translation; people can hear it more clearly if you make it appropriate for them, in terms they can understand. So be gentle, introduce things slowly and take time to understand them and make changes for yourself first. They will be drawn in by witnessing positive changes in you, and you will be invited to share.

Learning journal

To maximise the benefit from the activities it is useful to have a way of reflecting and capturing the learning. Find yourself an appealing notebook to have as a learning journal. In here you can do the activities and note anything that has struck a chord, or that you have further questions about, and reflections you have about your journey through this book. Enjoy the activities and the learning and benefits they will provide.

ACTIVITY: AIMS FOR THE BOOK

VISION

Start your learning journal with your aims for reading the book.

What's my aim in reading this book?

What would I like to get out of it?

What are my motivations for reading it?

Taking time to think about this now will enable you to direct your energies.

Begin and the impossible will become possible.
THOMAS CARLYLE
. . . .

PART 1: THINKING LIKE AN ECOSYSTEM

CHAPTER 1
Setting the scene

What is permaculture?

Ethics

Regeneration

The edge effect

Abundance thinking

THINKING LIKE AN ECOSYSTEM

CHAPTER 3
Design

We are all designers

Observation

Spirals of erosion and abundance

Limiting factors

Zones

Inputs and outputs

Design web

CHAPTER 2
Nature's lessons

Patterns

Principles

Systems thinking

Setting the scene

WE START WITH introducing some new ways of thinking that incorporate ancient wisdom, natural patterns and our innate abilities.

Permaculture provides a framework for this and we begin our journey with how we can see things from a permacultural perspective, which in turn comes from observation of nature. This part provides the underpinning ways of thinking that can then be applied to any system and adapted to its unique use for every individual situation or person. The rest of the book sets out examples of how these permaculture tools can be used in action.

We start with mapping out permaculture, its history and its future and the ethics at its heart. The last section of this chapter relates permaculture to the big vision of a positive future.

This part is intended both for the beginner and those familiar with permaculture; it lays the groundwork for the rest of the book.

What is permaculture?

The goal of permaculture is to create harmony with ourselves, between people and with the planet. Bill Mollison and David Holmgren[2] first coined the word in the 1970s in Australia. The sustainability they described wasn't completely new: much of the thinking is wisdom that our ancestors would have been well versed in, but this knowledge has been buried beneath the drive for productive and profitable agriculture systems and the thirst for fossil fuel economies.

There are as many permaculture definitions as there are permaculturists. Each person has developed their own ways of using permaculture and their relationship to it. Different thoughts, images, ideas and feelings emerge.

The central aim of permaculture is to reduce our ecological impact. Or more precisely to turn our negative ecological impact into a positive one.

PATRICK WHITEFIELD[1]

. . . .

1

Permaculture has limitless meanings, but here are some commonalities and key points to help us to understand it:

Permaculture:

- Uses nature as our guide
- Thinks holistically
- Is solutions based
- Is a design system
- Is based on co-operation and connections
- Creates abundance and harmony

The essence of permaculture is ancient in origin – taking inspiration from the civilisations of the world that have survived for thousands of years... However, permaculture is an integration of many skills and disciplines, brought together to design ways of living sustainably in the 21st century.

IAN LILLINGTON [3]

Using innate wisdom, new technologies and observation of nature's patterns our aim is to create holistic systems that enhance quality of life without causing harm or pollution. We can create beneficial connections through design to give more substance and stability, like joining random words to make meaningful sentences.

Permaculture designers use a succinct set of principles and techniques to establish homesteads and communities that provide for their own needs, require minimal care, and produce and distribute surplus food and goods ... permaculture emphasises relaxation, sharing, and working with nature rather than against it. Meeting our own needs without exploiting others is the primary goal.

HEATHER FLORES [4]

It will take time to reinstate truly self-sustaining systems globally though we can find joys and benefits on the journey. Permaculture has gained momentum and spread rapidly around the world with people hungry to nurture and heal degraded and polluted land. Hundreds of thousands of people have benefited and changed their thinking and lifestyles, also creating abundance around them.

There is not a single blueprint of how to get there. Each garden or person is unique and requires their own individual plan of action; there isn't one design that fits all.

Permaculture provides a set of ethics at its core, principles to guide us, techniques that assist us, methodical steps in a design process to achieve our goals, and a call to action. For each of the following parts we use one of these as a way of providing a permaculture context for understanding. In the next part we focus on ourselves and start to build our tool kit of techniques for design, observation and creative thinking. We then think about how principles can help us to understand our relationships in part three. In part four we use design as a framework for creating a more harmonious society. We come back to the core of permaculture using the ethics to help us feel connected globally in part five. In the last part we open up to actions we can take in our own lives.

Permanent culture

Permaculture originated from the observation of nature and, as it is easiest to replicate nature's systems in the garden most of the attention has been on doing just that. Growing food is one of the most powerful and tangible ways in which we can connect with the Earth and its cycles, and make a step towards living a healthier life. The main body of knowledge and experience therefore currently resides in land-based systems.

However, there is a growing realisation that, while enough skills, resources and techniques for widespread planet care and repair currently exist, there are other stumbling blocks that we have yet to overcome. What has been noted time and again is the ability of people themselves to stand in the way of positive action, right through from a personal to a global level. We can observe with individual, community and larger scale projects that it is our dynamics as human beings that ultimately dictates success or stalling. Well-meaning projects can come to a stand still if people aren't attended to.

Permaculture has evolved from being purely land based, to involving people in land based systems, to thinking about the invisible structures within community groups. The next evolution has begun to take permaculture into the heart of all our people based systems. There may come a time in the future where the word permaculture becomes obsolete as it becomes ingrained in our state of mind and behaviour to think in an integrated systems way. Similarly, perhaps we will no longer need to label food as organic because all of our food is grown in this way.

People, their buildings and the ways they organise themselves are central to permaculture. Thus the permaculture vision of permanent (sustainable) agriculture has evolved to one of permanent (sustainable) culture ... It can be used to design, establish and manage and improve ... all efforts made by individuals, households and communities towards a sustainable future.
DAVID HOLMGREN[5]

Applications of permaculture

Since the 1970s hundreds of thousands of people worldwide have adapted and experimented with permaculture and integrated it into their lifestyles and thinking. The effects have gone beyond just learning to grow their own food sustainably. From this initial step of accepting responsibility and taking action further leaps of empowerment become possible. Permaculture gives us the ability to look for the positives in any situation and create solutions. By thinking holistically and seeking the most productive and least polluting options we can provide yields for ourselves and protect resources for future generations.

The same thinking can be applied as effectively to our own lives and how we interact with others as for gardens. A permaculture garden is productive, healthy, vibrant, dynamic and able to meet its own needs; these are the same characteristics we would find in a natural system. Likewise permaculture people and communities can be productive, healthy, vibrant, dynamic and able to meet their own needs.

Permaculture has been used to design lives, homes, gardens, businesses, smallholdings, farms and ecovillages. It has been used in peace initiatives in Palestine, earthquake relief work in Haiti, soil and community regeneration in New

Orleans after Hurricane Katrina. It has been used in the centre of concrete jungles and reforesting deserts and is on the school curriculum in Malawi. We will hear more stories throughout from people using permaculture in their own lives.

Permaculture invites us to be a solution in the world.

Ethics

There are three ethics at the heart of permaculture: earthcare, peoplecare and fair shares. On the surface they are straightforward and can be used to guide our decisions and lifestyles. Are we caring for the Earth, are we caring for people, is our action fair? Each ethic has a range of meanings and subtleties that enables us to see more deeply into our choices, assess impacts and find options with multiple benefits. They help us manifest an attitude and way of thinking that leads us to develop skills and tools within each ethic. We can embody the ethics in our everyday thinking and behaving. They are not unique to permaculture; many cultures, religions and groups worldwide share them. They can be seen as 'life ethics'.

Earthcare

The earthcare ethic respects and preserves the biodiversity of the planet and creates new habitats.

The Earth is a living organism, able to self regulate, evolve and sustain the multitude of life upon it. The complexity of life it supports is staggering to comprehend. Permaculture is a way of valuing all life on earth. It asks of us to respect ALL life for its intrinsic value rather than just the plants and animals that we find useful or attractive. We must acknowledge that we do not own this planet.

Soil erosion, polluted water and air, extinction of species and melting ice caps are just some of the consequences of human actions. The quality of life of all species will further erode if positive action isn't taken. Earthcare activities look to halt this damage and reverse the effects. Modern farming practices are responsible in part. We can shift to more appropriate technologies to increase productivity and fertility while reducing chemical inputs and pollution. These include agroforestry, seed saving, green manures, compost and integrated pest management. How we manage woodlands, treat sewage, build homes and grow food determines whether we are positively contributing or further stressing the life support systems of the planet.

The environment is not separate from ourselves: we are inside it and it is inside us; we make it and it makes us.

DAVI KOPENAWA YANOMAMI[6]

Without caring for the Earth we as people cannot survive. We need to treasure wilderness, soil, forests, oceans and every creature. Everything on the planet is connected and all of our actions have ripple effects globally. We can care for the Earth by nurturing and valuing life so we can be proud of our contribution and the planet we leave behind.

Peoplecare

The peoplecare ethic asks us to care for ourselves and other people and meet our needs in sustainable ways.

There are different levels of needs to meet: physical, emotional, social, spiritual and intellectual. Currently many of people's basic needs are met in unsustainable, unjust and polluting ways. Permaculture can help meet basic needs of food, water and shelter in a sustainable way.

In groups and communities we can value and support diversity, accept individuals' needs and allow everyone a voice. We feel connected when working together for mutual benefit through authentic and effective communication. By doing this we are allowing people to be themselves and empowering them to realise their own potential. Reaching out and establishing links to create community infuses us with a sense of purpose and belonging.

Peoplecare can be like dusting and be more noticeable when it is not done. When we have our needs met and we feel secure and looked after we may take it for granted. When we aren't cared for we might feel impatient, aggressive, lost, anxious, or disconnected. These effects are felt collectively as well as individually and lead to further social problems. Peoplecare extends into social systems including healthcare and education.

The current state of the planet has arisen from the thoughts and actions of humans past and present. The ethic of peoplecare includes changing the thinking behind our actions. Once our thinking changes our actions will follow suit.

Look and listen for the welfare of the whole people and have always in view not only the present but also the coming generations.

THE GREAT LAW OF PEACE, CONSTITUTION OF THE HAUDENOSAUNEE (IROQUOIS) NATION

We all have first hand experience of peoplecare, how we look after ourselves on a daily basis, how others treat us and how we respond to people. Everyone has innate abilities to help with our peoplecare, and they can further be practised and improved. Some of the skills and qualities we need for peoplecare are leadership, openness, kindness, acceptance, curiosity, patience, tolerance, vision, motivation and sharing. Learning to listen and communicate effectively shows compassion and empathy as well as enabling decision-making, negotiation and conflict resolution.

People are wonderful, creative, diverse, resourceful and loving. Peoplecare allows us to connect with these inherent qualities, to shine and encourage others to do so. Respect, appreciation, love and joy begin with ourselves and expand out to other people.

Fair shares

The fair shares ethic promotes equality, justice and abundance, now and for future generations. We can summarise it as: some for all, forever.

It has two aspects to it. The first is *living within limits,* limiting our consumption and not exceeding natural boundaries or exploiting people with our choices. The second aspect of *giving away surplus* can seem contradictory at first to living within limits. However when we rethink the term living within limits as living in balance with the natural world and sharing in the abundance of nature, the two ideas live hand in hand. We do not have to live without when we harvest renewable resources and tap into nature's bounty, there is plenty to share around.

There are large gaps in society between the rich and the poor, and the opportunities available depending on your gender, race and nationality. These gaps breed resentment, lack of trust, complacency and exploitation.

There is enough in the world for everyone's need not everyone's greed.

GANDHI

· · · · · · · ·

The difference between needs and wants is fundamental to our consumption habits. Changing attitudes and redefining consumption, limits and surplus is needed to achieve fair shares. We are invited to live with an abundance attitude rather than a scarcity mentality. Spending locally, sharing and lending all help to distribute surpluses. Our energy can flow and we can contribute to the good of the whole in whatever way we can. A fairer world would emerge if we all lived on a bit less and gave a bit more.

Relationship between the three ethics

The current problems faced by the planet and people can be viewed as stemming from actions that have not been in line with one or more ethic. The loss of biodiversity comes from not protecting natural habitats and caring for the Earth. Mental illnesses from isolation arise when people are not cared for. Millions of starving children globally is due to unequal distribution of food, labour, surplus and control and contravenes the fair shares ethic. These problems are not the result of single actions and have complex cause and effect relationships.

The three ethics are drawn as overlapping circles without distinct edges as they interrelate and influence each other. The actions within one ethic affect the other two. When a problem occurs in one of the ethics, other problems arise in the others.

For instance our food choices affect our health and have repercussions for the places and people that grow the food. Large fields of monocrops, grown for a cash income, impact on the availability of land for growing local food and water for irrigation. Chemical inputs become a part of the soil or run off into water systems. These infringe on all of the three ethics.

To affect changes we need to change our thinking before we can sustainably change our behaviour. How can we create feelings of 'enoughness' so that we can share resources and wealth more equally? How can we enrich rather than poison the planet with our actions and choices? This requires us to shift patterns of thinking, both collectively and personally.

With the overlap and interplay of the ethics, practising our skills and being active in one area enhances our abilities in the others. For example improving our ability to listen to the land will help us to listen to people. Care is the answer, if we don't have care then what's to stop us trashing everything? True harmony is in the centre and cannot be achieved if one of the ethics is not met.

ACTIVITY– MINI TIME CAPSULE

Get some paper and an envelope. Write down your answers to the following questions. Don't worry about what you write or how you write it, just write what comes, whatever is present for you in this moment. Answer as fully as you can now, ensuring that you complete the task in one sitting, even if it might feel sparse, rather than leaving it half done to come back to.

What does peoplecare mean to me?

What peoplecare skills do I use regularly in my life?

How do I feel about myself right now?

How do I feel about my connections to other people?

How do I feel about the world?

Now seal it in the envelope and write the date on the outside. Put it somewhere safe, not so safe you'll never find it again. At the end of the book you can go back and read it. We often forget the journey we have taken, accepting the new scenery as normal. With this activity you will have a chance to reflect on where you started and see what's changed.

Personal responsibility

The prime directive of permaculture is to take self-responsibility. This is a groundbreaking concept in a global culture where we are constantly being bombarded with choices and products from around the world and governments making decisions on our behalf. Thoughts of 'it's all out of my hands', or 'nothing I do will make a difference' and blaming other people, parents, husbands, wives, the state, politicians or other countries are disempowering. Self-responsibility asks us to recognise our interconnectedness and apply our own free will to find ethical options. Being reflective encourages us to see the consequences of our actions.

> *The only ethical decision is to take responsibility for our own actions and that of our children.*
> BILL MOLLISON[7]

Responsibility is *response – ability*. We have the ability to choose how we respond to our circumstances and other people, how we look after ourselves, how we communicate and how we connect with our fellow citizens.

It can be an empowering, transformative shift when we take responsibility for our thoughts, feelings, what we say and what we don't say, how we learn and whether we change or not.

Regeneration

Sustainability

Permaculture is often described as designing for sustainability. However, sustainability has become a buzzword that is frequently used but not fully understood. Sustainability is defined by the Brundtland report[8] as "meeting the needs of the present without compromising the ability of future generations to meet their needs".

When we look at a natural system there is no work – all inputs are met by the system and there is no pollution – all outputs are used within the system, such as in a forest.

Economic sustainability focuses on achieving and maintaining economic growth. There is a big difference between sustaining our current lifestyles and living sustainably. Our current lifestyles require many inputs from fossil fuels and cheap labour from other countries. Land is stolen from ancient rainforests and pollution from our activities seeps into our rivers, is buried in the land and clouds the air that we breathe. On a personal level our bodies suffer from disease and stress; on a society level, crime and disillusionment are escalating and our local communities are eroding. Is this the lifestyle we want to sustain?

Living sustainably means non-polluting, non-harming and leaving resources for future generations and other species. Sustainable systems are ones that we can maintain. We can have different levels of sustainability that feed into one another: environmental, personal and social. These all overlap because we can find personal security in our social relationships, one leads to another and we can have none without a healthy planet.

Personal sustainability

Personal sustainability is the ability to sustain ourselves: our energy levels, health, and connections to our dreams and visions, other people and our higher self. People have responsibility to maintain their own physical, emotional, mental and spiritual health and avoid burnout. We need to have an understanding of our own needs and have mechanisms in place to meet them.

Social sustainability

A socially sustainable culture will have a common understanding of ethical behaviour. Social responsibility is woven into everyday actions; our lives filled with interactions that feed us, nourish our sense of self worth and encourage honesty. We are social creatures and it is not possible to do everything on our own, we need nurturing relationships for our mental well-being.

When we recognise our need for interdependence we are willing to support each other. It doesn't mean that we all have to be best friends; it means that we can respect, co-operate and co-exist with our differences rather than competing or trying to extinguish diversity.

What is culture?

Culture is the beliefs, customs, arts, institutions, practices and social behaviour of a particular nation or people. It is composed of internal thinking and external behaviours.

The systems we have for managing the Earth's resources and for how we interact with each other depend greatly upon our culture – its traditions, values and ways in which people organise themselves.

There are different layers to our culture. Race, class, language, education, locality and work all contribute to the environment we live in. Our cultures are a composite of our homes, family, work, community and wider groups that we belong to. Every person is a part of many groups and will have a unique set of cultures that they identify with. We have a family culture and a work culture as well as being part of a bigger community and part of even bigger groups such as age groups like children, teenagers or elders.

We often act from these cultural perspectives without necessarily being aware that it is our cultural conditioning that is dictating our thinking. For instance the time in the morning or evening that we consider is fine to phone people is conditioned and not the same cross-culturally. Each culture has preferences and aversions, beliefs and actions.

Shifts in cultural beliefs and actions occur around us all the time and can come about quite quickly. The mobile phone culture has taken root and spread rapidly around the globe. There has been a dramatic increase in the availability of organic food over the last decade and it is now more usual to recycle and compost food. Over the next ten years it may become as normal to reuse our grey water and buy second hand clothes. The current economy relies on products having built-in obsolescence but it could become the norm for items to be manufactured for disassembly and reuse or replacement of component parts.

Regeneration

Sustainability is the centre point where all three ethics are being met. However, we are so far outside of meeting the ethics that we need to make more effort to get there, than if we were already there and just maintaining this position.

We could think of sustainability as leaving no negative impact on the planet. At the moment there is so much negative impact happening that 'no impact' isn't enough, we need to have a positive impact. We could see sustainability as the mid point between degeneration and regeneration. We need to step up our regeneration of environmental and social systems to compensate for the damage.

Degeneration ----- Sustainable -------- Regeneration

The Great Turning

Joanna Macy[9] describes our present day culture of industry, technology and pollution as the 'Industrial Growth Culture'. This is the contemporary manifestation of a longer history of domination and separation. From here we have three options. The first is for 'business as usual', to assume that we can carry on with industrial and economic growth indefinitely. Many efforts are made to sustain this culture despite the negative effects experienced on environmental, social and personal levels. When we focus on the impact this is having on the world's resources, it is apparent that we can't carry on doing this forever and the second option seems likely to be where we see the breakdown of global systems in the 'Great Unravelling'. There would be great hardship during this process.

The third option is one of hope, responsibility and action. It is where we change the trajectory we are currently on, and shift our direction towards a 'Life Sustaining Earth Culture'. This is the 'Great Turning', the opportunity to turn our efforts to creating a sustainable culture that enhances life in our communities and for all species.

We are living in the time of the Great Turning
Turning away from making war
We are living in the time of the Great Turning
Turning back to natural law
Flowing with nature heals our spirit
Going against her harms us all
Rooh Star[10]

There are three areas of work needed to make the Great Turning. Firstly there are holding actions, such as protests and campaigning against the many damaging activities. Then there is the creation of alternatives and regeneration activities. And thirdly is shifting the way we look at the world and our values. In this book I deal predominantly with the second two, but I recognise the importance of holding actions as well. All three interrelate and support each other.

The edge effect

Edges of permaculture

When there is a sharing of beliefs, there is a sharing of culture. There are many disciplines and fields of activity whose aim is to create peace and harmony. Ian Lillington describes these as 'fellow travellers' on the journey towards a life sustaining Earth culture.

Permaculture is alive and demonstrates the same characteristics as an ecosystem: dynamic, growing and connecting. We could imagine a tree sending out new shoots as more people integrate their life experiences of earthcare, peoplecare and fair shares into existing permaculture knowledge. It is evolving and expanding as more information comes in and is assimilated through its permeable boundaries.

Permaculture shares edges with many other social groups; the more people that share the edge the bigger it is and the more exchanges there are. For example there is a big edge between permaculture and organic gardening. Some people think that permaculture and organic gardening are the same thing – they aren't, but there is certainly a very big overlap, the main belief being that nature knows best. There are a significant number of people who share edges between permaculture and shiatsu, yoga, reflexology and other body work and therapies. Two of the shared beliefs here are that care of the self is important to enable us to nourish others and that personal well-being is linked to the well-being of the whole. Branches of personal development share the belief that there is inner wisdom and unused energy that can be tapped into and released.

Jo Barker of Dynamic Equilibrium[11] integrates kinesiology, permaculture and life coaching to create a holistic way of finding sustainable solutions for individuals, groups and places. Kinesiology (or any energy medicine system) offers easy-to-learn techniques to release stress and maintain balance. The belief that brings these together is that through observation and listening we can find solutions to bring people's lives into balance. Jo says, "in any permaculture design we aim to help a system become more and more self sustaining and abundant. It is the same with a food garden and a person's life. I use permaculture, kinesiology and coaching to encourage self-reliance."

Some of the edges that are explored within this book are Nonviolent Communication (NVC), The Work That Reconnects, Transition movement and Neuro-Linguistic Programming (NLP).

The mutual belief between NLP and permaculture is that we can change patterns of thinking to change outcomes. I like to think of NLP as 'New Language Patterns creating Novel Life Possibilities'. NLP has provided useful information for part two in particular.

There are strong themes embedded in all of these shared beliefs of *care, nourishment, appreciation, connection and allowing*. The word allowing reoccurs many times. Through allowing ourselves to experiment, grow, experience, try, be, live and feel we connect to our authentic selves and make positive change in the world. Life sustaining culture could be summed up in one word – *abundance*.

> ## THE TRANSITION MOVEMENT
>
> The Transition movement started in 2004 as a response to the issues of peak oil and climate change. The movement is composed of many different initiatives; transition towns, cities, villages and bioregions. They are a way of facilitating the Great Turning through community action and connections. The basic idea is of bringing people together in their communities to build local resilience. Through this resilience we are able to avoid the hardships that might arise when we have to shift away from an economy dependent on oil. One of the key source inspirations is permaculture and hence there are many shared beliefs, including: local connections are beneficial; we need to reduce our ecological footprint; and together we can achieve more. We will go on to explore their potential role in society in part four.

In contrast, the thinking behind the industrial growth culture is linear, short term and based on fear and greed. Some of the main beliefs that stem from this are:

- Human beings are separate from nature
- The world is unsafe
- Power structures are good
- Feelings of self worth and our status come from material possessions
- There is a scarcity of resources

The last belief is paradoxical for the industrial growth culture: simultaneously acting like there is a scarcity (by being greedy and grabbing resources), yet also using resources as if they are infinite and we can use them up as we want.

ACTIVITY: SHARED EDGES

What edges do I share with permaculture?

What are the common beliefs and assumptions?

What skills can I bring to a more self-responsible Earth culture?

The common beliefs are patterns that we can use in our designs. Our skills are valuable resources to help with our designs.

Abundance thinking

Abundance versus scarcity

Central to an Earth culture and the fair shares ethic is the idea of abundance. The industrial growth culture has the opposing belief of scarcity. Scarcity versus abundance is fear versus trust. A scarcity mindset has an underlying fear that there isn't enough.

An abundance attitude trusts that our needs will be provided for. When we give of our time and services we are assisting the flow of energy, this allows the flow to return to us. When we are open to giving we are open to receiving. When we give we don't need to be concerned about the consequences of our actions or be looking for gratitude or pay back. With a scarcity state of mind we hold tight to our time, energy and resources and they can stagnate and pollute.

When I give freely of my love, my attention, my time and even my money, I am contributing to the overall health and growth of my community. It makes me feel happy and healthy, too. Such sharing is not a sacrifice but a celebration, an act of love that has an immediate ripple effect, sending happiness back to the giver, multiplied many times.

LIZ WALKER [12]

....

SCARCITY	ABUNDANCE
Fear	Trust
Greed/more	Enough/sufficiency
Hoarding and stagnation	Flow and evolution
'Mine'	Sharing
Competition	Co–operation
Undermining	Valuing
Either/or	Both/and

Resource use

We can get caught in the trap of hoarding resources when in fact there are some that stay the same with use, and others that actually increase with use. We can become protective of our possessions and not want them to be used like a child hoarding our toys when in fact they will remain the same even when played with over and over. There are other resources that increase with use; some plants that are harvested frequently can produce much more than when left, harvesting herbs promotes healthy and productive growth. Friendships also increase with use.

> *Elegant simplicity represents a deep, graceful and sophisticated transformation in our ways of living ... Elegant simplicity is not simple. It grows and flowers with a rich variety of expressions. Deep simplicity is a richly complex idea – forever clarifying, refining, opening and growing.*
>
> DUANE ELGIN[13]

There is some confusion about abundance and opulence. The excesses of the 'too muchness' world are not based on true abundance. Many environmentally conscious people want to move away from the spendthrift, wasteful attitudes and swing towards the scarcity mindset, believing that we have to do without to be 'green'. This is certainly the view the media presents, that being green means doing without, simplicity – a regression to a primitive lifestyle. Luxury, beauty and quality can all sit beside simplicity and being sustainable. We can invest in quality products that are going to last like a well-built tool or a pair of boots that can be resoled. We can create beauty and luxury around us that doesn't harm others.

Creating surpluses

It is within our power and abilities to create surpluses and abundance in our lives. Abundance is more than just material items; we can create abundances of self-esteem, confidence, practical skills, friends, local community, purpose, knowledge and time. This starts with observing what we have, seeing the surpluses and redefining what we have in terms of what we need. Appreciation and abundance go hand in hand. It is about making the choice to see the abundances; are we seeing the strawberries that we have in plenty or do we want imported bananas? Of course strawberries and bananas aren't the same, but abundance is about valuing what we have rather than focusing on what we haven't got.

This continues with active creation of surpluses; what can we make, what skills do we have to offer, what plants can we propagate, what can we harvest, what time do we have spare?

ACTIVITY: SHARING SURPLUSES

One of the ways to develop an abundance mentality is to practise giving things away.

What do I have around me – what are my surpluses?

Perhaps it is plants in the garden, items that you don't need, skills, time or money. Find a way to give some of this surplus away, offering your help, giving items to a friend, putting loose change in a charity box or propagating plants to share. Try and give something away small or large every week to keep momentum.

CHAPTER 2

Nature's lessons

THROUGHOUT THE BOOK I have used metaphors from nature to provide a two-way channel for learning. We can learn about ourselves through nature and about nature from knowing about ourselves.

One of the core ideas of permaculture is that nature is our guide and teacher. This chapter builds our understanding of the principles of permaculture, natural patterns and systems theory, and develops our ability to think like an ecosystem. People, as individuals and communities, are natural systems and when we can fluently think like one we are able to be more interdependent, adaptable, resilient and resourceful.

Patterns

Patterns in nature

All of nature is composed of interlocking patterns. Astonishingly the vast complexity of life is composed of only a small number of different patterns manifesting in an infinite variety of forms. These patterns are repeated at different levels all the way from atoms and cells to river beds and galaxies. Humans have long since used these patterns in their buildings, crafts, arts and technologies.

Each pattern has characteristics that serve a variety of functions. Copying nature's patterns in technology is known as biomimicry. Before inventing or creating anything we can ask ourselves 'how would nature do this?' For example how would nature provide strength or be waterproof?

The principles, which we will come to next, have come from the observation and understanding of the patterns underlying the functioning of natural systems. Nature is composed of structural patterns as well as patterns governing behaviour on an individual and collective level.

A lot of the structural patterns combine strength and beauty with efficiency of space through large surface area or extensive edges. Looking at the benefits of these characteristics provides us with attitudes that we can emulate in our design work towards a life-sustaining Earth culture.

Structural patterns

Pattern	Where it is found in nature	Human applications	Characteristics/benefits	Attitude as designer
Wave	Water Heartbeats Sound Sleep Brain activity	Music Bio-rhythms	Measurement of time Building of momentum Eroding Repeating but each one is different Pulsation	Constantly changing Accepting ups and downs Time for action and time for rest Waves of activity
Spiral	Snails Plant tendrils Inner ear Whirlpool Tornados	Herb spiral Corkscrew Springs Heating elements Seasonal living/ growth	Protection Acceleration or deceleration Can store energy Compaction Indefinite growth Supportive Efficient use of space Powerful Beautiful Concentrating or dispersing	Out a bit and round a bit Transcend and include Gradually improving or eroding Repeating to almost the same place Building on successes
Branching	Trees and plants – above and below Evolutionary tree of life Blood vessels Waterways Antlers Capillaries	Transport Family trees Website design Mindmaps	Spreading Covers large surface area Creates lots of edge Stabilising Anchoring Gathering Can travel both ways Resilient Increases diversity and spreads over a wider area Exchange and transport	Can cut off parts and the rest survives Useful for gathering or distributing flows of nutrients, energy, information, water, air from or to a large area Can reach out in stages
Lobe/ Honey-comb	Berries Hair and fur Reptile and fish scales Birds' feathers Pine cones	Roofing Jewellery Flooring Weather cladding Insulation	Lots of edge for exchange between parts Interlocking Can produce a large and strong structure from simple elements Uniform Protection Waterproofing Resilience	Small groups building to larger movement Protection and strength in numbers Multi-faceted More flexibility than just one large unit Modular Can sacrifice parts and the rest is undamaged
Net	Birds' nests Leaf and plant tissue Bramble thicket Coral Bone structure Sponge Spiders' webs	Barriers Hedge-laying Straw-mulch Cob walls Nets Woven cloth Knitwear Sieves	Strong and light Big surface area Permeable Spreads the load – distributes tension Catches things Strengthens and reinforces Interconnected Resilience Resistance Repairable Supportive and protective Efficient use of space Creates lots of edge	Making connections Spreading the work load Harvesting yields Swifter communication than a chain-of-command Many routes to the same places

Behavioural patterns

Like structural patterns, behavioural patterns are found repeated in nature, and each has characteristics and benefits that we can use in our design work. For example animals live in groups, families, pairs or predominantly alone. They exhibit different waking and sleeping patterns; diurnal, nocturnal or taking frequent naps. Each behaviour has evolved in relation to the whole environment including other animals. Structural patterns inform behavioural patterns, for example flocking is a manifestation of the lobe pattern; there is no leader, just many individuals responding to the same conditions. Where there is a 'pack leader' the branching pattern is more evident. Some examples of behavioural patterns and how we might use their characteristics in our design are listed below.

Pattern	Where it is found in nature	Human applications	Characteristics/ benefits	Attitude as designer
Flocking/ schooling/ herding	Starlings Pigeons Herring Grazing animals	Settlements Non-hierarchical teams Sports teams	Simple rules Shared leadership Minimising edge – less exchange with outside Protective Safety in numbers Interdependency	Safety in numbers Sense of belonging Solidarity Group trust Less effort Aligning with like minded people
Co-operative	Ant's nest Bee hives Penguins in midwinter	Workers' co-ops Intentional communities	Sharing of labour Sharing of resources Roles and specialisation Interdependency	Many hands make light work Working for the good of the whole Fair share of responsibilities and profit
Hierarchical structures	Gorillas Elephants Lion prides Wolf packs	Businesses Tribal communities	Quick decisions Chain-of-command Interdependency	Acknowledgement of hierarchies in experience, skills and knowledge
Family or pairs	Swans Gibbons	Nuclear families	Interdependency	Co-operation Commitment
Solitary	Tigers Bears	Freelancers Self-employed	Freedom Independence	Specialisation Finding your own niche

We see that interdependency is the common pattern in nature. Many animals have evolved to be dependent on others. Interdependency needs to be revalued in our societies.

Many of the structural patterns, such as branching and net have large edges or surface area. With flocking we see that it is beneficial to minimise external edge so that there is less vulnerability to predators, and in the case of penguins heat is conserved by less exchange to the outside while increasing the edge for exchange of body heat inside the mob. This illustrates that there are both advantages and disadvantages of increasing edge, and nature uses different strategies depending on the circumstances.

Likewise in our designs we can be strategic about the amount of edge we create. For example, vegetable bed shapes can depend on our watering and accessibility needs. Thinking about the advantages and disadvantages of creating edges in our working days, we can choose to insulate our activities or open up to new connections: there are some jobs that benefit from lots of edge to stop the boredom and others where minimum edge is important to maintain focus.

Patterns in people

Humans can be seen as complex sets of patterns overlaying and interacting with each other. We have patterns from a cellular level to organism to interpersonal to collective. Patterns of thinking and behaviour shape our lives. We learn through following patterns as children. As soon as we are born we recognise the pattern of a human face. Walking comes from observing and mimicking our parents, learning languages through following patterns of speech. From the early stages our daily routines consist of cyclical patterns: when we eat and play; active and restive periods. As adults our relationships and work lives exhibit more complex and flexible patterns. Patterns guide our lives enabling us to repeat actions quickly and easily; for example many people have a morning routine that gets them out of the house on time.

However, patterns can outlive their usefulness and we may become stuck in routines without questioning and improving them. The reason for the pattern in the first place may have changed but we still maintain it. An example of this is the 'QWERTY' layout of letters on keyboards. It was originally invented for the typewriter that was not able to cope with very quick typing (according to folklore, although people have different interpretations). We have since moved to computers and quick typing is no problem for electronic keyboards. We keep the QWERTY pattern because the time cost of relearning is deemed too high, even though in the long run it may save us time and energy.

Perhaps we have the pattern of a mid-morning snack in our daily routine that became a habit years ago when we had a light breakfast very early in the morning and had low blood sugar levels later on. Now, possibly decades later we may still be maintaining this pattern even though circumstances have changed and the original need is no longer present.

Many patterns are learnt from our parents, friends, society, books and television. Each culture has its own patterns. All of these have influence over our thinking and behaviour. Examining our patterns and where they have come from is the first step to creating new ones in our lives. We will return later to how we can shift stuck patterns and create new ones.

Pattern recognition

Patterns are all around us, although mostly taken for granted. Metaphors, songs, stories and proverbs traditionally help us access our understanding of underlying patterns. The use of archetypal behaviour in stories is commonplace. A familiar pattern when trying something new is for it to work on the third time – 'third time lucky'. The story of Goldilocks, amongst others, works on this pattern; the first chair was too hard, the second too soft and the third just right.

Using metaphors from the natural world helps us to see ourselves as part of nature. Our understanding of patterns such as spirals and waves is deeply intuitive because they are present within our bodies. When we connect with our own patterns and those around us we have a sense of belonging to something immensely ordered, vast and amazing. When we create using these patterns our creations are beautiful.

We can look at natural processes, cycles and rhythms to find functional patterns for our designs. Processes could include leaf drop in the autumn, seedling growth, hibernation, how bees collect nectar, or hunters bring down prey; any of these could provide metaphors that we can find useful in our design work.

We can also look to our own lives for patterns that we can use in our design. If we are embarking on a big project like building our home, we could think of how we have made a patchwork blanket, do jigsaw puzzles or cook meals to find attitudes and benefits that we can translate.

Andy Goldring, CEO of the Permaculture Association (Britain),[1] is using the lobe pattern as part of the organisation's strategic development. He likens all the organisations working for positive change to beads on a necklace that at the moment are scattered and thinking about their own bead. He asks how we can think about the whole necklace and strengthen the connections between organisations. "Through coming together we have strength in numbers and the potential to become the majority voice." The association works to grow the network; the connections between individuals and groups.

ACTIVITY: PATTERN RECOGNITION

Start with the structural patterns and find examples of wave, spiral, branching, lobe and net patterns in your environment. Then begin to identify where else these patterns can be seen in your own life and community.

Principles

One of the fundamental beliefs of permaculture is that nature is our teacher. The principles have been observed from nature as guidelines for how we can design sustainable systems. They have evolved over time with teachers adding their own interpretation and wording; this has resulted in over 50 principles in use.

In 2002 David Holmgren[2] redefined the principles and created a set of 12, each with an icon and proverb to reinforce the lessons embedded within them. This set has been used because the proverbs have an immediate hook in reminding us to access our innate wisdom and the icons[3] are useful for visual learners. Having the principle, icon and proverb together gives us three entry points to a fuller meaning.

The ethics provide us with the reasons we want sustainability, and the principles point to how to do it. They can be applied to any system from soil improvement to health, transport systems to communication. Throughout the book we will see examples of the principles in action.

The principles are not isolated. They interplay, oscillating in importance as the need and relevancy arises. For each principle there are self-reflection questions to help integrate them into your thinking. After a time, the use of the principles becomes second nature and you will see how they overlap and interact with one another.

The principles can be used like a lens to look through for problem solving or decision-making. There are different approaches to using the principles:

- Reflect on a problem or issue
- Generate solutions
- Choose from options

1. Observe and interact

In the garden we need to observe when fruit is ready to harvest, when pests are attacking our crops and what plants need attention.

Actively observing increases our awareness of ourselves, others and surroundings and stimulates our natural curiosity. As children our sense of awe and wonder pervades our perception of the world, then as we grow up we take things for granted until the world around us becomes an almost invisible backdrop for our lives.

Identifying our patterns of behaviour, preferences, contradictions and habits allows us to see what is going well and what might need changing. Our observations are first hand experience that we can interpret for ourselves, rather than second hand sources from books, the internet or other people.

Our observations are not static pictures of reality, they can provide us with insights into how to change the situation or ourselves. Interaction is vital – there is no point in just observing an accident waiting to happen – we also need to be able to interact and prevent it. Observation can prevent further problems downstream and save us time and energy in the long run.

What do I observe around me and with other people?

What do I see or feel in myself, what's my body feeling, what's my intuition saying?

What can I change?

ICON: *what do you see when you look at the icon? The icon can be seen as different things: a tree with a hole, a person with their head in the clouds, a peep hole through which one sees the solution.*

PROVERB: <u>*Beauty is in the eye of the beholder.*</u> *Everything has different viewpoints and it is up to us where we stand to look. When we look with appreciation we can normally find the positives.*

2. Catch and store energy

Animals store energy in their body before hibernation. In the landscape we can use dams and ponds to catch and store water. Solar panels catch the sun's energy.

Energy is all around us in different forms. Sleep and food are obvious sources of energy for our bodies. We need to get balanced amounts of them. Too much sleep and we can feel sloth-like, too little and we get frazzled. The consequences of too much or too little food are evident. It is not just the quantity we are getting, the quality is equally, if not more, important. We can rely too heavily on food and sleep to provide us with energy leading to imbalances. Energy comes to us in different forms, from physical exercise to stimulating conversations, from music to meditation. All of these things are nurturing and energy giving.

We need to work with our natural rhythms and energy levels for greatest productivity. When working with our passions energy flows more easily and we are more effective. Our capacity increases when we feel a connection and purpose to activities. Learning our biorhythms helps us to plan actions accordingly. Awareness allows us to be respectful of when we need to conserve energy.

ICON: *Sun in a bottle: can refer to a passive solar house, or preserving seasonal surpluses.*

PROVERB: *Make hay while the sun shines. It is easiest to work with the energy of the time. Or as new mums know, sleep while the baby sleeps. Niches in time and space open up and finding the best-suited activity produces the most efficient results.*

What gives me energy?

Am I making best use of my current energy levels and opportunities?

What activity would best suit this niche of time and space?

Is my energy flowing or blocked?

3. Obtain a yield

Grazing animals are continually obtaining a harvest. Expanding our idea of yields increases the potential for us to obtain harvests from activities. Job satisfaction, play, fun, friendship, growth and learning can be valued yields as well as more tangible ones such as money, time saved and material gains.

There is an infinite amount of yields that we could get from any system or activity: the yields are only limited by our imagination and information. In our gardens for example there are many weeds that could be harvested but we may not have the information about their uses. Even the yields from climax forests could be added to with educational activities and owl boxes, and the list of what else we could include is endless.

ICON: *A root vegetable. Edible yields are a measure of success.*

PROVERB: *You can't work on an empty stomach. Achieving short-term goals, getting results and meeting immediate needs entice us to work towards longer-term visions.*

If we don't harvest the yields we can't benefit from them; this is sometimes simply about us recognising and valuing them as such. We can increase the worth of the harvest by further processing or combining yields. By making fruit into jam we are adding value as well as *catching and storing energy*. Obtaining yields helps us to maintain motivation and momentum on our paths. Rewards provide incentives for us and are much more satisfying when they come from the work itself rather than externally.

What are the yields available?

Am I currently harvesting them?

Are there other yields that could become available?

4. *Apply self-regulation and accept feedback*

Our bodies regulate our body temperature, blood sugar levels and many more factors. Self-regulation is like adjusting the water temperature in the shower; small changes are needed, rather than swinging things too far in the opposite direction.

Being open to feedback, and learning to hear it without feeling criticised is important to our development as humans. Honesty and clarity are essential qualities in giving and receiving feedback. Feedback is not only about pointing out what is 'wrong' or needs changing, it is also about appreciation of each other and what we value about other people. By increasing our awareness we open up to growth and improvement.

We need the right scale so we get feedback and be aware of the consequences of our actions, with a global economy the ramifications are often out of sight.

ICON: *Earth: one large self-regulating system. Currently the planet is being exposed to rapid and extensive changes and this is throwing ecosystems into turmoil. People as a whole need to accept the feedback that the planet is giving us and self-regulate our actions.*

PROVERB: <u>*The sins of our fathers are visited unto the seventh generation*</u> *– not only do we reap what we sow but it has effects on future generations as well.*

Where am I receiving feedback from e.g. my body, others, written, verbal?

How can I monitor my progress?

What's working well?

What's not working so well?

What can I appreciate about myself?

5. *Use and value renewable resources and services*

All the energy to grow a forest comes from the sun and rain or from energy cycling within it. In contrast most of what we buy and activities that we engage in have used fossil fuels in either their production and/or distribution. Fossil fuel energy is a finite and expensive resource that will one day run out. Renewable energies such as solar, wind and water can carry on indefinitely.

Finding entertainment and activities that don't involve consumption of fossil fuels or pollution can benefit our purses as well as the planet. Creation rather than consumption is more empowering. Examples are going for a walk or playing games with children rather than buying more toys. Meeting our needs as close to home as possible minimises our use of transport.

People are renewable resources and we need to value and use their input. We can freely exchange knowledge and skills with others. We are renewable resources in ourselves and can choose to put our energy to good use.

ICON: *Horses consume only renewable resources, and could provide many services: pulling carts, ploughing ... manure is guaranteed!*

PROVERB: <u>*Let nature take its course*</u> *highlights the need to be patient and allow natural processes their own pace, reaping the benefits at the appropriate time.*

Where can I meet my needs with renewable resources?

What can I create?

Where can I cut down my consumption of non-renewable resources?

6. Produce no waste

There is no waste in a woodland, no bin bags awaiting weekly collection; everything is used within the system.

Recycling has now become a commonplace activity and is helping to reduce landfill. As well as reduce, reuse and recycle we can repair, refuse, re-educate, re-gift, replenish and rethink. For any purchase it is important to be aware of what the waste products will be. How quickly will the item become useless? Will it have a life after our use or will it go straight to landfill? These are questions to ask before any purchase. Buying items second hand gives them a new lease of life and saves them from landfill. Learning to mend clothes and fix items extends their life. We have other resources that may be wasted, such as our time. Where is our own energy wasted or blocked?

ICON: *Earthworm, the ultimate efficient recycler, aerating the soil and making fertility accessible to microbes.*

PROVERBS: *Waste not, want not* and *a stitch in time saves nine. Timely maintenance can significantly reduce waste, whether it is our health, relationship, tool or an item of clothing.*

Where is my time being wasted?

How can I prevent this?

What needs maintaining in my life?

7. Design from patterns to details

Every tree has the same pattern of roots, trunk and leaves but each has different details resulting in thousands of different species.

There isn't one blueprint, a single design that fits all. Each garden and person is different and needs unique solutions. When designing any system we can look at the overarching patterns of success from other systems and translate them, finding the details that are appropriate.

Our patterns influence our lives and interactions with others. There may be patterns of communication, thinking and behaviour that are helpful in some areas of your life that could be taken and converted for use in other places.

When planning meals we look at our overall preferences and aversions as the patterns that then get made into specific recipes – the details.

ICON: *Spider's web: every spider's web is unique, but the pattern is universal.*

PROVERB: *Can't see the wood for the trees. When concentrating on the details we can miss the bigger picture of what is going on.*

What are the patterns at play here?

What are the useful patterns and what would I like to change?

Am I getting lost in the details and not paying attention to the bigger picture?

8. Integrate rather than segregate

The beehive is a classic example of creatures working together. We can seek to create beneficial relationships in our lives, integrating skills and combining different aspects. The connections between elements in a system are as important as the elements themselves.

Being inclusive and welcoming when we work in groups allows everyone to participate and decisions can be made by the community. Everyone's aptitudes and abilities can be identified and utilised within a group and given an appropriate role. Combining skills and energy with others increases our capacity many-fold. Integrating head, heart and hands empowers us to reach for our potential.

ICON: *An integrated system composed of interlocking parts: people linking arms. Separately they are meaningless but together they become significant.*

PROVERB: *Many hands make light work. Moving a wardrobe by yourself can be impossible, with two or three people it is achievable. Together we have power to move mountains.*

Are there aspects of my life I can bring together?

Which of my friends could I introduce to each other?

Are there different aspects of my community that I could help bring together?

9. Use small and slow solutions

Trees don't grow overnight. We need long-term thinking in permaculture design; putting the effort and time in the planning stages will get us further in the long run.

ICON: *Snail carrying spiral home on back. The spiral is capable of incremental growth – bit by bit.*

PROVERBS: *Slow and steady wins the race and the bigger they are, the harder they fall, remind us that quick, big fixes are not necessarily the best or long lasting.*

Don't try and do it all at once. Starting with realistic expectations keeps change steady and manageable. Pacing ourselves, setting small steps and bite size chunks can turn our visions into reality.

Crash dieting may seem to be working well initially but it is difficult to maintain and such diets often end up with more weight going back on when we start eating properly again. Small and slow changes to our diets and eating habits for instance will increase our health and vitality and shift more weight in the long run than crash dieting.

When we are dealing with other people working towards win/win solutions can take more time in the short term but will provide better outcomes in the long term.

Is there a small step in the right direction I could take today?

Where am I likely to trip up if I go too fast?

10. Use and value diversity

Diverse systems are more resilient and stable. If we have a monocrop then we could lose it all to a disease; having a multitude of crops means we can carry some loss. By having at least three ways of meeting each important need we are safeguarding ourselves from losing everything.

When working in groups we can recognise and incorporate everyone's innate talents and abilities, providing us with a wider range of possibilities than if we were all thinking the same. Acknowledgement is needed of others' strengths and weaknesses and different ways of thinking and behaving.

ICON: *A humming bird sipping nectar from a flower illustrates nature's biodiversity allowing many species to fill different niches within the same habitat.*

PROVERB: *Don't put all your eggs in one basket emphasises the dangers of relying too heavily on one thing. Having contingency plans in place can protect us against loss.*

How many roles do I have?

Can I create a diversity of activities?

What areas of my life would benefit from more diversity?

11. Use and value edges and the marginal

The interface between two ecosystems is the edge; it is an active and productive space. Edges are not sharply defined boundaries in nature: a forest perimeter peters out gradually, a riverbank blends into the field, the sea moves with the tides. These fuzzy edges are dynamic places of interest that share and amalgamate characteristics from each of the adjoining places, as well as having a distinctive ecosystem with its own creatures.

We naturally find, use and create fuzzy edges in our lives, like gradually fading out when singing a lullaby to a baby.

We learn most when we are at the edge of our comfort zone. This *stretch zone* is dynamic and productive. By being aware of our boundaries we can gently stretch ourselves into the new. Being open to other viewpoints and ways of doing things we allow new information in and expand our knowledge base. Being conscious of times we are on an edge, then appreciating it for its characteristics, allows us to be brave and challenge ourselves, perhaps leading us to new and exciting possibilities.

ICON: *Shows a world defined by edges, day and night (sunset or sunrise), land and sky, natural and built, soil and water.*

PROVERB: *Don't think you are on the right track just because it is a well-beaten path. This illustrates how the most obvious is not always the most important or correct. There are many unsustainable habits that are commonplace in our society such as putting waste food in landfill. Just because everyone else does it, doesn't mean there aren't preferred, viable alternatives.*

Where are the edges of my comfort zone?

How can I expand these limits?

How can I reach out to people on the edges of society?

12. Creatively use and respond to change

On bare thin soil nature will quickly colonise, with pioneer plants. These plants often have the characteristics of being hardy, producing lots of leaf litter and setting seed quickly. These improve conditions for plants that need more shade and soil, and barren fields can eventually become forest. This process is called natural succession. Groups or settlements will have a natural succession and flow of people over time, from the hardy pioneers to whole communities.

ICON: *The butterfly. Change is inevitable for us, just as the caterpillar has changed to a pupa and then a butterfly.*

Change is inevitable and often beyond our control, influence and even comprehension – how we deal with it is important. We need to be flexible and adaptable, building skills that enable us to adjust to situations. Instead of resisting change we can consciously observe and explore it, seeking the gifts it brings. When circumstances shift we can be curious as to 'now what' and trust and reflect on how we can learn and grow. From non-attachment to the past or present we can be open to new possibilities in the future. In top-down thinking there is a tendency to change too much too quickly. Before changing anything observe first and think hard – this links back to the first principle *observe and interact*.

PROVERB: *Vision is not seeing things as they are but as they will be.* This relates to the first principle: how we view things is important. We can use our imagination to vision our lives and the world as we would like.

How can I use the change for my advantage?

Where and how am I resisting change?

What gifts did the last big change in my life give me?

What do I vision for my future?

Systems thinking

Scientists have spent many decades looking at the world to find the basic building blocks of life, the 'stuff' that the world is made of. They looked at individual parts or things and often ignored the connections between them. Although many advances were made there still remained large gaps in the understanding of the complexity of the world. This brought about a shift in thinking: looking at things as wholes and the relationships between them. From this, Austrian biologist Ludwig von Bertalanffy founded systems theory, which he described as a 'way of seeing'.[4] It moves us from thinking about 'stuff' and 'what' the universe is made of, to the 'process' and 'how' the universe is made.

In *Thinking in Systems*, Donella Meadows describes a system as "a set of things – people, cells, molecules, or whatever – interconnected in such a way that they produce their own pattern of behaviour over time."[5]

Properties of systems

Systems occur in all parts of the universe, from biological systems within our bodies, to social systems and entire ecosystems. There are four key properties[6] that all systems hold regardless of their size and complexity.

(1) Each system has emergent properties

We cannot understand any system by seeking to comprehend each component. When elements interact with each other there is a flow of energy between them, perhaps in the form of nutrients, water, food, or information. Synergy is when the sum of the whole system is greater than the sum of its parts: 1 + 1 = 3.

We have the individual elements and we also have the relationship that adds further complexity and characteristics. Many parents will identify with having to manage not only the demands of each child but also the dynamic between them, which can create more work. The whole is not predictable from looking at the parts, because we do not know what the relationship and flow of energy is between them or how that will influence each part. From this synergy of interactions new properties will emerge. We cannot predict the wetness of water from looking at oxygen and hydrogen molecules separately. From neurons, consciousness and creativity emerge. The number of possible relationships increases exponentially with the number of parts.

(2) Systems can self-stabilise

Systems have the capacity to stay the same. They will tend towards equilibrium, a baseline of functioning. This is achieved through negative feedback. For example our bodies will maintain a body temperature of approximately 37 degrees. When the temperature goes outside of these limits, either above or below, signals will be sent and the body will react by either cooling or heating the body. The temperature will come within the limits after a bit of sweating or shivering and the signals will be turned off. This kind of feedback is also known as self-stabilising or balancing feedback. Systems need to be open to receiving the feedback. For ourselves we need to keep our senses and awareness open, otherwise we will miss information.

When there are frequent fluctuations it is like riding a bike with constant adjustments to keep the system in 'dynamic equilibrium'.

(3) Systems can evolve in complexity

Systems can evolve through self-organisation in response to changes in the environment. Systems are not static, they are dynamic and ever-changing. When a group of people come together they self-organise, creating more complex relationships and flows. A garden develops an intricate web of connections.

Self-organisation is evident in a swimming pool, where people adapt to each other's movements, and the comings and goings of other swimmers.

(4) Each system is a holon

A holon is a system that is whole in its own right and part of a larger system. They are living systems within living systems. A lichen is a system that is part of the system of the tree, which is part of the woodland, and this too is part of the wider bioregion, continuing to include weather systems and the entire planet. Our people systems are built up in the same way: we have our individual systems that might be part of a family system, a street, a neighbourhood, a town, country, all the way to a global system. We are in more than one system at any time. We might be part of the family system and the workplace, community group and neighbourhood. Each other member will also be part of more than one group demonstrating how everyone and everything is ultimately connected in some way.

The most marvellous characteristic of some complex systems is their ability to learn, diversify, complexify, evolve. The capacity of a system to make its own structure more complex is called **self organisation.**

DONELLA MEADOWS[7]

. . . .

Systems are nestled within each other like stories within stories, flowing, unfolding and expanding.

Elements are systems in their own right and systems don't have borders. But to facilitate thinking we artificially place boundaries and name things 'systems' or 'elements' depending on the appropriateness of scale and the context.

Hope for the Great Turning

These four properties give us confidence that the Great Turning can happen:

1. We don't know what emergent properties there might be from many people coming together to participate in the Great Turning. It may take just one extra person to create a majority to create an Earth culture; not just in terms of numbers but effects.
2. Feedback from the actions of the industrial growth culture is causing a rethink of behaviours in some places.
3. As the community of people coming together for the Great Turning grows, our systems, tools and skills for earthcare and peoplecare will evolve and develop in complexity.
4. As everything is connected all of our positive actions will have ripples elsewhere.

Resilience in ecosystems

If one element of the system is not working then the whole system is affected. An ecosystem that is adaptable and flexible and is receptive and responsive to feedback will be more resilient.

Resilience is the capacity of an ecosystem to tolerate disturbance or change without collapsing. This does not imply that the ecosystem has to return to its original state; it will have the ability to recover, adjust and bounce forward to a new state rather than back.

Allowing systems to demonstrate their own evolution

In practical terms what does it mean to allow a system to demonstrate its own evolution? As permaculturists we set up systems within our designs. A system is an association of elements that together perform a function. We are either setting up new systems or looking to improve what is already there. We are setting up conditions that allow the system to grow in complexity. We are likely to be trying to increase productivity and obtain yields.

We need to allow systems to grow in the direction they want to, and follow the course that is natural to them, rather than imposing this from the outside. An acorn can grow into an oak tree; we can't change this or determine its growth pattern but we can help by protecting and feeding it. Systems often exceed the expectations of the designer as unique properties emerge. We can monitor what is needed for growth and productivity and what might be limiting them. When something is limiting, we may need to wait for balance and a natural solution to occur, and *let nature take its course*. Or it may be appropriate to intervene. The system needs to be allowed to respond to feedback: intervening too early can inhibit the system's inherent ability to self-organise.

If we think about the swimming pool analogy again, the swimmers organise themselves within the pool, but the staff might create some conditions that make that easier: by opening and closing lanes, restricting the number of people or the time allowed in the pool. This might evolve over time with changes to opening hours or times for different people. The staff would just be dealing with conditions and wouldn't actually be involved with the swimmers directly unless of course there was the need.

The philosophy behind permaculture is one of working with, rather than against, nature: ... of looking at systems in all their functions, rather than only asking one yield of them: and of allowing systems to demonstrate their own evolutions.

Bill Mollison[5]

When the systems we are talking about are people systems then this 'allowing' means giving responsibility and ownership to the people involved. It is allowing them to reach for their potential and to constantly rethink what this might be. To stand back and observe rather than try and influence is the aim.

When we dictate our viewpoints and try and control the direction of growth it can be oppressive. When the West imposes its routes for development on indigenous cultures it is interrupting their own natural course of evolution. When animals are bred simply for yields, diseases and dysfunctions are more prevalent. We are forcing evolution to go at an unnatural speed or in a direction that it doesn't necessarily want to go.

We can take this to philosophical extremes with regards to allowing systems to demonstrate their own evolution and never do anything. On the ground, what it means is to observe first, and to think before intervening. Long-term responsibility for our intervention needs to be part of the thinking.

Systems within the human body

Within the human body there are several major systems, and other minor ones each with different functions and various components that work together to fulfil them. In permaculture design we move from finding out about the functions or needs – what are we trying to achieve with the design? We then think about what systems could fulfil these needs and then what components or elements the systems could consist of.

We saw from the properties of systems that they are holons and exist as whole in themselves and part of a bigger whole. In our bodies the lungs are part of the respiratory system and a system in themselves, composed of bronchioles, which are made of different cells, and can also be considered as one organ or element within a system.

Some of these elements are part of more than one system; the mouth for example is part of the respiratory and digestive system. The systems serve different functions of the body, and are composed of elements that communicate with each other to provide the function efficiently. The systems also interact with each other, to make a bigger whole – a person.

Systems in this book

There are systems within this book, interrelated and separate. They consist of separate elements that work together to fulfil the functions. Together they make the whole of the book. The systems could be seen as metaphors for those in the human body.

The ethics are the heart. The principles are the blood, transporting nutrients. The activities are the muscles, allowing for movement and stretching. The illustrations are like the senses, giving rapid communication. The quotes and poems draw in the emotional body. The design web is the framework, the skeleton providing support and protection. The interviews have provided food and nourishment. And the breath has been the interdisciplinary work, the fuzzy edge of sharing. The words are the skin, holding it all together. You, the reader, are the next generation, integrating this knowledge with your own unique skills and experiences and taking it forward.

The elements within each system relate not only to the other elements of their system, but also to the other elements around them. An activity relates to all the other activities as well as the text in the chapter. How well it relates will depend on where it is, amongst other factors. In this way the book itself is a living example of permaculture design.

Nature knows best how to make these connections. Linking things up in this way is thinking and acting like an ecosystem, and is the essence of permaculture design.

CHAPTER 3

Design

IT IS ONE thing to vision a positive
future, it is another to know the steps
and feel empowered to get there.
The different aspects of design given in this chapter are tools for us to
use in design work and provide us with varied ways of achieving insights.
The design web in the last section provides a cohesive framework for
attaining our goals.

We are all designers

Design can seem like an exclusive word, something that we somehow have to be
trained to do. On the contrary, we are all innate designers. When I ask the question
on courses "who has designed something before?" only a few
will say they have. I then ask who has planned the layout of
their living room. Mostly everyone has at some time and they
use criteria such as the resources they have, flow of people
through the space, activities in the room and the location of
certain items in relation to others, such as sofa and fireplace.
All these factors are taken into account on an intuitive level
and a design or plan arises. This type of designing is known
as black box designing – where the process is not transparent. Our lives are filled
with design opportunities from planning our day to running projects, organising
fitness programmes to revision timetables. Most of these we do without recognising
ourselves as designers.

*Design is putting together what
we have in order to deliver the
values we want.*
EDWARD DE BONO[1]

From understanding nature's lessons of principles, systems and patterns we
have already increased our ability to make more informed decisions and lifestyle
choices. Permaculture design is an open box framework that pulls these all together
in methodical steps towards our goals.

Why design?

Designing is like planning a journey; we are more likely to get there if we know where
we are going. The more information we have, the more effective the expedition. When
our design is a transparent process we are able to engage others. It saves us time,
energy and mistakes. By applying a step-by-step method and organising ourselves we

can minimise any feelings of overwhelm. A design can inspire action and be a vehicle for manifesting our visions.

What is design?

In its simplest form design has 3 steps:

1. Observing where you are
2. Awareness of where you want to get to
3. Identifying the steps to get there

There are of course complexities to add to this picture that we will come to in due course. When travelling we would research the costs and time implications of the different options and who our companions might be. We might listen to the radio as we drive to check on traffic jams and choose an alternative route. We could have contingency plans in place for delays.

Observation

Observation is an on-going process throughout design and in life. It is essential for us to observe so that we know where we are, what effect changes have had and how we and other people are feeling. Observation widens our awareness and happens through all of our senses: seeing, listening, feeling, tasting and smelling.

It is easy to look without seeing. Watching the world zoom by from a moving car or in miniature behind a television screen, we can forget how to see the detail and observe in wonder like a child. How can we see the patterns in nature, or the person behind the face? How can we reflect on our own progress and be open to feedback?

Most of the time when we see we also interpret, we make assumptions that lead our thinking. Can we perceive like a child? As if we don't know the story behind what we see, as if we don't know the creature buzzing from flower to flower is a bee collecting nectar to make honey, or that the yellow flower will turn into a puffball of seeds to float on the wind. It is a skill to see our observations in the present, without imagining the past, predicting the future or thinking we know the outcomes of our adventures: to see without judging or thinking what we see is static, true or unchangeable. It is important for us to think about how, what and why we observe at the outset. The initial observations are necessary for us to tune into what is going on. It is essential to start our journey knowing where we are. Through these observations we can gain a deeper understanding of what is needed with the design. Slowing down and opening our eyes and ears begins the process. A useful skill to develop is the ability to stand back from what is happening and just observe. Putting our judgements and assumptions to one side enables us to perceive more fully, with objectivity and perspective.

One of the challenges we may encounter both when we are designing for ourselves and for others, is that initially when we open up to observing what is going on, we can become aware of a problem previously hidden from view. When we bring it into focus this may provoke feelings of guilt or embarrassment. Other people may be annoyed with us for allowing the problem to get so bad. It may seem like a step backwards at first and we feel like we are worse off because we now know how bad things are. However, in the long run it is an entirely necessary step.

As we progress in the design, observation allows us to receive the necessary feedback from our actions. We can plan specific times when we stand back from our work and reflect on our progress. We can mark milestones or have regular times to check–in, like taking a photo from the same spot every month to see the change in the garden. Through conscious observation we may see changes that might otherwise be invisible to us.

During the process of designing we can be observing ourselves (and others) by asking 'How do I feel?', 'What's going on inside of me?', or 'What are my energy levels?'.

Observation is as much about paying attention to the periphery as focusing on the centre. Seeing who is being left out of discussions, what's happening at the edges of the day in my family, where thoughts are wandering off to… These will provide us with useful information, and perhaps point us to a problem on the horizon that we might then be able to avert.

If we don't take time to observe, we are in danger of heading off in the wrong direction, trying to fix something that isn't broken or neglecting what needs attention. We miss important clues as to what is appropriate, and simple ways to improve the quality of the lives around us. By observing where our energy leaks are, we can design ways to improve the channels for energy, flowing to a bigger vision.

When we begin our design we cannot predict what the emergent properties might be, like forming a band and getting a magical sound. Keeping open to observation allows us to be responsive to this.

Biotime diaries

Biotime diaries are a way of collecting observations that allow us to look for patterns. Recording observations over time will give a better insight into why things are the way they are. While we are recording the data we do so as objectively as possible: without assumptions, judgment or manipulating the information. We can try not to make assumptions about why things happen, and look for relationships at a later time.

Biotime diaries were originally used to note natural phenomena, such as rainfall, temperature, the day the first daffodil came out or the last frost of the year. If this data is collected over a period of years it can be used for comparisons. Expressions such as *oak before ash, you'll get a splash, ash before oak you're in for a soak*, arose from making the connections between which leaves come out first and the rainfall that summer.

If you use biotime diaries for yourself on a daily basis, you can note your energy levels, the food you eat, the quality and quantity of sleep, your moods, concentration, confidence or any other factors that are relevant to you. You might want to note the quality of interaction with family or friends. Find a simple way of recording these, so that the diary is easy to maintain. After time this can start to show connections between things both internal and external that we may have not previously linked.

	M	T	W	Th	F	Sa	Su
Food	good	Med	poor	v.good	. . .	. . .	. . .
Energy	6/10	4/10	3/10	6/10	. . .	. . .	. . .
Sleep	8hr	7hr	6hr	7hr	. . .	. . .	. . .
Mood	☺	😐	☹	😐	. . .	. . .	. . .

Gary Finch, a permaculture teacher, started a biotime diary as part of a design for his own life while doing his permaculture diploma. He records the feeling he had when he woke, the quantity and quality of food, exercise, mind–body activities such as tai chi, his energy through the day, the amount of water he drank and concludes with his thoughts for the day. He also notes any excessive consumption, things he is not doing, zone 00 activities (see page 43) and anything towards any of the three ethics. Not wanting to do all of this every day, he decided to do it every nine days, so that he would not incur any bias from doing it the same day of the week.

After doing this for over a year he has noticed various connections between his eating and exercise patterns and energy levels. For example, when he eats sandwiches for lunch he has less energy during the afternoon and after work than if he eats just fruit during the day. He has observed that when he keeps properly rehydrated through the day his energy levels are better and his emotional health is more balanced. He has also been able to observe that the amount of exercise he has is more influential on his energy levels than the amount of sleep.

He has recently evolved his system and is now recording observations with the phases of the moon, rather than every nine days. This is easier to remember and he is hoping to get interesting information about how he is affected by the moon cycles and the seasons. He records them on A4 sheets, which have space to record four years' worth of information on them, so he will be able to compare one year to the next, enabling him to identify bigger cycles within his life.

He says, "Doing the diary has allowed me to put theory into action. I can observe my habits and the impact they have on my life. I record what happens if I change my behaviours. I can then make choices about what I do and take self-responsibility. If I am feeling low I can think about why this might be. I have enjoyed making observation a habit in my life."

ACTIVITY: BIOTIME DIARY

Keep a diary for a week recording your energy levels on a scale of 1–10 in the morning, afternoon and evening, and the food that you have for breakfast, lunch and dinner and any snacks. You may want to add other relevant information, but not more than you can manage to record for the week.

At the end, have a look back over the week and see if any patterns or connections emerge. You may decide to continue this and add further information.

Spirals of erosion and abundance

Our aim in permaculture is to turn spirals of erosion into spirals of abundance and productivity. This can be applied to human systems as well as natural ones.

Erosion

All around us we are faced with problems: little ones, big ones and ones that can seem insurmountable. The world is becoming more and more complex around us and we can feel smaller and smaller in the face of it all. One of the ways of identifying what is happening around us is to think in terms of erosion. Erosion is usually associated with natural resources such as soil, but it is the gradual destruction, reduction or weakening of anything. It describes something that has been useful becoming less useful.

Not all of these things are eroding everywhere, but generally around us we can see erosion of:

- Natural resources – soil, forests, clean air, water, biodiversity.
- Social structures – relationships, communities, public transport, traditional wisdom, care of the elderly.
- Personal capacity – knowledge, practical skills, experience, self-love, freedom from debt, connection with nature, time to be.

Some of these things could be regained with the right strategies and resources; others will be lost forever.

We don't usually just wake up one day and find a big problem that needs solving. More often than not there is a gradual worsening of the situation. This slipping away from the richness there once was taken for granted or only perceived from the periphery. There can be a major event in our lives or in the news that brings loss to our full attention but it generally doesn't come from nowhere, there has been a build up of circumstances.

Problems interact with each other in the same way systems do. To make effective change we need to know the cause of the problems. This is a far more complex issue and sometimes we may be looking at the symptoms rather than the causes. Some factors initiate the erosion and others just perpetuate it; the effect is cyclical. These are known as spirals of erosion or vicious cycles.

Spirals of erosion

Each revolution of the cycle returns us to a place slightly worse than the last. With this spiral of apathy, the overall health, energy, confidence and self-esteem of the person are being eroded.

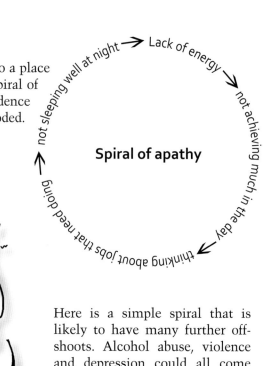

Spiral of apathy

Interpersonal

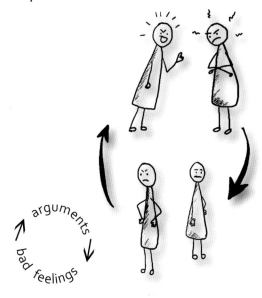

Here is a simple spiral that is likely to have many further off-shoots. Alcohol abuse, violence and depression could all come into the picture and have further ramifications. The negative effects are cumulative with each cycle. These spirals can become routine; one thing follows another and we come to the same place, making a pattern of behaviour, which we keep following as we are creatures of habit.

There are larger scale spirals of erosion as well. One in society is

Globally we see the spiral of

Symptoms versus causes

When we experience a headache the pain is actually the external symptom and not the root cause. The headache could be caused by too much sun, dehydration, stress, an allergic reaction, or a much more serious problem. Taking a headache pill may mask the pain and provide relief but this only treats the symptom. Looking for the root cause and treating this could provide relief *and* prevent the problem reoccurring.

Spirals of abundance

What we would all like in our lives are spirals of abundance where each time we go round the spiral, our well-being and productivity increases. The accumulation of yields provides further momentum and there are knock-on benefits creating further spirals of abundance.

The spirals of erosion oppo-site could look like this if they were turned to spirals of abundance.

The spiral of apathy turning to a spiral of achievement:

The spiral of argu-ments becoming a spiral of communication:

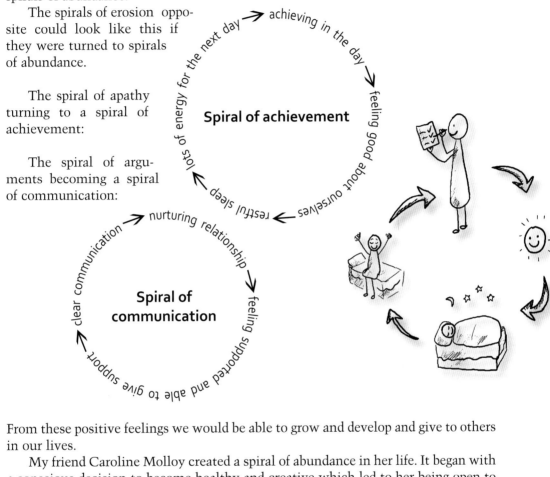

From these positive feelings we would be able to grow and develop and give to others in our lives.

My friend Caroline Molloy created a spiral of abundance in her life. It began with a conscious decision to become healthy and creative which led to her being open to learn about permaculture. This provided a community of like-minded people who further supported her to become more healthy. This pathway has led her to training to become a permaculture teacher, bringing the skills from her previous work in the trade union movement.

Points of intervention and transformation

We have identified the erosion that is occurring and the abundance we would like to have; we now need to think about how to turn one spiral into another.

The first time I felled a tree my first reaction on trying was 'no way have I got the brute force needed to do this'. Luckily my chainsaw teacher was on hand, not for any physical help but to guide and reassure me that it was achievable – by me – I just needed to find the 'sweet spot'; the point at which it was possible. By finding the exact position and using the momentum of the tree rocking back and forth to do the work for me I was able to bring the tree down without breaking my back. Likewise to break these spirals of erosion we need to find the 'sweet spot', the point at which we can intervene and start to turn the spiral. There are also likely to be places where it is particularly difficult to break the spiral; for example trying to stop it dead in the middle of a blazing row is likely to just inflame the other person more! Attacking the root of the problem is ideal in the long run but it may be advantageous to soften other places first.

The idea of leverage points is ... embedded in legend: the silver bullet; the trim tab; the miracle cure; the secret passage; the magic password; the single hero who turns the tide of history; the nearly effortless way to cut through or leap over huge obstacles.

DONELLA MEADOWS[2]

Just as I used the energy of the tree rocking to bring it down, we can use the energy of the spiral to transform it: after an argument, when everyone has cooled down you can use the situation to express true feelings and come to a deeper understanding.

After observation we can think of many ways and places that could be turning points, and evaluate which ones seem appropriate for the people and the situation. It may be that two or more could be used simultaneously.

Possible points of intervention

Each of these actions either deflects one of the stages of the spiral of erosion or provides us with a link to the spiral of abundance, or both.

Turning a spiral of apathy into a spiral of achievement:

- Set small goals
- Write a list for the next day
- Get support from a friend
- Increase energy with yoga, exercise or walking
- Do something before bed to help sleep such as drinking chamomile tea or writing down your thoughts
- Achieve one task before bed

Turning a spiral of arguments into a spiral of communication:

- See the bigger picture
- Agree to disagree
- Set agreements on how to discuss
- Argue constructively and respectfully not abusively
- Make interruption-free space to listen to each other's feelings
- Proactively work on the good feelings

Design

Observing and identifying spirals of erosion in our lives is the first step to turning them around. Sometimes the spiral turns slowly and we may not even be aware of the gradual effects that are occurring. Keeping a biotime diary will help to build awareness.

From identifying points of intervention we can then use other design methods to identify resources and opportunities that can aid us. These points of intervention may not be immediate fixes; like with felling a tree, there is some rocking back and forth and it can take a while before it is committed to the change. Our actions may initially just slow down the spiral; for example there could be longer gaps between each argument. This application of the brakes allows us to put more things in place to further turn the spiral. Conversely sometimes a little nudge in the right direction can be all it takes to turn it around.

We have done the three steps of design:

- Recognise what the spiral of erosion is
- Vision the spiral of abundance we would like
- Identify steps that lead us from one to the other

We can design ways to transform our problems into spirals of growth, regeneration and well-being in all aspects of our lives.

Limiting factors

Invisible and visible limiting factors

The next complexity of design arises in making the steps to achieve our spiral of abundance. There are likely to be things that stop us from immediately making the interventions. Limiting factors are any leaks or blocks in the system that slow us down or stop us getting where we want to get to. Anything that limits growth and productivity can be called a 'limiting factor'. Where is the dripping tap? Where could the energy flow better? It is through identifying limiting factors that we can assess which areas we need to focus on in our design. The leaks need to be plugged and the blocks overcome.

Limiting factors can be physical or invisible. When we are thinking about land it is easy to identify physical limiting factors: climate, soil, size of land and aspect all affect the productivity and dictate the foci of the design. The invisible limiting factors often come from the people who are gardening on the land – their energy, skills or communication within the group. External limiting factors might include red tape from

officials, land tenure or planning permission. Both external and internal limiting factors need to be identified and resolved.

Money and time are the most often mentioned limiting factors. "If only I had the money I would…" "I don't have the time to…" While this may be true in many cases there are also many situations where it is not time or money that is the fundamental thing stopping us, but confidence, motivation, skills, support, inspiration, momentum, processes, moods or space.

Until the base limiting factors are addressed we may move forward but not as much as we would like. We sometimes fix one higher up and wonder why things are still not shifting. Like a leaky barrel, we need to address the lower-down limiting factors to stop the energy leaking out and make progress. If we manage to access money but time is still limiting us we could look at how we could use this resource to minimise our time constraints, for example by employing someone or paying for childcare.

It is the invisible limiting factors that often slow us down the most, mainly because of our blindness to them. Within relationships, work places and any groups there are invisible limiting factors such as communication, decision-making processes, group dynamics and conflict that greatly diminish effectiveness. There may be other distractions that limit us by upsetting our focus and pulling us off course. Honesty is needed to identify all the limiting factors. When we know them, we can design ways to work around them or to minimise their impacts.

Limiting factors are not static, they can change over time. In the garden they can change seasonally: in the spring we can be limited with the number of pots we have to sow seeds; in the summer water can be our limit; in the autumn we can run out of space; in the winter, sunlight and warmth limit growth. They can change more quickly than this as well.

Addressing limiting factors is like strengthening the weakest link in a chain – another link now becomes the weakest one – or peeling back the layers of an onion, another limiting factor appears, and it may make us cry!

Building blocks of design

When we do a risk assessment for an activity it is not to deem it too risky to do but so that we can work around the risks and find strategies to deal with them if they happen. Likewise the aim of identifying the limiting factors is not to shatter our confidence or motivation for doing the project but to build in ways to dissolve them or lessen or remove their impact. We don't need to develop a preoccupation with our limits.

When we have established what the limiting factors are, these then become the foundations – the building blocks for design. The more candid and explicit the limits are the more real the solution is. The aim of the design is to minimise, side step or negate altogether the influence of the limiting factors to allow more potential for growth and productivity.

When friends, Helen and Jim Morris-Ridout were building their home there were plenty of opportunities for them to confront their limiting factors and design around them. Helen reflected, "Without our training in permaculture we may well have given up at times. But we knew there were solutions to every problem we encountered and we just had to find a way around them." One of their biggest limiting factors was the challenge of how to balance family life and still make progress on the building. Jim said, "For me it wasn't an option to either not see my children or not get on with creating our home, both had to happen." He resolved this by finding jobs that he could do with his sons around and teaching them safe ways of using tools for themselves. His eldest son loves carpentry and is more proficient with tools then most seven year olds.

Scenario	Limiting factor	Design needs/solutions
Community garden	Money	Fundraising, selling plants
Exercise routine	Motivation and stamina	Get friend involved for company
Wanting promotion at work	Not getting along with your boss	Developing relationship with boss
Community group	People to get involved	Awareness raising event
Transition town group	Group dynamics	Effective meeting techniques

ACTIVITY: DOING THE ACTIVITIES IN THE BOOK

What may stop me from doing the activities, or somehow limit the potential productivity of them?

What are my limiting factors?

Everyone will have their own limiting factors. Some examples may be understanding, time, lack of confidence, motivation, seeing the relevance or resistance to change.

There may be things inside of yourself or external influences pulling you off in a different direction. Dig a bit deeper here and ask yourself – what else may get in my way? There may be concerns that you have about change that are underlying your resistance. Or it could be practical considerations such as reading the book in bed at night.

Look back at your aim for reading this book and think about what could stand in the way of you reaching it.

For each of the limiting factors and concerns think of at least one way in which they could be worked around. Then decide which strategies you could put in place now, and which ones you can use later if and when you need to.

Zones

Zoning is a conceptual design tool used for managing our own energies. Radiating out from the centre are zones zero to five. Zone 00 is the self at the centre. On a land based design, elements that are in need of most attention are placed nearer to the home and yourself than those that need less frequent attention. Placement varies according to how often they need visiting or how often we need to visit them, with those that need to be checked every day closest to ourselves, saving us energy. Zone 0 is our home, zone 1 is the immediate garden, 2 and 3 would be main crops that need less harvesting and maintenance and larger areas of pasture. Zone 4 is managed woodland. Zone 5 is the wilderness zone that we would only visit to learn lessons from nature and not to interfere.

In our homes or office we can use this concept on a smaller scale to assess our energy flow. The idea is that items closer to where we need them will get more attention paid to them. Just as we water plants more frequently that are right outside our back door, urgent and important tasks are more likely to get done when within our sight. If we want to play the guitar more, having it close to hand will make it more accessible. Conversely we can relocate items to a further zone if we want to focus less on them.

For instance we will reach for chocolate biscuits less often if they are on a high shelf out of the way than if they are right next to the teapot. Having to actively get the TV out makes us pause and think about whether we actually want to watch something or are turning it on out of habit.

ACTIVITY: DISTANCING THE DISTRACTION

Think of two things in your current lifestyle, one that you would like to do more of, and one you would like less of. Now think about where these things are in relation to you and your movements through the day. You may have the answers already, or perhaps you need to observe yourself over a few days.

Whatever you would like less of is a distraction that you can remove or distance. If this isn't possible find some barrier, or way of making it more difficult to get to; this could be as simple as a cloth over the television. This is a way of breaking our patterns of behaviour.

To test this theory out, move something from one of the cupboards in your kitchen that you use frequently; this could be the oil for cooking, wooden spoons or the tea jar. Over the next few days observe how often you open the cupboard it was in to reach for it without even thinking. (You may want to let your other house members in on the experiment as they will also be reaching into the same cupboards and may get annoyed!)

Now, think about what you would like to encourage in your life, reading, playing music or eating healthy snacks. Where can you place these so you can visit them more easily?

Zones of people

Zones can also help us to map out our connections with other people in our lives. Each zone has defining characteristics, although they are not fixed and do not have distinct edges.

Zone 00 – ourselves.

Zone 0 – partners, spouses, children, people we live with, people we see most regularly.

Zone 1 – friends and other family.

Zone 2 – neighbours, work colleagues, acquaintances, schools, clubs, where there can be common bonds and understanding, or assumptions and motivations.

Zone 3 – community of interests and locality, friends of friends, shared cultures.

Zone 4 – national.

Zone 5 – global – the wilderness – people we are unlikely to meet; this zone contains the largest number of people.

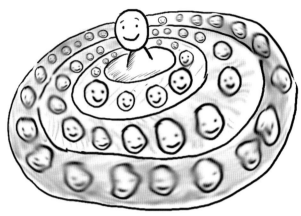

Which zone people are in, shifts over time. People are not always in the zone you would like them to be; some closer and some further away. How we manage our relationship with these people may depend on which zone they are in. Our range of peoplecare skills and ability to relate to people within each zone varies. Some of us have compassion and understanding for people in zone 5 and can dedicate our life's work to people in other countries, many of whom we will never meet. Others spend their energies supporting a close-knit family.

Zone 00

This is the place we have most impact. We are central to all that we do and if we do not manage our own energy well then this will have a ripple effect through the other zones. We need to be in good working order to have most effect. It is within our inner landscape that we can cultivate compassion, love, understanding and motivation; from this we can nurture and encourage others.

Inputs and outputs

All systems require inputs and produce outputs. The inputs are the needs of the system, and the outputs its products or yields. In a natural system the inputs come from the sun and the rain. The outputs are used either within the system or by another living system. Leaf litter for example is incorporated into the soil by organisms, and hence it is a local, sustainable resource.

If the inputs required are not met then work is needed to meet those needs. A garden may not have enough rainfall so work is required to water it. Domesticated animals are not able to forage for themselves and need feeding.

Unmet inputs = work

If outputs of a system are not used they become waste or pollution. Leaves falling on tarmac are not used and become pollution, manure from battery farms is not used in the system and is a pollutant.

Unused outputs = pollution

Everything we do has inputs and outputs associated with it. For example, we have to put time, energy, planning and money into a business. If these things cannot be provided by the system itself then work is required to meet the need. If we need a website design and we don't have the skills, then we need to bring this in from the outside.

We would also get things out of the business: wages, products or services. Outputs of our actions can either be yields that we can and want to harvest such as friendships, connections and job satisfaction. There may however be unwanted outputs such as stress, wasted time and material waste. If we have outputs that are not used or wanted then they become pollutants.

When we set up a new project, garden, business or home, we will put more in initially and our yields will be lower. Over time we will be aiming to increase our desirable outputs and decrease our inputs. In permaculture we adopt the 80:20 principle. At the beginning of a design 80% of our time and resources are put in with the planning and set up and 20% is put into the maintenance of the system. For example, if when planting trees and perennial crops, time, care and thought is taken about which species to use and when and where to plant them this effort is rewarded by good yields over time.

Examining our inputs and outputs for any given activity is a useful tool in evaluating where our energy is best placed. For any task or project we can ask: what are we putting in versus what we are getting out? This brings us to another principle, *minimum effort for maximum effect*. When deciding where to place our efforts, we look for the smallest action that will have the biggest change. An

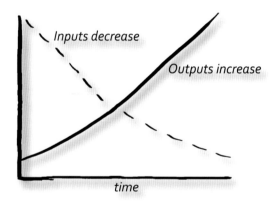

example of this might be if we are tidying our homes, we could spend a lot of energy tidying one shelf, or we could use the same energy and clear the floor making more of a noticeable difference. This isn't to say the shelf doesn't need doing later, but if limited energy is available, pick the action of most effect.

In order to decrease the inputs we can look for ways to meet these needs from within our systems. If we have a gap in our needs, they are either filled externally by work, or activity. Unmet needs can leave us with unwanted feelings and emotions and take us into a spiral of erosion.

To fulfil needs we have to design more elements into our system, replace them with elements that meet more needs or create more connections between elements.

In a family, work may be needed to care for or entertain children. There may also be an unused output of the children's energy, that if unused can bounce around the house being a noise pollutant. In order to deal with this, a good design would consider how outputs of one part of the system can be used by another part. Can we make connections between the children where the energy of one is used to entertain the other?

This leads us to two more ecological principles:

Multiple elements for important functions – or more simply – have back-ups. If something is important find more than one way of meeting this need. In this way if something breaks down or doesn't work then we have back-ups. This doesn't mean have three televisions, it means have three different ways of relaxing.

Many yields for every element – everything in your system does more than one thing. Having friends over for dinner for example meets the needs of eating, socialising and relaxing. If every thing fulfils three functions, then we need fewer things, more of our needs are met within the system, and there are less inputs from outside.

Design web

We now have all of the components to do more thorough designs. The design process is key within permaculture, to facilitate change and turn our ideas into reality. The design web is a framework created specifically for people-based designs. It is one interpretation of the design process. This is the process we will focus on although it is not the only way of approaching permaculture designs.

It can be used for a wide variety of designs, from our own personal health to our family life, from community groups to schools, from healthcare systems to international development projects. Whoever we are designing for is 'the client' or 'clients'. This may be ourselves, a family, group or organisation.

The web has 12 anchor points, each focusing on a different area to build up a detailed, holistic picture of where we want to go and how we are going to get there. The questions given here are general and open ended; they can be adapted to fit whatever you are designing.

Anchor points

VISION – allow yourself to dream and create goals

PAUSE – incorporate times of rest and rejuvenation

HELPS – identify the things that are going to help

REFLECTION – evaluate progress

LIMITS – identify the things that might block your path or keep it small or slow it down

APPRECIATION – focus on things to be thankful for

Design Web

PATTERNS – identify the helpful and unhelpful patterns

MOMENTUM – how to keep going

IDEAS – gather inspirations

ACTION – make a plan for getting things done

INTEGRATION – bring it all together

PRINCIPLES – look through the lens of each one

VISION
allow yourself to dream and create goals

What is my ideal?
What are the abundances I would like to create in my life?
What are my wildest dreams?

HELPS
identify the things that are going to help

What are my motivations for changing?
What resources do I have within me?
What external resources are available?

LIMITS
identify what blocks the path, what might keep it small or slow it down

What's holding me back?
What are my limiting factors?
Why would I not want to change?
What concerns do I have?

PATTERNS
identify helpful and unhelpful patterns

What are the current patterns of thinking, behaving and interacting?
What spirals of erosion can I identify?
What would a spiral of abundance look like?
What patterns from nature, other people or different activities could help within my design?
What patterns of success from another area of my life can I translate into my design?

IDEAS
gather inspirations

What creative, adventurous, wild and wacky ideas do I have?
What big, little, practical, routine ideas do I have?
What seeds of ideas do I have?

PRINCIPLES
look through the lens of each one

If I look through the lens of each principle what do I see?
What does it tell me about my current state?

What ideas does it give me about the direction I want to go in and how to get there?

INTEGRATION
bring it all together

How can I integrate the information already gathered?
What are my needs within the design?
What systems could be put in place to meet those needs?
What elements would each system be composed of?

ACTION
make a plan for getting things done

What am I going to do and when?
What resources do I need?
What yields and benefits am I going to get?

MOMENTUM
consider how to keep going

How am I going to maintain momentum?
How am I going to build and increase momentum?
What support might I need to keep moving towards my vision?

APPRECIATION
focus on things to be thankful for

What can I appreciate about myself?
What can I appreciate about other people and the world around me?
How do I feel supported at the moment?

REFLECTION
evaluate progress

What is the current situation?
What is going well?
What is challenging?

PAUSE
incorporate time for rest and rejuvenation

How can I recharge my batteries?
How can I make times of rest and quiet a built-in part of my design?
How can I rejuvenate myself?

These anchor points can be visited in the sequence appropriate for the design. After each anchor point there are many directions you could move in. Where to go next is governed in part by what arises in each step. The design can become an intuitive movement for the designer, or a dance between the designer, the clients and the design where one step naturally leads on to another. For example you may want to capture your *ideas* after spending some time *visioning*, or exploring *patterns* may lead you to think about the *limits.*

You probably don't know all of the answers to these questions at first; the answers may take time brewing. Your vision may be hazy at first, you may not be sure where you want to go, and so through revisiting it several times through the process you can add more detail and texture to it. You can dance in and out of stages without getting stuck waiting for something to feel complete before moving on, knowing that you can return when it feels right.

Solutions can emerge from any of the anchor points. While looking at our limiting factors it may become immediately apparent how to overcome them, or we could have inspiration from appreciation of ourselves.

Peoplecare is embedded within the process, including *Pause* for rest and *Appreciation* anchor points. Giving time and space to design is an act of support and nurturing.

Natural patterns

The design web follows a natural pattern. Webs spread the load, catch things, make connections, are strong, light and repairable and create lots of edge. The more steps are made, the more connections and resilience the design has.

All parts of the web could be connected with each other; this is a key difference between this and linear design processes. There is a lot of scope for seeing how one part of the design influences every other. Our *vision* sparks ideas, *limits* dictate our *actions*, and *appreciation* can provide *momentum*. We will look in more detail at these connections in the final part.

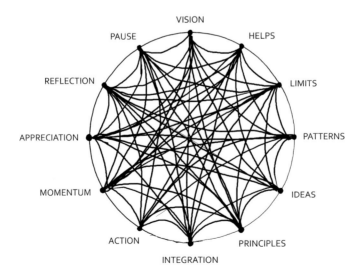

Once established, the design will catch skills and experience as well as the yields of the design itself. That is, we learn through doing and we increase our design skills for future designs, the more we reflect on the process the more we learn. Reflections can be harvested with sharing, group awareness and recording of the process.

A spider is aware of the vibrations in its web showing there is something caught. In order to make the most of our design we too need to be aware of the vibrations made. We could get so carried away with designing that we don't notice that there is already a yield. Observation is a constant throughout.

Phases of life

The design web also represents systems embedded within systems. Each anchor point is a holon, a system by itself; it is also part of a bigger system, the phases, which in turn are part of the whole design.

The anchor points are in four phases reflecting the phases of life we go through as a person.

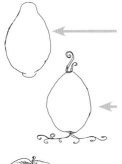

Growth phase: *Vision*, *Limits* and *Helps*; these are the anchor points of the child. The phase is represented by the seed, showing the potential and what is going to help or limit growth.

Exploratory phase: The next phase is of the apprentice, the young adult, learning, thinking and expressing. It is represented by the roots, reaching out, searching and exploring with *Patterns*, *Ideas* and *Principles*.

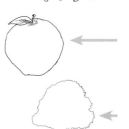

Productive phase: The adult stage of deciding, doing and producing is represented by the fruit, where we are looking for yields from our design in the anchor points of *Integration*, *Action* and *Momentum*.

Reflective phase: *Appreciation*, *Reflection* and *Pause* are the introspective and insightful stages of the elder, represented by the mature tree.

Design methods

As well as approaching each of the anchor points as a series of probing questions there are other tools we can use to gain insights. A lot of the activities are based on the anchor points, tailored to a specific issue. You will notice that some of them have more than one anchor point symbol with them showing how the anchor points can blend or follow on from each other. We will build up our toolbox of how to use the design web and then expand on each of these anchor points in the final part. We will look at how we can use different tools and methods when designing for ourselves, with other people, in larger systems or for other cultures in the following parts, alongside a real-life design.

PART 2: LOOKING DEEP INTO THE CENTRE

CHAPTER 4

Our internal landscape

The importance of zone 00
Observation of ourselves
Needs
Self-identity
Beliefs
Patterns
Edges and transitions

LOOKING DEEP INTO THE CENTRE

CHAPTER 6

Being at our best

Reaching our potential
Being effective
Our home environment
Being creative
Thinking tools
Right livelihoods
Real wealth
Empowerment and self leadership

CHAPTER 5

Health and well-being

Health and healing
Physical health
Emotional health
Healthy mind
Spiritual health

CHAPTER 4

Our internal landscape

THE PREVIOUS PART focused on how we can think about the world differently from a permaculture perspective. In this part we focus our attention inwards – looking deep into the centre of ourselves. For many people this is where the journey with permaculture really starts, with changes to our attitudes and thinking and opening up new possibilities.

Within these chapters are tools and techniques that release energy, build our capacity and embed permaculture thinking and design. They help us to recognise and use the resources we already have. There are plenty of activities here to build our experience of using the design tools. We are then able to apply them to other situations.

This first chapter focuses on ways in which we can connect and reflect upon our internal landscape, in particular our needs, beliefs and patterns.

The importance of zone 00

Self-care is vital on our pathway towards a positive future for all. It is tempting to see all that is going on in the world and want to try to save the planet, save humanity and generally put our energy into work outside of ourselves. There is plenty to be done, there is no denying it, and it can seem selfish to spend time caring for ourselves. However, if we don't care for ourselves, is someone else going to do it for us or is it going to get left undone?

We may not be paying attention to our own self-care because it feels self indulgent, or perhaps we are worried we will fall behind in our work. Whatever the justification the end result is that when we put ourselves last (or second) the time comes when our bodies or minds will scream for attention with resentment, illness and burnout. Giving all our time to others and seldom to ourselves is ultimately not personally sustainable.

The proverb *we can't pour from an empty jug* reminds us that we can only give if we have filled ourselves with energy. On aeroplanes we are instructed to put our own oxygen masks on first before assisting anyone else including our own children. We can be of no help to anyone else if we run out of oxygen.

Pippa Johns, a permaculture teacher and mother, spoke to me about how personal sustainability is built into her life, in everything she does including her relationships with her husband and children. It determines how she spends her days and ensures she builds in enough self-care time. Using design, her aim is to be thriving and growing as a person, developing and learning about herself. She checks in with herself and listens to her body and what her needs are in the moment.

In the long run, leaving yourself out of the equation is the most selfish thing you can do.

NANCY KLINE[1]

· · · · · · · · · · · · · · ·

We inspire through demonstration, our light kindles sparks in others. When we lead by doing and our actions are congruent with our words and values we motivate others on their journey. How we listen and respond to ourselves echoes how we listen and interact with other people. When we respect ourselves, others are more likely to respect us. Nurturing ourselves regularly gives signs of self worth and value, which increase our self-esteem. Learning about ourselves informs us about the world and other people; we learn empathy and can spend time listening to others and seeing their needs.

Serving people, taking care of creation and nurturing the spirit do not demand different courses of action. Service to the world and care of the soul are one and the same thing.

SATISH KUMAR[2]

· · · · · · · · · · · · · · ·

If we cannot change ourselves then how can we want or expect the rest of the world to alter? When we change one person in a relationship the dynamic shifts. We alone can transform ourselves and through this we can change the world. Our growth and development will alter the environment around us.

Self-care leads to caring for others, planetary care and care for other beings. We need to find a balance between productivity and self-care that allows us to be the best for the world and ourselves. Part of the work of the Great Turning is to see things differently and this work involves how we see ourselves. We need two wings to fly – our own inner sustenance and outer work in the world. Our inner work is for the collective as well; what we do for ourselves we do for the greater good.

Observation of ourselves

When we are attentive and responsive to ourselves and build up a balanced picture we are able to fit an integrated design to our lives. Solutions that come from within and are tailor made will be longer lasting.

Observing ourselves helps us to determine our own rhythms and to work more effectively. Keeping a biotime diary will provide us with indicators of our energy flows and influences on it. Taking time to read our inner landscape saves us from taking wrong turns or losing our way.

We can recognise our own early warning systems, such as the signs that show just before illness or losing our temper or other symptoms of our needs not being met. We can then apply the principle of *a stitch in time.* We start to see the connections and patterns, and any spirals of erosion that we may be caught in. We can look at our daily lives and see where we have energy leaks; this could be time, money or emotional energy.

Observation isn't just about noticing the problems: the positives in our lives are equally relevant, and we can also include a stocktake of our resources and helpful patterns in our life. We can become more aware of our internal and external resources and how we might put these to use. These are all part of the *helps* anchor point in the design web.

Not only is zone 00 the place of most influence, it is also the richest place for us to access the resources we need. We are our own greatest assets with talents and qualities that can be used in a multitude of ways. We all have thinking skills and proficiencies with people, technologies and ourselves. Transferable skills are ones that we can take from one situation and adapt and integrate with other skills in new situations. Employers are increasingly recognising that the expertise used to manage a household can be brought into the workplace.

Self-observation brings man to the realisation of the necessity of self-change. And in observing himself a man notices that self-observation itself brings about certain changes in his inner processes. He begins to understand that self-observation is an instrument of self-change, a means of awakening.

GREGOR IVANOVICH
GURDJIEFF[3]

. . . .

Observation activities can be carried out as and when we want to deepen our self-knowledge or to provide additional support for a situation. All art forms including painting, drawing, collage, sculpture, movement, dance and music provide access to our inner worlds.

These activities can all be adapted for use in focusing on different areas of life or our whole selves. For example, we will see how pattern recognition can help with thinking about transitions in our lives and for identifying learning patterns. The observation activities can show new perspectives, helping us see who we are in the world and the choices we have made. The more we use them the more we open up this channel of communication and become conscious of our own emotions and needs.

Linda McDermott, a yoga teacher, says, "Yoga encourages self awareness, this needs to filter into the whole of life not just on the yoga mat, from day to day, moment to moment. There is often the tendency to observe with judgement, to complain to oneself about the traits that we observe. Much of the work for me when I teach yoga is around helping people to truly love themselves – to have compassion and self-acceptance."

Insight is seeing for the first time that which you knew already.

SWAMI NISCHALANANDA

. . . .

Through self-awareness we can know what our needs are, to care for ourselves better. Held within each of us are the answers for our being; sometimes it is just a matter of asking the right questions.

Through observation we can look into the centre of ourselves and know where to focus our design, what our motivations are and what is holding us back, and connect with our inner wisdom and guidance.

ACTIVITY: LISTENING TO OUR BODIES

Lie or sit comfortably with your eyes closed. Take three deep breaths. Briefly think about your movements through the day, taking yourself through them in sequence to arrive in the present moment.

Then take your awareness to your left hand – each finger in turn. As your awareness is held in each finger notice if there is any tension there and send a message through to release it. Then work your way up your arm, releasing any tension in your wrist, elbow and shoulder. Then move down the front left side of your body releasing tension in your chest, belly, hip, knee, ankle and foot and then up the back of your leg.

Then take a moment to notice any difference in feeling between the two sides of your body. Then follow the sequence from your right hand to the right buttock and then continue up your whole back paying particular attention to any tension in your shoulders. Continue up your neck and around your head and face.

When you are at your face take another few deep breaths. Listen to where your mind is, where your emotions are, what is happening in your body. Listen to it all without becoming engaged in your thoughts – let them float by.

Needs

At its core the peoplecare ethic is about meeting people's needs in sustainable ways.

When we are not able to sustain ourselves there is a gap. The gap between what is and what we would like represents a need. Often we might notice the gap but do not look too deeply at what will actually nourish us, and just fill the gap with whatever captures our attention in an advert, or a habitual means of gratification: smoking, sugary snacks, television, alcohol... Maybe we want to indulge in some self-care but don't have the opportunity so we overindulge in junk food. We might look to fulfil the need with something that ignores the precision of our feeling; perhaps we take extra sleep when we are actually missing creative expression, or have more food when deep down we want conversation.

The idea of needs may have connotations for some people; they don't want to be a 'needy' person or 'in need'. Or they think people are acting greedily if pushing for fulfilment. As humans we all have requirements for our basic survival and others that allow us to thrive. We cannot deny them or sweep them under the carpet; they govern our behaviour and that of others.

Several people have written their theories about needs. Maslow proposed a hierarchy of needs, where our energy and attention is with the lower levels until they are met. His first level is our physiological need for food, water and physical comfort. With that met, we move to needing safety and security. The next level is for friendship and belonging. After this we have esteem – for ourselves and others. When all of these needs are met we can strive for self-actualisation – reaching our potential.

Max-Neef[4] stated nine basic human needs that are common across all age groups, cultures and time, although the strategies for meeting the needs change. The nine needs are subsistence, protection, affection, understanding, participation, leisure, creation, identity and freedom. He agrees with Maslow that our need for subsistence and food and water is primary. He then believes that the other eight needs have equal pull on our attention.

The Nonviolent Communication (NVC) movement initiated by Marshall Rosenberg,[5] cites our needs at the core of our communication with each other. Robert Gonzales[6] has called this 'the living energy of needs' that is within each one of us. Our needs at any one time are fluid and dynamic; when we eat we stop feeling hungry but that need doesn't stay met, we soon feel hungry again. Similarly, other needs flow in and out of being met. Even just becoming aware of the unmet need can help to fill the gap at times. Our needs all interact with each other and paying attention to one will help others. We can observe ourselves confusing 'needs' with 'preferences' and learn to be more flexible.

All of these theories have something to offer in our understanding of when we are feeling at our best or not quite right. Looking at our needs helps us to identify where we can improve our lives.

Needs in design

The *integration* anchor point gathers up the information to determine the needs of the design. We can use the terms needs, functions and purpose interchangeably when it comes to design. When we know what the needs are we can then think about ways in which we can meet them, and the systems and elements we can put in place. We can think of at least three ways of meeting each need, ensuring that we have back-up plans. Likewise we can find activities that give us many yields and meet more than one need. Max-Neef describes these as synergistic satisfiers: taking a walk in nature with friends meets the needs of connection, participation, understanding and leisure.

From understanding our needs we can look beyond into what systems would take us into regeneration and thriving.

ACTIVITY: WHAT ARE MY NEEDS?

What needs do I have in my life?

What systems do I currently have in place to meet them?

What systems could I put in place?

We may well not have all of the answers at the moment. This is the start of an ongoing process of observation and exploration.

Self-identity

Where does our self-identity come from?

Our self-identity and our authentic selves may not be the same things. Our identities are formed over our lifetimes from the moment we are born. Our primary experience is from our connection to our parents. Between one and two years old we start to associate with our name and realise that this identifies us as a unique person. Our name is often an anchor for our identity. As we get older our identities come from the cultures we live in, both the smaller cultures of our families and the larger context of our schools, social groups, countries, religions and any other groups we belong to. Experiences, hobbies and interests combine and replace each other to become part of our evolving self-identity. In our adult life we often associate most with our job and home.

Our identities are often formed in relation to others. Daughter, mother, father, brother, sister, husband, wife – all of these identities are roles that are defined in terms of who we are to others. The roles we take on combine to become part of our identity. These roles may have fuzzy edges. There is a continuum between playing music and being a musician or painting and being an artist. There are some things that we do, but do not consider ourselves proficient enough to fully identify with that role, shying away from the label. We can identify with certain qualities that we have, such as being a generous, kind, angry or focused person.

Our self-identity has many layers. Our past, present and future selves are intertwined to make who we are. We are all much more than we are aware of, and our identities flow fluidly, so that the fixed idea of 'one self' is an illusion.

Gifts and the shadow side of self-identity

It can be useful to have a self-identity to know who we are in the world, to be able to distinguish between our own actions and those of others. Max-Neef includes identity as one of our human needs.

Having an identity also has a shadow side – it creates a division between others and ourselves. Me and you, us and them, I am separate from you, what happens to me doesn't happen to you, and what happens to you doesn't affect me. This dualism separates us from the reality that we are all interconnected. By over-satisfying the need for identity we can become self-absorbed and distant from our needs for participation and understanding, engaging with others less.

We can get trapped in labels, boxing ourselves in and forgetting that a role is just a small part of our bigger, dynamic and fluid selves.

Collection of stories

Our lives build up like a collection of stories on the bookshelf. We can get into the habit of retelling the stories that are perhaps limiting us in some way. We travel down the well-beaten track, reinforcing stories. There will be other stories of our lives that we need reminding of, times when we were creative, courageous and exceeded our expectations.

All the experiences that we have had in our lives – the trials and tribulations, the highs and lows – form a rich bank of learning. Every friendship and relationship, the people we have loved, our role models and the ones we have fought with, provide us with growing edges – ways to move forward. Experiences can be remoulded into ones that enhance our self-identity and esteem.

The stories of our lives can build self-identity and beliefs. These can lead to expectations we have of other people, the world and ourselves. Our behaviours and thinking will be directly influenced by our expectations, hence creating our experiences. These will then add to our stories and reinforce our self-identity.

For example, if our experience as a child has led us to believe that we are a shy person, then we will expect to be shy at a party with new people, and our behaviour is going to mirror this belief of ourselves. We may not initiate conversations and spend more time watching than engaging. As we leave the party that perception of ourselves is reinforced.

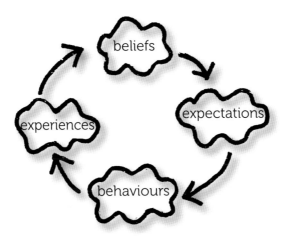

ACTIVITY: RIVER OF LIFE[8]

Draw or paint a river of your life, (or any creative approach to the river theme; waterfalls, hot baths or rapids). Show the turning points and significant events. For this exercise you are not trying to retell the whole of your life, and it needn't be accurate in terms of time spent in different experiences. For example a two week holiday climbing mountains could hold more significance to you than five years of a job you did. Represent the story of your life that

you would like to remember; the highlights and the periods of growth and experience. Remind yourself of the times you felt full of life and joy, the times when you were your best self.

Comfort zones

Every person has a unique shape of comfort zone. There are skills and experiences we feel comfortable doing. For some people it is within their comfort zone to drive in busy cities, to talk in front of a room full of people, to dance on stage and to play music in a band. Someone else may be able to talk fluently in French, carry heavy loads, facilitate group meetings, knit jumpers and cook for large groups.

For each of these activities there will be a level at which we are comfortable and confident and a time when we feel stretched. We may be comfortable talking to a group of 20 people but a group of 50 will make us nervous. Outside of our comfort zone is our stretch zone, a place where we might start to feel jittery, need to concentrate more and prepare thoroughly. Beyond this is a place of unknown that can make us feel extremely nervous. The edges between our comfort, stretch and unknown zones are not clearly defined, they can expand and contract over time. Riding a horse may have been an everyday occurrence many years ago but now, when it is once in a blue moon it feels like a big experience. Your comfort zone has the potential to expand again if it has done so before.

We generally like to stay within the familiarity of our comfort zone. Even when our comfort zone is no longer comfortable we can still feel resistance to move. Imagine yourself in a lovely hot bath; after a while the temperature drops but still you want to stay in, it can turn lukewarm and you know that you have to move and go through the cold to get to the warmth of being dressed. Perhaps you are in a job that you don't like but are used to; it has become like a baggy old jumper that doesn't suit you any more but is familiar. Our friends and family may be attached to us staying as we are. If we change they might also need to adjust, so there may be external resistance to change as well as internal.

We have cultural comfort zones as well as individual ones; behaviours that are acceptable within one culture may not be in others. In some cultures it is perfectly normal for young children to learn to cook with sharp knives. The distances we are prepared to walk may be more due to cultural comforts than individual physical abilities. In the West at the moment it is as if we are sitting in the cold bath, resisting the shift to a regenerative Earth culture. With changes coming we will need to expand our cultural comfort zones and the more we are able to do this as individuals, the easier it will be to do this collectively.

The edges of our comfort zone are fertile places for growth and expansion and the more we explore these edges the more we are able to develop into being our whole selves.

Expanding our identity

Our identities change over time, we need to keep in touch with what is current in our lives and not hold on to the identity of the past.

The way we perceive ourselves links with who we are but it is not exactly the same. Moments of stillness – we are human 'beings' not 'doings' – help us to tune into the bigger picture of who we are, outside of the roles and responsibilities that we currently have. Others often see us differently from how we see ourselves. Our perceptions and identities are subjective and shifting. We can choose to associate with the parts that serve us, and think about the aspects that are limiting us. We do not have to hold on to them; they can be dropped.

When we become aware of our identity and how it influences our lives we can begin to determine the direction we would like to take. Fresh experiences, breaking away from cultural identities and meeting new people all open up different horizons and invite change. Imagining a 'future self', how they might be and what they might say, allows us to expand our vision of ourselves. With an openness and commitment to change, anything is possible.

Beliefs

We all have beliefs about the world. They are patterns of thinking and we then recognise similar patterns and make sense of what is going on around us. Our beliefs are the glasses through which we look at and interpret the world and the rationales behind our behaviours. Our personal beliefs are linked to the beliefs held by our cultures. And our collective beliefs influence the whole structure of our society.

Some of the beliefs we hold will serve us well, others may be holding us back in some way. The beliefs we have can provide us with motivations and be part of the *helps* anchor point or they can be *limits* holding us back.

Self-limiting beliefs

Self-limiting beliefs are beliefs that we have about ourselves, other people or the world we live in that are no longer useful to us. When something is considered true and fixed it can be a self-limiting belief that stops us growing.

Some examples of limiting beliefs we may hold about ourselves are 'I'm not good enough', 'I'm crazy', 'no one likes me', 'I can't sing, dance, do maths, draw…' Beliefs we may hold about other people include 'they are better than me', 'they find things easier', 'they are happy', 'I can't trust anyone'. World beliefs could include 'you can't change anything', or 'successful people are persecuted'.

Self-limiting beliefs can be like cliff edges in our thinking, dreams and actions. We will only go so far and then stop. Sometimes we don't even start on the path because we imagine the edge in the distance.

Where do they come from?

We have attachment to the stories of the past giving them weight, authority and substance in the present and expecting them to continue into the future. They may be just that though – stories of the past (told in voices other than our own; our parents, teachers, peers or society) that we have internalised. We are fed views from the media; 'happiness comes with this product', 'your body needs to be this size and shape...' We are given feedback from others: 'you are clever, good, slow, stupid...'

When we start to view them as beliefs from outside or from our past we can ask ourselves the question of 'what do *I* believe *now*? What is true for me in this moment?' If other things around have changed then the context, if not the content, has also changed.

We can start to see exceptions to them, times and situations they have not been true: 'I can't draw – except for trees'. Consciously seeking contrary evidence, finding exceptions and building on them can rock the foundations of the belief.

Consequences of our beliefs

Believing is seeing; we see what we believe to be true. We all like to be right and can usually find evidence to support our beliefs. The phenomenon of only seeing what you already believed to be true is known as 'confirmation bias'. The opposite of confirmation bias is seeking the new – looking for new possibilities and information.

How we interpret and interact with others is influenced by our beliefs. If we believe everyone is better than us, our actions will follow this belief in our body language, tone of voice and choice of words.

Our beliefs determine how we show up in the world. We can take this further and ask ourselves how the belief 'I'm not good enough' affects the healing of the planet. It may mean that we don't speak up about the injustices we see around us.

Beliefs have given us gifts in the past. For example the same belief, 'I'm not good enough', has perhaps kept us learning and pushing ourselves forward. A belief of 'I'm different' may have allowed you to stand out from the crowd and find your own voice, however it could also have kept you from fully connecting with other people. Acknowledging the gifts allows us to recognise the yields we may have gained, integrating rather than segregating this aspect of ourselves, at the same time freeing ourselves from its limitations.

Why shift them?

Self-limiting beliefs can be like a glass ceiling preventing us from going any higher in our lives. We can get stuck in the same patterns. Limiting beliefs are invisible limiting factors, holding us back and preventing us from being who we could become. In designs we would look at all of the limiting factors and use these as the basis for our design. We may address other limiting factors such as time, money and support, but if we still have in place a belief that we don't deserve them, we may not make use of the resources and it still feels like we are swimming through treacle to realise our design. These are the *limits* in our design that demotivate and hold us back.

How to shift them

Sometimes it can take a lot of energy to free us from these beliefs. Other times just naming them can be enough for them to evaporate; they can be like roots that wither and die when they are brought to the surface. When we bring up one belief it can bring others up with it like pulling threads on a jumper.

Nancy Kline[9] proposes the idea of incisive questions. The aim of the question is to shift the belief out of the way and then see what happens. When the belief is parked then we can see what is truly wanted. 'If this wasn't the case, then what?' Another great question for cutting through any self-limiting beliefs is 'if you knew you would succeed what would you do?'

We may need to release the emotional charge attached to the belief, letting go of the emotions that arose from the words (of the teacher that told us to mime in the back row, rather than sing, for example) so that we can move on.

We can stop repeating the belief and feeding it more energy. We may still have that place of self-doubt but we don't need to visit it, we can keep the door closed and break the habit. There is a traditional Native American story of a boy who has two wolves inside of him, fighting for his attention. He asks his grandfather which one is going to win; he receives the reply that whichever one he feeds will be the winner.

Reframing the belief

The language we use can present beliefs as immovable facts. We can reframe information in a different way that allows movement and anticipates change. This is a potent way for the beliefs to lose their grip. The language we use helps to create the reality around us. We can shift our consciousness with the words we use.

Self-beliefs love the sweeping statement words such as always, never, all and everyone; even changing these to often, rarely, most and some people creates a shift. Other words used with limiting beliefs include can't, should or must.

Self-limiting phrases	Reframing phrases
I can't do this...	I need to work on...I can't yet
This won't happen...	I haven't seen this happen yet
I always...	I sometimes...
How could I be so blind not to see that before	It's great to have opened my perception to that now
I'm stuck	I'm at the edge of discovery
I don't have the answers	I can look for the answers
I'm not confident enough	I'm looking for ways to build my confidence

Chris Dixon teaches permaculture and runs a smallholding in Wales. For the last 20 years he has kept a biotime diary of the weather. And, yes, Wales is wet. However, he has observed that there is generally a break in the rain at some point in the day allowing a quick trip outside to feed the animals. Now when someone says 'it always rains in Wales', he counters this with 'it is extremely rare for it to rain all day in Wales'.

Turn your face to the sun and the shadows fall behind you.
MAORI PROVERB
. . . .

In the same way that we turn limiting factors around to become building blocks of design, we can reframe our beliefs.

Gremlin

Our internal gremlin is the voice within that stops us doing what we intuitively want to do. It is the culmination of thoughts and feelings over our lifetime. Our gremlin likes us to stay within the familiarity of our comfort zone. It works on the assumption that where we are is a secure place to be. Its aim is to keep us safe, protect us and maintain the status quo; however it may do this in ways that are no longer appropriate for us. When we were young we put structures in place to make us feel safe, but at thirty we don't need the protection mechanisms of a five year old to rule our lives. As children we were told not to talk to strangers. It was good advice then but as an adult we want to be able to connect with new people. Our gremlin can block our actions, doubt our capacities and find excuses for us. It has a knack for homing in and amplifying our self-doubts. Our gremlins put the foot on the brake while we are trying to put our foot on the accelerator.

Our gremlin has been on every course, read every book and had every conversation that we have had. It knows the language to use and the buttons to press. New ideas you come across can be grasped and turned on their head to suit its needs. It is reading this book with you. The principles, like anything can be taken to unhelpful extremes. We could use the principle of *creatively use and respond to change* to avoid sticking to any plans or making commitments. Just as we are about to make the big leap and leave our job, our gremlin could come in with *small and slow solutions.*

Our gremlin's voice will get quieter as we find the truth of our own being. But it will evolve with us; as we move past it at one door, it will find another door to guard. Its messages become subtler and we need to increase our awareness. As we move on it loses its attachments and will find other things to cling to. We need to develop the ability to stand back and observe ourselves without judgement. Then we can look objectively and check for the validity of our internal messages. Is the caution appropriate or is it working against what I truly want for myself?

Another word for the gremlin or saboteur could be the slug – the bane of every gardener. The slug has a place in the ecosystem but when it is amongst our newly planted seedlings it is a pest. Similarly this internal voice has a function and can be an ally in warning us about dangers, playing the devil's advocate role and being a reality check, it can also help us to access our creativity, imagination and spontaneity.[10]

The gremlin may speak in the voice of the over-indulgent parent: 'There, there you've had a hard day, it's OK to have a beer/cigarette/chocolate'. The over indulgent parent keeps us lazy, allows addictions to continue and lacks the discipline needed to instigate and maintain change. Or it could be the critical parent saying 'you don't have the strength/stamina/will power to change, I knew you couldn't do it'. The critical parent can find any flaw or weakness almost before it happens and destroy confidence.

The gremlin may set unrealistically high goals, then declare your attempts a failure. It can work more subtly and sound reasonable in its request to defer actions – 'until the time is right/Monday morning/you have more support, time, energy, money…' Our gremlins will undermine us to prove our self-limiting beliefs.

We can counteract the gremlin voice, by becoming a nurturing parent to ourselves: one that will encourage us to move forward and work for our higher self, pushing us on when the going gets tough, because they believe that we can do it. The voice that shows us the best path for our long-term picture as well as short-term needs.

Abundance beliefs

Many of our limiting beliefs are rooted in the scarcity mindset. They are based on lack and competition. Tapping into abundance thinking creates beliefs in growth, potential, plenty, sufficiency and trust. Beliefs can emerge such as 'I trust myself', 'The universe will provide', 'I have enough', 'I can grow', 'I can adapt to change', 'I have the skills, strength, motivation…' Stating these beliefs and looking for evidence of their truth can eclipse our limiting beliefs.

We can do anything we want – individually, collectively, personally and environmentally – if we believe that we can.

Roz Savage

Patterns

Our beliefs lead to our internal thinking patterns and our external patterns of behaviour. These influence our lives and our interactions with others.

We like the familiarity of our patterns; they provide us with mechanisms for getting through the day efficiently. Patterns can be useful pointers to us; we get hungry at certain times so we know to start cooking in advance. Our lives are composed of interlocking patterns, for instance, eating patterns that fit around patterns of work and rest and connect with our family and cultural patterns. Patterns can be traditions, addictions, habits, and routines of thinking, feeling, behaving and interacting. Our brain is a pattern-recognising organ; it will find the pattern and repeat it if possible.

Sometimes patterns can arise with just one action. Where we sit the first time at a meeting, on a course or in a restaurant could be just because it was the last seat; next time though we may be the first person and still sit in same place, now it's familiar. Moving seats changes the scenery, perspective and connections in groups.

Patterns arise from our cultural background, learnt from our parents and society either implicitly through mimicking behaviour or overtly through instruction. Patterns can reinforce and perpetuate themselves.

We may have inherited traditions that were appropriate for past circumstances. A friend was cutting the ends of a joint of meat to go in the oven and put them against the edges. Her partner questioned why she did this. "I don't know, my mum always did this," she replied. Following this up with her mum, she received the same answer. The question then went to her grandmother, who laughed and explained this was because she had a small oven and this was the only way it would fit!

Differing patterns of thinking and behaviour can cause friction or confusion with other people. We have different rhythms to our days and when we are not able to follow our own rhythm it can cause an inner conflict that can be expressed internally or externally. We perhaps have different sequences of doing things and can't make sense of how someone else does something. A funny example of this was given by a friend on an NLP course; she had a sudden light bulb moment when she realised why it had been troubling her for 25 years of marriage that her husband put his socks on first when getting dressed. We all had a good giggle hearing his rationale was so his toes didn't get caught in his pants.

Patterns need to be changed when they are no longer useful to us, or fit the current circumstance. If there is no underlying desire to let go, then there will be no lasting movement despite any rational thoughts.

Addictions

Addictions are patterns in our lives that have been taken to extremes and are damaging our well-being. We understand the message 'smoking kills'; it is in front of us each time we pick up the packet of cigarettes and evidence is easily accessible, yet we can trick ourselves and know one thing and do another.

We numb ourselves through addictions of smoking, alcohol, drugs, television, food or internet. The quality and quantity of the experience with some of these determines whether they are nourishing or polluting our systems.

We have patterns of how we meet our needs. For any unhealthy activity, think about the need behind it; this then helps us to see other ways of meeting the need. For example, smoking may have the need of breaking up the day, having a stretch and move from the desk, having five minutes to yourself. This can take us into design, where we consciously look for healthy and beneficial ways to meet our needs.

ACTIVITY: SITTING WITH THE DESIRE

When reaching for the biscuits ask yourself, what is it I really want now? Perhaps it is water, or a sit down and you are just filling the gap with a biscuit out of habit. Take a pause, sit with the desire for a moment and see what is the need behind it. Think of at least two other ways of meeting the need, then make a conscious decision about what you are going to do.

Creating new patterns

We can become stuck in patterns that we might not even realise are unhelpful, or that aren't necessarily bad in themselves but there are more effective routines. We take a familiar route to a friend's house because we know it gets us there and it is within our comfort zone. But then we are told about a different much shorter, quicker route. We realise that we have actually been wasting a lot of time and energy. We mustn't assume that our patterns can't be improved. The well-beaten pathways in our brains are not always the right track.

Changing old patterns is likely to provoke feelings in us. We may well have emotions attached that need to be acknowledged. Change can be daunting and stressful, but it is no use just wishing for a different life and a better world and continuing to do the same things. If we want to improve then we need to be ready to change.

I met a woman, Genevieve Ellison, who works in Antarctica. For six months of the year it is dark for 24 hours a day, and for the other six months there is continuous daylight. It was fascinating to hear stories of what happens personally and collectively when the external cues of dark and light were gone, disrupting the usual patterns of sleeping and eating. This was an extreme way of testing and releasing patterns!

Releasing patterns can leave a gap. It is typical for someone to replace one unhelpful addiction with another: the drinker becomes the over-eater, smoking is replaced with gambling... Letting go of the old pattern is more effective if consciously replaced by something that is known to be helpful, such as exercise or an art project.

Patterns in one area of life are reflected in other areas. It can therefore help to shift things indirectly by working on patterns in a different area, and tackling issues side on. Practising non-attachment to material possessions can help us to let go of difficult relationships from our past for example. Changing small patterns in our lives will start to shift the rigidity of our comfort zone and allow us to experience change in a non-threatening way. It will also bring to our attention how often we are on automatic pilot. Examples of some easy pattern changes might be brushing our teeth with the opposite hand, trying different meal times or combinations of clothes.

There may be useful patterns of communication, thinking and behaviour that can be used in other areas. This is a key way of using the *patterns* anchor point.

After actually doing something new we can reflect on how it feels. Is it challenging, exciting, refreshing? There are times with children when we don't want to do something as it might set a precedent. We can turn this on its head for ourselves in just trying something once, to break the mould and open our mind to doing it again. We can use all our resources to achieve it once – just to know it is possible.

Where would we like to be, what would that look, feel and sound like? Visioning the new pattern and the benefits it would bring help spur us on. Phrasing it in positive terms provides a hook, rather than reminding us of what we need to forget. For example if you are trying to give up smoking it is more helpful to vision healthy lungs, than to repeat the message 'I will not smoke'. Saying to ourselves 'I will not eat chocolate today', is just going to get us thinking about chocolate, but saying 'I will eat healthy snacks' is positive framing.

All or nothing thinking and behaviour is a common trap to fall into, for example thinking, 'I won't be able to give up smoking entirely so there's no point cutting down and I won't try at all'. Initially it can help to set boundaries within the day or week to try a new pattern, exercising one day a week, or delaying the first cigarette of the day. The edges can be expanded once it feels comfortable to keep to these boundaries. Another way of expanding the edges is to increase the gap between actions, allowing space for something else to occur. This starts to break the connections between actions.

We need support and willpower to establish a new pattern until it has become anchored in our life. We can notice the changes that are occurring and the knock-on effects, and use the momentum of these changes to do more. It might be that initially we do not see the benefits: we might need to find acceptance of the disruption and see this as part of the process, a phase that we need to pass through. Like redecorating, changes can bring about a mess initially. Or perhaps we feel like we are not moving anywhere, just returning to the same point, but if we think of spirals we are slowly moving out, rather than just returning to the same point.

Our ecofootprints are linked to both individual and wider societal patterns. We have habits of how much we put our heating on, how often we wash our clothes and the food we buy and eat. In order to reduce our footprint and create the Great Turning we will need to change many of our patterns. What is present in the world today is the outcome of individual and collective patterns – change these and you change the outcomes. With improved patterns we open up alternative ways of seeing and being in the world.

> ### TECHNIQUES FOR SHIFTING PATTERNS
>
> - *Consciously replace with a helpful pattern*
> - *Shift things indirectly by working on other patterns*
> - *Do something new and reflect on how that feels*
> - *Envisage the new pattern*
> - *Set boundaries in which to try the new pattern*
> - *Translate effective patterns from other areas of your life*

An Autobiography in Five Chapters

Chapter 1) I walk down the street. There is a deep hole in the sidewalk. I fall in. I am lost ... I am hopeless. It isn't my fault. It takes forever to find my way out.

Chapter 2) I walk down the same street. There is a deep hole in the sidewalk. I pretend I don't see it. I fall in again. I can't believe I'm in the same place. But it isn't my fault. It still takes a long time to get out.

Chapter 3) I walk down the same street. There is a deep hole in the sidewalk. I see it is there. I still fall in ... it's a habit. My eyes are open. I know where I am. It is my fault. I get out immediately.

Chapter 4) I walk down the same street. There is a deep hole in the sidewalk. I walk around it.

Chapter 5) I walk down another street.

Sᴏɢʏᴀʟ Rɪɴᴘᴏᴄʜᴇ[11]

• • • • • • • • • • • • • • • • • • • •

Edges and transitions

Edges are interesting places. Moving beyond the edge of our comfort zone and creating new patterns requires us to move from one place to another. Transition is the state of moving from one edge to another, where we are in neither the old nor the new place. It can be a quick transition or it may take time. We may pulsate between reaching the edge and stepping back into our comfort zone before we are fully able to make the transition. We can be carried in the momentum of the transition zone or it can become our new comfort zone and we can forget that we were actually on our way somewhere else.

The edges might be physical spaces, places in time or our mind. They may seem seductive or scary to us. We may enjoy the movement or feel uprooted. It can be unsettling especially if you don't know what the new place looks or feels like. Edges are fertile places where there is huge potential for abundant growth.

In crossing boundaries we may experience internal resistance, shown in different ways: we might feel tired, agitated, irritated, wired, afraid or have physical aches and pains. We may experience resistance from others: discouragement, anger or diversions. These are all part of the *limits* anchor point, the things that are holding us back, the reasons why we don't want to change. We also have the *helps*, the motivations that are pushing us forward and the exhilaration of the new.

Process of change

Old place	Edge	Transition	Edge	New place
Comfort	Exciting	Unstable	Landing	Comfort
Boredom	Challenging	Dynamic	Finding our feet	Stability
Security	Vulnerable	Disorientating	Challenging	Relief
Stability	Dizzying	Potential	Impatience to	Calm
Calm	Eye opening	Productive	settle	Putting down
Safety	Shock	Uncomfortable	Daunting	roots

When we recognise all these stages as the process of change it is easier to sit with the emotions that arise and know that they will pass.

Transition initiatives are based on the premise that change is inevitable and by actively stepping forward into that change we are more able to direct it to a life-sustaining culture. The Transition movement recognises that support is needed for us to go through this transition because of the emotional journey it will entail. Together with many others, Sophy Banks has been involved in the Transition Network from the early days and has been instrumental in holding the vision of 'inner transition'. Alongside the changes we need to make in our social systems and behaviours are shifts to our internal landscapes. Initiatives often have a group where people explore what the internal Transition might involve – for individuals and families as well as organisations and communities. Names include 'Inner Transition', 'Heart and Soul', 'Spirit of Transition' and others. They also often create places and systems of support, understanding that the journey of Transition and change can bring up all kinds of feelings and responses.

When we come to the edge we see different realities and possibilities. Moving to the edge of modern culture we are more able to see the opportunity for the Great Turning.

ACTIVITY: EMOTIONS OF TRANSITION

This is a chance to practise pattern recognition, which is so useful in permaculture design.

Think about a transition you have been through: moving house, changing partner or job. Reflect upon your emotional journey.

Can I recognise a pattern with other times I have been through a transition?

We need to find our way to the centre of the Self in our lifetime, but the centre is not a destination: it is a journey ... When each person is able to discover their medicine they are more able to make their contribution to the whole, and this makes us stronger as a people.

WINDEAGLE AND RAINBOWHAWK[12]

CHAPTER 5

Health and well-being

OUR HEALTH AND feelings of well-being are central to our ability to contribute to our relationships, work and communities.

There is of course a huge wealth of information out there about health. In this chapter we open up a way of looking at our health through permaculture glasses and using design tools to increase our well-being.

We think about four aspects of health: physical, emotional, healthy mind and spiritual or intuitional health. These all overlap and influence each other.

Health and healing

What is health?

Health is the balanced functioning of our bodies. Being healthy is to be able to access and flow with internal and external energies. In a healthy state we are in tune with the rhythms of life, living our dreams and content with who we are. We are joyful, aware, expansive, balanced and at ease with life.

Well-being is freedom from pain in our bodies, mind, spirit and emotions. We need to look after ourselves on all of these levels to stay healthy and fit. Listening intuitively and being aware of our bodies provides us with the knowledge of what is appropriate for ourselves. When we are self-observant we can act to divert illness, acting for prevention and timely maintenance rather than cure.

The doctor of the future will give no medicine but will interest his patients in the care of the human frame, in diet and in the cause and prevention of disease.

THOMAS EDISON

....

What is ill health?

It is important to know what we don't want and how this arises. When we have blockages in our life they can manifest as ill health in our bodies. Often what we notice in ourselves as illnesses are in fact symptoms of something else. When we are not following our own joy and passions in life – not being authentic – we feel lethargic and lacklustre. The word disease could be read as dis-ease, when we are out of alignment and not at ease with the world or with ourselves.

Stress is a state of tension; when we are beyond the elastic limits of what we can cope with, our physical systems will also struggle to cope. Stress has its usefulness in certain circumstances – it can get the adrenaline pumping to meet the deadline, or make the presentation – but there is an edge at which the level of stress is no longer beneficial. Sometimes we are so beyond our capacity that we are no longer learning and growing and our bodies experience difficulty.

The stress itself then produces different symptoms in the short, medium and long term. These symptoms can create further stress. Stress can lead to sleepless nights for example, which can decrease our ability to cope and exacerbate the initial stress, leading to a further spiral of erosion. In tackling this spiral we need to look for both points of intervention and ways of treating the root causes.

There are three aspects to stress: firstly is the external stimulus; this leads to an internal response; which then produces symptoms of stress. At each of these stages we may be able to alter things. Can we change the situation or choose a different one? Then our internal response is based on subjective interpretation so seeing it differently will change our response. Finally, we have a choice in how we deal with the symptoms of stress. Stress may be a healthy response to the circumstances we find ourselves in. Often though it is dealt with in an unhealthy way.

There's nothing wrong with butterflies in the stomach, You just have to get them to fly in formation.

ANONYMOUS

. . . .

We can reduce stress through laughter, exercise, singing and social contact, but it is unrealistic to expect our lives to be free of stress. We can aim to use the tension rather than avoid it. We have to *let nature take its course* and accept the challenges, emotions and timescales of our situations. Stress is a symptom of the circumstances of our lives and how we are responding to them rather than a cause in itself. Our responses to difficulty relate to our attitudes to edges and stretching, our self-beliefs and comfort zones.

Healing

While we can try and avoid illnesses, accidents and traumas they are a reality of life and we need to know how best to recover from them. There are different levels of healing: emotional, physical and energetic.

When we heal we become whole. To do this we need to integrate the new experience into our being rather than suppressing it or pushing it away. Accepting our part in the healing of the Earth and acknowledging the connection between our own healing and the healing of the planet is part of the inner transition work.

A cranial osteopath described her work as holding the person in their discomfort so that the body thinks 'this is wrong' and a healing response is provoked. Other healers and therapists concur that the person themselves is responsible for healing and it can only come from within. The healer is there to help the person access their own healing but cannot do it for them. We can only make an invitation to heal. Our souls know the medicine we need – our own song for healing.

In the 20 years since Rod Everett has been practising and teaching permaculture he has only visited the doctor a few times, mainly to get a diagnosis of symptoms. Homeopathy, herbs, pressure points and specific exercises have helped to balance his body. He believes everyone can unlock their potential for healing. We can enable ourselves as healers by knowing the resources we have internally available to us, and exploring the gift of healing.

Medicine

Medicines can be anything that promotes healing. Medicines were traditionally seen as preventatives as well as curatives. In modern cultures medicines are mostly viewed as drugs that we take to cure an illness. They often have side effects that can in turn need treatment with further drugs. There are times and places for allopathic medicines and we could be too rigid with wanting to use renewable resources when in fact we need a drug or intervention to save our life. But complementary medicines are generally more gentle on the system, and rather than just suppressing the symptoms they work to shift underlying causes, whether on a physical or emotional level.

There are many ways we can relax and lift our spirits; hot baths, music, singing, walking the dog, being in the garden, meditation, yoga, tai chi, cooking, reading, dancing and companionship. We can research our own personal treatments to maintain healthy body, mind and emotions and rebalance ourselves. The methods that we use can interrelate and become a whole system of self-care.

The five best doctors in the world and no one can deny are Sleep, diet, fresh air, sunshine and exercise
ANONYMOUS
. . . .

Physical health

Exercise

Keeping our bodies moving is a natural state. Our modern lives allow us to keep still for much longer than we would have done in our ancestry, so we have to create opportunities for exercise. How we move our bodies has been developed over the years of sitting at school and office desks and is unlikely to be fully natural and freely flowing. If we watch children moving we can witness what it's like to move freely with the whole body. Our bodies get caught in habitual patterns; just starting small such as walking at a faster pace can help to break these.

We might say that we want to improve our health but we have limiting factors that slow us down. One of these might be time in our lives, and we need to find ways of incorporating exercise into our existing daily and weekly routines. Cycling to work, walking to school, taking stairs instead of lifts, parking further away, stretching at our desks or walking faster, are all steps to creating energy in our bodies and building momentum that might lead us on to other forms of exercise.

Nutrition

What we put into our bodies determines what the body can do – it's not rocket science. When we choose our food, unless we are growing our own, we have to interact with bigger systems that may have something other than our best interests at heart. Supermarkets are more interested in profit than health. Most of our food choices are not made on a nutritional basis but are influenced by geographical, social, political, religious, psychological and economic factors. We have to weigh up availability, cost and nutritional value while being bombarded with advertisements and special offers. It's hardly surprising that the rate of obesity is increasing so rapidly in the West.

The nutritional requirements of humans are quite simple but there is a huge diversity of ways in which we can meet these needs. Different foods represent different things to us, beyond just their nutritional value. Typically we seek 'comfort' food, or associate certain foods with security or love. Advertisers play on these associations.

We will have developed patterns of the foods we choose, methods of eating, preparation, number of meals per day, time of eating and size of portions from when we were small children. These habits come into being and are maintained because they are practical or symbolically meaningful to us. They can be very ingrained and it may take a while to shift to more appropriate patterns for our current lifestyle. Ecological and economic factors change availability forcing change of habits. New foods and recipes are discovered, widening our choices. When we share food with friends and family we also share our habits.

Whatever we eat has short, medium and long-term effects. A lot of the food we are sold tempts us on the short-term taste effect. This is indicative of the short-term thinking that dominates the industrial growth culture and has created many problems for the planet. Short-term effects are felt within the first hour: the taste, the feeling in our stomach, and the change in energy. After that we move into the medium-term effects: how do you feel in an hour or two, do you want more, have you got more or less energy, do you feel bloated? And then the long-term effects: is it excess fuel that your body is going to store as fat? What is it doing to your internal systems? There are also effects outside of ourselves: where did the food come from, what is the packaging and where is it going? Unfortunately it is the long-term effects that we pay least attention to. When we start to ask ourselves these questions we can learn to self-regulate more effectively. Using the biotime diary can help us to get in touch with how we feel after different food types. The next step is to interact with those observations.

Preparing food

Cooking with fresh ingredients has more nutritional value than processed food; generally less sugar, salt and fat. The process of cooking also has value and enjoyment in itself and is not just about the end product. Growing, preparing and cooking the food extend the experience and bring more satisfaction, incorporating other needs of participation and connection as well as exercising our design skills and creativity.

Rest and relaxation

Rest and relaxation are important parts of maintaining our systems. They have benefits for our physical and emotional bodies. Our energy follows a wave pattern and periods of rest and renewal are as necessary as the activity. If you are taking some time out to relax then there is no point in feeling guilty about it and thinking that you 'should' be doing something else. Sitting and doing nothing and just daydreaming for 20 minutes is a valid part of self-care. The dream state is a powerful place to be in; it is the edge between our conscious and subconscious[1] minds and allowing time for this integration by just sitting and being is valuable. Expanding the edge between sleep and activity allows the lessons of the subconscious to surface and take root. Being fully present and conscious that this is your time to relax will help you get the most out of it.

Take a moment to note your reaction to the idea of sitting and doing nothing for 20 minutes. Try it now and see what happens.

For many people sitting in front of the television is their main form of relaxation. Sitting may relax the body but what we are watching determines what is happening to our emotions. When we plug ourselves into the TV we are denying ourselves time to just be and dream, to reflect on our day and be in our own thoughts or to be creative.

What form of rest or relaxation do you take daily and weekly? How long do you spend weekly relaxing? Having regular times and activities gives us signs of self-worth and increases the benefits.

Alice Walker talks of the pause, "the moment when something major is accomplished and we are so relieved to finally be done with it that we are already rushing, at least mentally, into The Future. Wisdom, however, requests a pause. If we cannot give ourselves such a pause, the Universe will likely give it to us."[2]

Many of us have first-hand experience of illnesses or cars breaking down, or other ways we have been forced to take time to rest. If we design these periods of rest and rejuvenation into our systems, with the *pause* anchor point, then they might happen less often in unplanned ways with other difficult side effects.

Sleep

Sleep is vital to our physical and emotional health. It allows the subconscious mind to process our day's events and integrate new learning.

We will have inherited beliefs and assumptions about sleep; these could be cultural beliefs as well as personal ones. Personal beliefs we may have about our own sleep patterns are 'we can't get to sleep at night without...', 'we can't get out of bed easily in the mornings', 'we can't get to sleep if we are cold', 'we can't nap in the day'. Again we need to ask ourselves if these beliefs are currently useful to us and if there are exceptions to them.

If we experience a 'sleep problem', can we turn it around and make a solution out of the problem, by using the characteristics to our advantage? For example if we have trouble getting to sleep at night because we have too many thoughts going around our heads can we write them down and catch some of the ideas? Could we relax and enjoy the edge between our dream state and conscious thoughts when we wake in the middle of the night and listen to the messages this time holds for us?

Sometimes it falls
A flake at a time,
Into your life while you're
asleep
STEPHEN PHILBRICK[3]
· ·

Emotional health

Negative emotions

Many people's lives are peppered with anger, fear, worry and guilt. Can you imagine the difference in our communities if people felt joyful, confident, hopeful and peaceful on a regular basis? Two things become apparent here. Firstly, how affected we can be by the emotions of others and secondly how these negative emotions can almost be connected up into a spiral of erosion: worry leading to fear to anger to guilt and maintaining momentum to spiral into more and more negative feelings. It would be hard to distinguish the cause and the symptoms. There are likely to be other effects on our health and relationships such as disturbed sleeping and eating habits and arguments, that would in turn further compound these feelings.

Negative moods are giving us messages from the subconscious mind; they are letting us know that something is out of balance, a need is not being met, perhaps the need for time alone, being heard or rest. Taking time to find out what that message is helps to change the moods.

Our energy can shift rapidly. This is particularly true with children; they can be out walking and saying how bored and tired they are one minute and the next they see a cat ahead and run off. We could be sitting at work trying to plough through our jobs and we get a phone call inviting us to a party; suddenly we are excited and have energy. Equally it can dissipate rapidly; a sarcastic comment from your boss and you might deflate instantly or be thrown into confusion.

Our emotions and our energy levels are linked. Our emotions can follow a wave pattern and it isn't necessary for us to expect to be totally joyful all the time, but when we get stuck with feeling low then it is good to have some way of pushing ourselves up again without resorting to something artificial that is unhelpful to our health in other ways, such as alcohol.

Weeding and pruning are part of gardeners' processes to keep a balance. What emotions can we weed or prune out of our lives, making space for the ones we do want?

Anger

Anger is a symptom of something else going on. Anger can arise from a physical hurt, shame, teasing, unfairness, fear, misunderstanding or embarrassment. We can develop anger habits; circumstances, people or timings provoke the same feelings over and over again.

We can use the energy behind the emotion to motivate us to do something. We need to find ways to integrate and transform the energy rather than suppressing it. When it has no outlet anger is likely to be turned inwards and cause illness or explode out into the world creating more problems.

Anger about injustices in the world has provided the energy for action to change them. The bumper sticker 'if you're not angry you're not paying attention', reminds us there is much in the world to be upset about. Many permaculturists have their roots in campaign movements fuelled by anger at what is happening in the world. Permaculture has led them to being proactive in finding solutions.

> *There are many problems in the world to worry about; permaculture helps us to focus on the solutions.*
> ANDY GOLDRING

Worry

There are times when we find ourselves caught in mental circles. This could be from worrying about something, replaying conversations or gossip, or being caught in a loop of indecision.

These loops can be exhausting, taking our energy away from taking any positive action. They may be spiralling and the situation gets blown out of proportion. We can get caught up with imagining and second-guessing what the other person is thinking and interpreting their comments and actions.

We need to stop and find the learning or growing edge. What can we learn from what has just happened? How does it affect me in this moment – not the future or the past? We can write down why we are worrying, what we might like to do differently and possible courses of action, focusing on the lesson and then letting it go.

> *Worry is like a rocking chair: It gives you something to do, but it doesn't get you anywhere.*
> ERMA BOMBECK

It can be beneficial to imagine a big STOP sign in your mind, a barrier coming down in your thinking, switching the tracks of thinking and getting off the negative thought train.

Joy and happiness

How can we grow happiness in our lives? Small amounts of joy can quickly dispel a lake of anxiety, if only we could bottle it. We all need to find our own ways of building up our reserves and being able to access them at times to bring ourselves up. Being joyful and happy can motivate ourselves and others around us.

We could use the design tool of inputs and outputs to gain a better understanding: what are we putting into our emotional bodies? Daily news, soap operas and crime programmes are going to filter down into our emotions. What other influences are we surrounding ourselves with? And what is coming out in our lives – family arguments, sleepless nights, nightmares, self-criticisms and fear?

Are there inputs that we could stop to curtail the negative emotions? What would we need to put in to get more positive emotions out?

When he is teaching Qi Gong, my friend Paul Eagles suggests we give ourselves permission to be unreasonably happy. There are cultural norms and limits on how much is 'right' to feel and express. What other permissions could we give ourselves – permission to be less than perfect, make mistakes, experiment, love, be creative…

Cultivating confidence, self-esteem and trust

Our confidence, self-esteem and trust are all interlinked and can be increased by expanding the edges of our comfort zone. When we give ourselves feedback in the form of self-appreciation rather than self-criticism, we might reflect and improve instead of feeling regret and guilt.

Life unfolds for each of us and within each experience lies an infinite amount of possibilities.

ANONYMOUS

....

We make decisions every day, all day; what to wear, what to cook, where to go, how to speak to people. Every decision that we make sets us on a different path. Different decisions have a variety of short-, medium- and long-term outcomes, so while something may seem to be not the best thing in the short term it may be that further down we arrive at the place we were aiming for. It is virtually impossible to tell what all the outcomes of our actions will be further downstream.

Saying to ourselves 'I *should* have done this' or 'I *should* have known better' undermines our confidence. The word 'should' implies lack of choice and responsibility. It ties us to the past instead of allowing us to be in the present and plan for the future from where we currently are. Replacing *shoulds* with *coulds* allows us to see that there were in fact many other possibilities that may have given us different outcomes. We can feel that other options were open to us and think about what might have been without implying we were in the wrong for not taking them.

A useful principle that can shift our attitude significantly is *the problem is the solution.* Each situation we find ourselves in has a unique set of characteristics. Focusing on how to use these characteristics to our advantage rather than trying to change them can lead us to a satisfactory conclusion. Within there somewhere is a solution, we just need to be open to finding it and recognise it as such.

This principle invites us to seek the blessing in disguise from the outset. For example, if an event is cancelled, how can we use the time we now have available – what gifts arise from the new situation? How can I turn it around to make the most of it – what are the positives, the advantages? How do I utilise the plus points? If I was to think of this as a great thing that was happening to me what would that be like? This involves changing perceptions and reframing the situation. Altering plans provides new opportunities and opens doors into unseen scenarios.

Our lives follow a branching pattern; each decision we make opens new doors ahead into different scenarios previously unseen. Only if we stay still do we restrict our potential to learn and grow.

Building trust in ourselves builds our resilience for the changes and challenges we face.

Healthy mind

One of the main aspects of a healthy mind is to be continually learning. We can increase our ability to learn new skills with some simple self–reflection and awareness techniques. The learning cycle continues throughout our lives, not just in formal education settings. Starting a new job, embarking on a project or becoming a parent are all learning opportunities. Improving our peoplecare skills of self-care, communication and creativity all follow similar patterns of learning. Understanding these can save us time and effort and increase the health of our minds.

Learning to learn

One of the primary beliefs of home education is 'if children can motivate and think for themselves they can learn and do anything they choose to'. It is more important that they know how to learn than knowing specific facts by rote. Once a person knows how to ask questions, research, use their memory and integrate the learning into their lives, they can apply this to any new skill.

Questioning is a sign of curiosity, intelligence and dynamic engagement. Questions show that you want to integrate the new information with existing knowledge and your map of the world. It is not accepting the information as static but allowing it to be expanded upon. There are many questions in this book to stimulate self-reflections and the search for your own answers. The questions are an invitation to slow your reading, and turn the book into a conversation in which you can learn much about yourself.

Looking beyond content to process

When we want to learn a particular skill we can look to people already doing it. This is looking at the details of what people are doing and trying to find the patterns of their success, the underlying principles that they use in their work.

From reading a book to attending a workshop, we can look deeper than the content to the underlying structures and processes that either engage or bore us. To improve our business skills we could look at successful businesses. All around us are living examples of peoplecare in action to learn from. For anything you want to do you can look at the deeper level of what others do. You can see what the metapicture is that makes them successful and apply this to your own situation.

Learning from our mistakes

Asking ourselves why things do not work provides us with as much information as recalling how and why they worked well. We can learn from the mistakes of others as well as our own.

When something doesn't work quite in the way we expected we could use this as a learning opportunity. This is starting to break the mould of success and failure. These mistakes are not failures in our lives; they are opportunities for us to try something new, problem-solve and improve our skills. We can harvest the feedback from the experience to provide us with rich information and a better starting position in the future. What could we do differently next time? How could we improve? What are the patterns of what we did that could be different and what are the details that could be changed?

Gemma Suggitt, a gardener, says that permaculture helped to liberate her from her self-confessed perfectionism. It has allowed her to see that it is OK to break rules, experiment, copy other people's ideas, and do things her own way. It allowed her to see that there was more than one way of doing things, and it might not work out the way she planned in the garden, but that is OK.

Competence cycle

The competence cycle shows how we move through four stages from not knowing at all about a skill to it becoming second nature. This could be anything from patterns and principles to listening and facilitation.

- **Stage one – Unconscious incompetence – 'blissful ignorance'**

When we first come across a skill we have no idea how to carry it out, it is all a mystery to us. We see the finished product but have no idea of how to get there. We may have heard the term 'principles of nature', but have no understanding of what that means.

In stage one people can be complacent, static, defensive or in denial. They may be in their comfort zone and happy in their place of ignorance. They could be in a state of anticipation and expectation of something new.

- **Stage two – Conscious incompetence – 'the door opens'**

In this stage we are shown how to do something and become aware of what we don't know.

Moving to stage two may be overwhelming. People can feel shocked, panicked or embarrassed and have a sense of urgency when they see how much there is to know. There can be excitement and a hunger and eagerness to know more.

- **Stage three – Conscious competence – 'awkward know-how'**

We learn how to do a skill and can accomplish it ourselves with concentration.

This stage brings highs and lows with growing confidence punctuated with times of humbleness. There can be satisfaction and frustration. The concentration needed is tiring and we can be either self-conscious or arrogant.

- **Stage four – Unconscious competence – 'second nature'**

After practice the skill becomes second nature and we are able to do it without thinking about each individual step so much.

When we have moved to stage four we can feel relieved, confident and relaxed. We may forget the previous stages we have journeyed through and not value the skill, feeling bored and complacent and insensitive to the incompetence of others. We may become stale in our skill and think we know it all and the passion for learning may go out or we may be buzzing with enthusiasm to share.

When we learn another aspect of the skill we go round the cycle again. We can be in more than one stage at a time. We may have reached stage three with driving a car, but still be at stage one with parking. The stages are more of a continuum that we move through rather than distinct steps.

What is illustrated here is the connection between our emotional health and our ability to learn. It is obvious that there are emotions here that would push us on and inspire us to continue learning and there are others that may make us give up. We have been through this cycle numerous times in our life, from learning to walk and riding a bike, to science classes at school, from learning an instrument to our first job.

These build our beliefs about ourselves as learners. When we enter a new learning context these beliefs can trigger the same emotions, leading us to a positive or negative spiral of learning.

This is an opportunity for us to practise pattern recognition on our habits of learning. There may be one particular stage that we habitually stop at. Some people may find that they don't want to learn new things; they do not want to have that feeling of not knowing so they stay in stage one and are averse to new skills and experiences. For others as soon as the door is opened in stage two they run in the opposite direction. For some people it can be too tiring being in stage three and they don't want to do the practice that it would take to move them to stage four. Some people can get to stage four but then get bored and do not maintain or exercise the skills they have gained.

Awareness that these are the emotions associated with each stage of learning and not necessarily down to our own weaknesses can be the first step in breaking unhelpful patterns. Just knowing this to be a natural cycle helps to stay with the learning process.

It will normally be a mix of emotions that are stirred within us. We can now also look for the accompanying emotions that could drive us forward and not just focus on the ones that are pushing us away from the learning. We can prepare ourselves in advance and look for support to help us through a particular stage. We can accelerate the natural succession through the cycle by focusing on the positive emotions, practising and getting support. By shifting to positive learning patterns we can cultivate a healthy mind and make it fertile for new growth.

There is a further stage that not everyone will automatically progress to.

- **Stage five – Reflective competence – 'the wise owl'**

In this stage we can take in the whole cycle of learning like 'the wise owl'. By consciously going into the stage we are able to reflect on our learning journey and empathise with others. Taking time to reflect provides us with a useful pattern for any other skill we learn, the *limits* we had to overcome and the *helps* that have supported our journey. We can show self-appreciation for our efforts.

To most effectively pass on the skill we need to go to stage five, where we can break it into components for someone else to follow. In this stage we can be creative with the skill and develop it for ourselves, not just learning from others, and maybe finding new ways to share and teach it.

Spiral of abundant learning

We want to create a spiral of abundance learning where:

Multiple intelligences

Howard Gardner[4] first proposed this division and highlighting of multiple intelligences. Within each of us is more 'intelligence' than is measured merely by the standard intelligence tests. Intelligences are a set of abilities and skills that can be developed and improved. We each have all of these intelligences to some extent, although some may be more in use and others latent. The more stimulation, the more they develop, and increasing one intelligence helps to stimulate the others. Developing the full range will assist in our long-term learning. He uses the terms 'intelligences' and 'talents' interchangeably. Some people will have a naturally high intelligence in particular areas. What is valued and therefore encouraged and stimulated varies across human cultures and even from family to family.

Permaculture is an integrating approach that can stimulate all of the intelligences. At the end of this part we will consider how we can use them when we are designing for ourselves.

Spiral of abundant learning

we want to learn more → we learn → our confidence increases → we make use of the information → the new skill or information is valued →

- Musical – Sensitive to mood and emotion and enjoys rhythm.
- Linguistic – Good with language, patterning and systems. Can think in metaphors.
- Kinaesthetic – Good timing, good control of objects and body. Proficient at handicrafts and sport. Uses body to assist learning.
- Self-intelligence – Self-motivated, strong sense of values, high self-knowledge.
- People intelligence – Relates well to others, good mediator and communicator.
- Visual and spatial – Ability to think in pictures and mental images, maps and charts.
- Mathematical and logical – Likes precision and enjoys abstract and structured thinking.
- Naturalistic – 'Green fingers' and affinity with animals.

ACTIVITY: MULTIPLE INTELLIGENCES

Draw your own spectrum or rating for your intelligences. Appreciate the talents you have.[5]

Spiritual health

Another aspect of our health is our spiritual well-being. This is not necessarily aligning ourselves to a religion but being aware of a bigger picture, of life outside of ourselves and our control. We could think of it as our intuitional health.

Humans like to create clearly defined boundaries and this has contributed to our perceived separation from nature. We like to define our 'self' as something distinct from 'the wild' or the 'other'. This has resulted in alienation from other people, other species and the Earth. Edges are not impermeable barriers, however they are entrance and entry points, passageways between two 'selves'. When we eat an apple, at what point does it become a part of our 'self'? When we connect to nature and other people, we recognise our interconnectedness.

You are closer to God's heart in the garden
Than any place on Earth
DOROTHY FRANCES GURNEY

There are environments that encourage and support us to open up to a spiritual perspective. Places of worship and retreat centres hold the space that allows us to open up to the possibilities, and we can then carry this awareness and attitude back into our daily lives. A spiritual robustness is expressed through the daily living of a spiritual path. Spending time with nature as our spiritual teacher encourages an appreciation of death and life cycles.

There is something infinitely healing in the repeated refrains of nature –
The assurance that dawn comes after night and spring after the winter
RACHEL CARSON[6]

We need food for our soul as much as for our bodies. We may find this through music, art, sacred places, dance, walking in nature, being with animals or deep connections with people.

Realisation of ourselves beyond time, words and body provides the foundation for spiritual health. It is easy to get caught up in 'little' world experiences, the day to day running of our lives; expansion into 'big' world perception allows us to see the beauty, connection and order in the world. Giving thanks and expressing our gratitude for the lives we lead and all the gifts it presents us with opens our hearts. The *appreciation* anchor point incorporates this into our designs.

A spiritual perspective encourages us to be mindful of a bigger picture and timeframes beyond our human perspective. The Great Turning may take another 200 years to fully move into a life-sustaining Earth culture, but this is still a blink of an eye in planetary terms. Connecting with the bigger picture reminds us that we are just a part of this journey.

Our breath is unifying and is the connection between our internal and external worlds, and connects every living being. Each breath is as unique as every wave lapping on the shore.

We know the Earth has a very long breath of life, much longer than ours.

Davi Kopenawa Yanomani[7]

ACTIVITY: BREATH MEDITATION

Take deep breaths. With the first breath feel the air filling your lungs. With the second breath feel it in your abdomen. With the third breath feel it filling your entire body. Continue to breathe with your awareness on it filling your whole being. With each breath, as you breathe in imagine you are breathing in strength and energy; as you breathe out imagine any discomfort or tension leaving your body. With the next three breaths think about one thing in your life you are thankful for.

Focusing on our in-breath we will not find a distinct point of entry into our being; it is a continuous flow from outside the body to inside the body. Imagine your breath going out into the world, connecting with every living being.

CHAPTER 6

Being at our best

WITHIN EACH PERSON is a vast untapped source of energy. This energy has the potential for healing, creativity, wisdom and many other hidden talents.

Improving our well-being is one of the steps we can take to release this energy. This chapter continues to explore ways in which we can block energy leaks, be more effective and create a nourishing environment, enabling us to achieve more. We then look at how we can open up to our creativity. We consider our own abundance with right livelihoods and real wealth. The chapter ends with thinking about what it means to be empowered and our own leader. These can all become systems of growth, expansion, change, clarity and new horizons in our lives.

Reaching for our potential

We can all soar to great heights. This possibility exists within each one of us. For some of us we may already be stepping into our potential; for other people it remains latent, unseen behind the curtain. The inner world is as vast as the outer; there is an infinite, expansive universe within each and every one of us. We can reach for our potential through observation and design, unfolding the possibilities of our being.

Our potential is unboundaried; we cannot reach or fulfil our potential because there is always somewhere further we can take ourselves. We are also perfect in ourselves in the moment, just as a baby is no less perfect than a fully-grown adult.

Our expanded being may have a completely different form to our current selves. It may not be just more of the same; a bigger you, like a sapling to a big tree. A caterpillar changes into a butterfly, a grape seed turns into a vine. We may find ourselves different from who we are now. This of course is scary to our gremlins who may stand guard at the threshold. We may find ourselves under pressure from our gremlin to stay where

And the day came when the risk it took to remain tight inside the bud was more painful than the risk it took to blossom.

ANAIS NIN

. . . .

we are. As a seed germinates the outer shell has to crack and is lost to the earth, so too our growth and learning may involve us letting go of previous attachments that no longer serve us, like shedding skins of the past to allow us to shine. This creates clarity for our higher visions.

The difference between what we do and what we are capable of doing would suffice to solve most of the world's problems.

G ANDHI

·········

When we are at our best, we can serve the world and allow ourselves to fully contribute. Our own potential links with the potential of others and the culture we live in. By reaching towards our potential we are encouraging others to do the same. With ourselves as we are, there are a certain

amount of possibilities and ideas available to us. As we grow these possibilities increase. As we all grow and increase our collective potential the possibilities increase even more. We don't know what technological and interpersonal solutions are in the space of the collective potential that may allow us to live sustainably in harmony. Being at our best will enable us to participate in the Great Turning and help it to happen more quickly.

Soaring high

Beyond stillness
Within me the fire
Welcoming me into its dance
Of beauty, passion and fierceness
Flickering without,
Within,
Beyond.
I see no mystery,
Eternity
Unanimous in its greeting,
Beyond the full moon
I soar
In the space and stars,
Unfolding wings
Crushed and stiff
With inactivity
Breaking free
Of the prison
Inside of me
I know not how or why
I just know
And now it is time,
Time to fly
To unfold these wings
And set free
My beauty
My power
My strength
My glory

In a flashing rainbow
It escapes
Into the blueness
So ready and willing to take me
Able to caress me
And hold me in the vast hands
That can embrace
All life
All death
All beyond
And within,
The fire burning
Transforming
Holding the matrix
The web beyond
Within and without
Connections brewing
Vibrating in the currents
Flowing flourishing
Recreating
Soul fires
Flickering
Flaming
Enhancing
Restoring

Soaring high
Shining bright.

Being effective

In order to be at our best we need to be doing what we want to do and be efficient at it. Time is often cited as one of our main limiting factors. We all have the same amount of time in the week though some people make better use of it. In our daily lives most of us have ways we waste time. By looking at how we can save time we open up to thinking about the bigger picture of what we would like to achieve. Even small savings of just one hour a week can bring benefits. An hour of music or yoga a week would make a difference to our well-being. Time saved could have an impact on our earthcare systems. This could be as simple as just having enough time to make lunch instead of having to buy food with packaging, or a much bigger project.

Effectiveness is producing a desired or intended result. In order to do this we must be clear what the desired outcome is, otherwise we could end up somewhere entirely different. We also need to pay attention to the wider impacts and the inputs it takes to achieve our result.

When we are in the flow and being clear and decisive everything can run smoothly and we have a sense of achievement. We see the bigger picture and can focus on the details. We are thriving and able to complete tasks and make progress. We are unhurriedly able to juggle the tasks we give ourselves successfully and maintain a high standard of work. We have clarity and spaciousness in our lives.

Leaks and blocks

Identifying where we are losing time and energy will help us to remedy the situation. These leaks to the system prevent us from being fully effective. Observation of where the drains are can help us to stem them.

Some patterns of leaks of energy that are often observed are:

- Overcommitting
- Wasting time on unimportant activities
- Being late
- Losing things
- Lack of organisation
- Forgetting appointments and arrangements

Before taking on any new projects, consider in advance how big they might grow. It is easy to sow lots of seeds – they are little and it is a quick task – but then they need watering, a small, daily task. Soon they need planting out, which is a bigger job... And we mustn't forget to have time to harvest. If we sow too many seeds then we will find ourselves with more than we can properly care for. We need to sow an amount that we can maintain and nurture.

Sometimes we need to clear the decks before taking on board any more. If we have a backlog of seedlings that need planting out it may be useful for us to do this rather than sowing other seeds. When one part of the system is overloaded it can create blockages in other parts of the system.

If we are over our time budget we need to do some pruning. What can we move from our list? Can we ask someone else to do it, or say no in the first place?

Procrastination

Procrastination can take on different forms. What is it we are actually doing when we procrastinate? Procrastination can be a way of avoiding facing up to our responsibilities. The mind gym[1] identifies five main messages our gremlin can say in order to avoid the task at hand.

- Complacency – 'I can do it anytime, it's going to be easy so I don't need to do it now'.
- Avoiding discomfort – 'I'm not going to enjoy it, it's going to take ages, I'll start another time'.
- Fear of failure – 'I won't be able to do this, I won't get it right'.
- Emotional barriers – 'I'm too stressed, too tired, I'm not in the right mood, the time's not right'.
- Action illusion – 'I'm busy so I must be making progress' (although busy doing something else).

Procrastination is a symptom rather than a root cause. The cause may be fears, resentments or anger about the task. There might be fears of failure, change, being open to criticism or that it won't be perfect. If we just don't do something we eliminate the chance of failure and the opportunity to test ourselves. The resentments may be around feeling that it's not supposed to be your job, resentment of authority making you do the task or resentment of yourself for agreeing to do it.

There are small tasks that we put off, that may not have long-lasting consequences, but these can create a pattern for the bigger steps that we would like to take in our lives. How are you procrastinating about being at your best?

What techniques do we already have to deal with procrastination?

- Recognising spirals of erosion and finding points of intervention
- Measuring our inputs and outputs
- Reframing our beliefs
- Observing ourselves
- Building confidence in ourselves
- Appreciating what we have done
- Turning our limits into building blocks for design
- Using principles to reflect on the problem or find a solution

ACTIVITY: NUMBERED LISTS

Create a list for the day. Order the first six priorities on your list. These can be quite small tasks, and if the task is a big one it is best to divide it into smaller achievable chunks.

Complete the list in sequence. Keep with the first task until it's finished, then move onto the next one without reading the rest of the list. Continue until you have finished all six. Congratulate yourself and then number the next six things.

This method allows us to maintain focus, stops us procrastinating between tasks, and allows the subconscious to start working on the next task, so we are more ready for it.

Focused energy

We can identify when we are using focused or unfocused energy and assist in acting accordingly. If it is unfocused then we either need to attune ourselves to the job in hand or consciously decide to put it aside for a while and do something else.

> *Sometimes using tiny amounts of focused energy can move mountains, whereas masses of unfocused energy would not move a single stone.*
>
> JULIA CAMERON[2]

Our projects have different paces of growth and momentum. There are times when trickle-feeding jobs and taking chunks off them is beneficial and other times when it is good to conserve energy and take a proper break, coming back to it with full energy and focus, and complete the task.

There are other times when applying conscious effort and focus is necessary. In meditation the urge to move, open our eyes, and allow our thoughts to wander is there, and we need to keep coming back to our breath and drawing our focus in. Sometimes we need to stay seated at a task and resist the first, second and third impulse to get up.

There is a balance to be made between structure and flow. Sometimes we go where the energy is, doing things when we are in the mood and able to concentrate on the task. Other times we need to be disciplined and just do what we have to do and sit with the task until it is complete. We need to find the appropriate strategy for the situation and ourselves, and keep watch for our gremlins looking for an excuse or a way to procrastinate.

A big step forward to being an effective person is to know when to take a rest, reflect and nurture oneself to return with focused refreshed energy, and when this would be avoidance and it's more honest to stay with the task in hand.

Investing in ourselves

When burning wet or unseasoned wood we only gain a fraction of the potential energy, so we burn more to get less. When stocking our wood stores, it is best to get ahead of ourselves ensuring a supply of well dried wood to make most use of the available energy. This pattern is the same for other areas of our lives where we can end up chasing our tails trying to keep up. Keeping on top of things reduces stress, linking with our health. Spending time designing, blocking energy leaks and creating efficient systems can make best use of our energy in the long run.

When looking to buy solar panels we are told how long it will take for them to pay for themselves. This is the point at which the outputs exceed the inputs. As we saw previously, when we design systems we are aiming for the outputs to increase over time and the inputs to decrease.

We could think about how long it takes to pay back investments we make in ourselves. At what point would we be saving more time than we invested if we were to learn shorthand or to touch type, upgrade our filing systems or make other improvements?

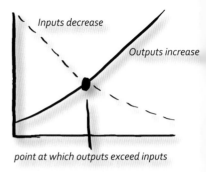

Inputs decrease

Outputs increase

point at which outputs exceed inputs

Our home environment

How can our homes encourage and support us to be at our best? Our environment is the physical edge between our internal and external worlds. It is the edge, the place of interaction with others, particularly if we share our home. Our physical environment affects our emotional environment and vice versa. It reflects our inner processes and both the positive and negative patterns in our lives: patterns of variety, hanging on to the past, unfinished projects, unity, growth, relaxation and play.

The space we live in can be fertile ground for thinking, health, creativity, positive relationships, work, learning and love. Or it could be a place of chaos, frustration and bad memories, with mini avalanches occurring whenever you try and find something. To improve soil condition and enhance fertility in the garden we would aerate. Dust and clutter could be seen as the pests and diseases of the home that restrict our growth.

We might be living in the past, emotionally connected to our memories through physical items, or living in the future: 'I'll make/do/read that when I have time'. Clutter is a product of procrastination, we put off dealing with what's in front of us: we'll put that cup away later; we'll do our filing another time. This is not being kind to our future selves.

Moving items on can be like pruning our lives. When we prune fruit bushes the plant is then able to put more energy into the remaining fruit, producing less but bigger fruit. The first step with pruning is to take out any dead or diseased branches. This could apply to anything that is broken – fix it or ditch it. Next we look at what branches are crossing over and rubbing each other. What is crossing over in your life and stopping you doing something else? Is there no floor space to put your yoga mat? Would you like to move home or go travelling but are too weighed down to do so? Our material assets can be used to pseudo-satisfy our need for protection and identity, but may inhibit our need for freedom, creativity and leisure. Pruning is not going to kill the plant and likewise moving stuff out of your life will actually enhance growth and allow space for new influences and experiences.

What beliefs do you hold about your environment and belongings? I remember reading 'a messy room is a creative room'. Another slogan found on mugs is 'a clean house is the sign of a wasted life' – is it? Or is it actually a waste of time looking for your keys buried under a pile of washing?

The words 'getting rid of' can be sticky in themselves and need reframing. Changing this to 'moving things on', or 'creating space' allows us to feel more positive about it. Regifting is my favourite way of moving things on. Moving into an abundance mentality allows for more flow of energy around us.

Beware of the gremlin presenting us with traps such as 'getting rid of things produces waste!' There are limits to what we can keep and find useful; it is not feasible or desirable for us to keep every yogurt and margarine tub. Storage is not recycling!

How to clear clutter

As autumn draws close trees send toxins into their leaves. As we let go of things we can imagine the toxins – the bad habits and painful memories – going with them. In the river of life activity we edited and remembered the highlights of our life. This is the same method on a physical level; we are left with the highlights. Clearing clutter becomes a cathartic, healing process.

We can expand the edges of tidiness and create new patterns by slowly increasing the boundaries of order. This leads us to another principle *work out from small well-managed areas*: success in small areas encourages us to continue as capacity allows. Thinking of our home in zones allows us to prioritise the areas to sort out.

For a while it may be necessary to stem the flow into your home and increase the pathways out. This may present us with many opportunities to practise saying no to things. We wouldn't want to make this a permanent state to be in – saying no to new things/projects/experiences in your life – but it may be a vital step to take for a while.

Motivations for change can come from focusing on what we are going to gain. Letting go of the past gives us space to expand into new horizons and allows for the 'now' in both the literal and metaphorical sense.

Potential exit routes:

- Donate books to the library
- Swap clothes with friends
- Charity shops
- Freecycle
- Local schools, kids' clubs or home-educating groups
- Friends, family, neighbours
- Putting things outside your house with a 'please take me' notice

ACTIVITY: ENERGY FLOWS

A permaculture design method is to map energy flows. You can do this for what comes and goes in and out of your home. This will provide you with useful information about where all this stuff is coming from and how you might be able to restrict items coming in. Mapping the pathways out of your house will also help to see how many places you can pass things on to.

Letting go
Releasing
Free to be me
Standing as new
In the present
Of myself

Being creative

Creativity

Everyone is creative. We continually construct our lives in new, meaningful configurations. Every conversation holds the potential to be innovative. We have a right to be creative; it is a natural part of our humanity. Opening up to our creativity allows us to become more resourceful in our daily lives and access some of our stored potential.

Imagination is more important than knowledge: knowledge is limited, imagination encircles the world.

ALBERT EINSTEIN
. . . .

Being creative is bringing our imagination into expression. We could expand our concept of creativity to include gardening, dressing, cooking and talking, to help us see ways in which we all live creatively – it is not just for some 'artists' to be creative. Creativity can permeate everything we do – if we let it. We can integrate both ways, being creative in our practical activities as well as efficient with our creative projects.

Permaculture is a creative process asking us to use local resources in new, unique, appropriate ways. We can use our ingenuity to create gardens, jobs, incomes and communities. Problems provide opportunities for us to be creative in finding solutions. When designing, the more inspirations we have in the *ideas* anchor point the more options we have to choose from.

Helping us to be creative

By blocking our energy leaks with being more effective and creating more space in our environment, we are gifting ourselves with the time and space to be creative.

Inspiration can arrive at any time, but there is also a lot to be said for putting the time in. It is a place of potential to turn up and be present to whatever arrives. When the ideas flow we need to be able to *catch and store the energy*, having a notebook to hand to sketch or write.

There are times of day when we feel more creative or are able to see new ways around an issue we have been pondering. We might notice a pattern in this; when we are driving, or in bed at the beginning or end of the day, while washing or exercising... It is often at the times when we are relaxed and have space for daydreaming that ideas surface. Walking or riding a bike requires us to use both sides of the brain and integrates thinking from the right and left side. Under stress the connection between the two hemispheres doesn't work so well and we function from our dominant side. The left side deals with logic, language and time. The right side holds imagination, intuition and creativity.

Stimulus to kindle ideas can be found all around us: watching other people or looking at the stars; listening to music or the waves on a beach; feeling the wind and rain on your cheek; a feeling in your belly watching a film. Snippets of conversation or opening a book at random can stir the imagination.

We can use metaphors found in pictures, natural objects and weather types to observe ourselves and access deeper meanings to our own thoughts and feelings. 'What fruit would describe how I felt today? If I were a tree where would I live? Which of these pebbles on the beach represents my future?' We can find meanings in the colours and textures, patterns and sounds. These sorts of questions can bring fun images to mind.

The icon for *integrate rather than segregate* holds little meaning in its individual parts. When brought together as a whole however we might see people linking arms and a star in the centre. Meaning can be created through its connections and organisation. If we find ways to cross-fertilise ideas it can give rise to unique combinations.

Our projects have different stages of growth. There are underground processes at work; like mycelium creating connections in our mind, we can prepare the soil and enhance this with food for our creativity such as ideas, stimulus, information and our environment. Sowing the seed of the idea comes next; when we draw down inspiration, we may have to wait for germination time. Next comes the watering, nurturing and growth stage. Finally comes the ripening and harvesting, sending it out into the world and reaping the benefits.

We have probably all come across the phrase 'thinking outside the box'; it may not be apparent though what shape it is. We can look at the characteristics of edges to help us to look for the edge of the box and move beyond it. The edge is a place of dynamism; it can be uncomfortable and we may feel the resistance, but it is also a productive, creative space. The edge is the place of innovation and discovery.

Tara Joy, a friend and wonderful painter, describes reaching this place with a painting where she can't do what she was planning and thinks about abandoning it. Sticking with it though and looking for the potential and growing edge she breaks free and it invariably leads her to a beautiful, unexpected place. She is now using that metaphor and experience from her art while setting up a reforestation project in India. Whenever she feels the resistance of the edge and thinks of giving up, she looks for a new route into the unforeseen.

There is delight and pleasure to be had in the process as well as the end. We can creatively use and respond to change and be open to new directions that emerge. Our lives feel a corresponding expansion as we release the infinite possibilities of our own being.

ACTIVITY: RANDOM ASSEMBLY[3]

This technique is used in design to break us free of our usual patterns of thinking, described here in terms of garden design, but the technique could be adapted to different designs or played with in many circumstances.

On paper or card write down all the elements in your design. On different coloured paper write down prepositions (words that describe relative positions such as under, inside, far away from). Now choose two elements and one preposition. You may come up with some funny ones such as the chickens on top of the rabbits. Think about how this might work and the interesting effects of this. This might lead you to ideas for a double layer hutch, or a chicken run on stilts. Keep going choosing three more cards. The more ideas the better. This is a great game to play with other people, especially children.

A thought breaks

A thought breaks
Washing over me
Percolating through my experiences
To catch a metaphor.
Ideas pushing forward
Flowing in the current
The distance coming into focus
The horizon beating its wings closer
Shimmering to be felt
Behind the mist of consciousness.
Whispered dreams in the night
With images fading with the dawn light
Outstretched fingers grasping at the fruit
To bring it to awareness
To show to my mind.
Shaping wafts
Like flames flickering into fire
Our dreams into reality
Our thoughts given power.

Thinking tools

Thinking tools can help us to expand our creativity and increase our effectiveness. By changing our patterns of thinking, our outer behaviours and systems are also transformed. By improving the way we think we can increase our quality of life and produce more effective solutions. Our design work benefits from improved analytical, reflective and questioning skills as well as generating more ideas to choose from. These tools are also useful for working and designing with other people.

Tony Buzan and Edward de Bono have produced large bodies of work for developing our thinking skills. Tony Buzan is best known for mindmapping.[4]

Mindmapping

Mindmaps are visual representations of information. They follow a branching pattern that mimics the structure of information storage in our brains. It is an open form of representing information allowing it to be continually added to. Their non-linear approach makes many edges for our subconscious to keep working away at, while the map remains complete in itself at any time. The design web follows the same pattern of creating thinking edges while allowing us to see the whole picture.

Mindmaps represent systems within systems. Each branch of the mindmap is a holon; it is complete in itself while still a part of a greater whole. The information is captured in a concise form that allows our brains to work on many different aspects at one time. Mind maps make it easier when we are trying to recall information, because they work with our visual as well as our conceptual brain.

Mindmapping is useful when juggling lots of roles in our lives and seeing how they interrelate. They can be used as alternative list writing to increase our effectiveness. I create a mindmap for every month showing each of my areas of activity including personal and family as well as work. It helps give me a sense of where the balance is

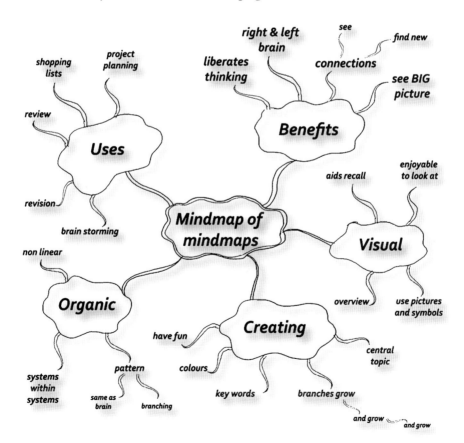

over the coming month, and shows that I might be overcommitted if it won't all fit on the page!

Mindmaps allow us to be creative and access both sides of our brain. When Leonardo de Vinci was asked how he was so inventive he answered 'everything is connected in some way to everything else'. Mindmapping liberates our thinking and allows us to see existing connections and make new ones.

ACTIVITY: MINDMAP OF SELF

Create a mindmap of yourself. Some suggestions for branches on the map are your past, present, future; your hobbies, likes and dislikes; friends, family; home and work.

Through the creation of the mindmap new connections, overlaps, ideas and patterns may emerge.

Parallel thinking

This traditional story reminds us to seek beyond our own experience for a more complete and deeper understanding. Edward de Bono[5] has developed parallel thinking tools where we examine an issue from different standpoints and integrate multiple perspectives.

The first of these is called a PMI, Positives, Minuses and Interestings. Whatever the issue or problem, we initially focus on all the *positives*. Next we look at the *minuses*. Lastly we can look at the *interestings* – anything worth commenting about that doesn't necessarily fall into either of the first two categories. For example we may be considering going jogging each morning. The *positives* may be getting fit and fresh air. The *negatives* may be less sleep, it is weather dependent and it's still dark in the mornings in winter. The *interestings* may be the feeling in your muscles.

The second technique is Six Thinking Hats, which we will come to when we look at decision-making in Part Three.

In Rajasthan in India six blind men visited an elephant belonging to a prince. They had never felt an elephant before and were excited by the opportunity. Outside of the palace afterwards, they discussed what they had felt and quickly fell into an argument. "It was like a rope," said the one who felt its tail. "Nonsense it was like a wall," replied the man that touched the belly. "You are both wrong, it is like a snake," retorted the one who felt its trunk. The man who touched its ear thought it to be a fan and the man who felt its leg was convinced it was like a tree trunk. "It was sharp like a spear," assumed the last man. While they continued the debate, the prince rode by on his horse. He stopped and listened and then declared them all to be right. "But" he warned them, "You each know only part of the answer of what the elephant is like. You need to take heed of what the others are saying and then you will know the whole truth."

Right livelihoods

Having a livelihood is an important part of being human. A 'right' livelihood means it is 'right' for us as an individual, it suits our needs and is in line with our ethics. It also means it is 'right' for others: that we are not harming or exploiting other people or the planet. Our job can provide many functions in our lives. Beyond financial gains it might also provide a connection with other people, a way of using and developing our skills or contributing to the world. Our jobs can be our delight, passion and play.

What would it feel like to do what we love and love what we do every day? We need to find our joy and purpose in life and ways to satisfy a whole range of ethical, intellectual, social, emotional, physical and financial needs. There may be a transition phase where we can volunteer or apprentice to build up our skills.

Poly-income streams allow us to have *multiple elements for important functions.* Our current culture promotes people having one full time job. A poly income would be where we have yields from different sources. Joe Atkinson is one amongst many permaculturists who have designed themselves a poly income. He works as the learning co-ordinator in the Permaculture Association, a gardener and permaculture teacher, and is developing mentoring at the University. He says, "A poly-income can yield an incredible diversity of rewards that I believe would be difficult to find in a single job. I am able to connect the inputs and outputs of one job with another. For example, my gardening informs my teaching and vice versa, and this informs aspects of my job as learning co-ordinator. So, in a sense, each element forms a kind of symbiotic relationship with the others to provide mutual support and development, much like in a natural system." At the beginning in particular, he found the switching between jobs required a high degree of personal organisation and investment in time management activities. Hc also found that in order to change, he needed to go on an inner journey to challenge the mindset of the rat race he had been conditioned with.

There is a risk of all of the streams becoming rivers and being overworked. If this is the case we can regift one of the opportunities to a colleague.

We can weigh up the inputs and outputs for our work. A word of caution: we may be so busy thinking that it's not about the money and accounting for the yields of satisfaction, enjoyment and worthwhileness of the work that the financial side can get left out or sidelined. A balance can be achieved where it's a 'both/and' situation – the satisfaction and the money – rather than 'either/or'. Doing work that inspires us, and gaining financially from it, is a winning situation.

*Don't ask what the world needs
Ask what makes you come alive
Because what the world needs
is people that are alive.*

HOWARD THURMAN
. . . .

To strive for leisure as an alternative to work would be considered a complete misunderstanding of one of the basic truths of human existence, namely that work and leisure are complementary parts of the same living process and cannot be separated without destroying the joy of work and the bliss of leisure.

E.F. SCHUMACHER[6]
. . . .

In your work you must feel
1. *That your existing skills are being utilised*
2. *That your skills are being improved*
3. *That your work is of benefit to the wider community*
4. *That you get your just rewards*
Anything missing and the work will leave you unsatisfied.

MERRICK[7]
. . . .

Desire lines

In a landscape the desire lines are the places where people want to walk. Generally people like to take the shortest route cutting corners across the grass. A landscape architect told his team to just turf over the whole area in the courtyard connecting freshly built apartments instead of creating paths. After a couple of months they returned to see where the desire lines were – i.e. where people wanted to walk – and over the rough mud tracks that had been created they built the paths, exactly where people wanted.

In our own lives we have desire lines that appear by virtue of us wanting to travel that way often, time that is effortlessly spent. Where are the desire lines appearing in your work, with people, places, hobbies? What do you enjoy spending time doing? Who do you like spending time with? When and where do you feel you are best using your skills? Desire lines often occur subconsciously, but paying attention to them can inform us of our true wishes and longings and lead us to our right livelihoods.

You can ask yourself 'what do I really want?' Ask yourself repeatedly until an answer comes. It is OK to not know what your purpose is. This is a place of power and potential. It could be that the next step you need to make is to slow down, stop and think.

Real wealth

When we think of wealthy people we generally consider the money and assets they own. Real wealth looks beyond money and asks what we value. The word 'wealth' comes from Latin and combines well and health.

Wealth extends beyond our bank accounts and there are many ways in which we can be well off. For example in the majority world there is often a richness to communities that has been eroded in the West, where we are buffeted by technology and material wealth and no longer have to be dependent on one another and often don't even know our neighbours.

Real wealth asks us what we value in our lives that brings us well-being. Ways in which we may be wealthy could be in our relationships with family, friends and our community. We have wealth in our basic needs of shelter, water and food. Having freedom of speech, to make choices and to move around is valuable. Our skills, creativity, inspiration, humour, knowledge, time and ideas contribute to our real wealth. Culture, entertainment, safety, being loved, health, living in nature, and space are of value.

It is not just what we have ourselves but the resources that we have access to. Social structures such as healthcare, schools, library and transport are of value. Nature is an abundant resource providing for our needs.

The fair shares ethic encourages us to look at the equality of opportunity and voice in the world as well as the distribution of material wealth and control.

Eight forms of capital

Our real wealth, just like our bank account, is not static; it can grow or be depleted. Ethan Roland[8] identified these eight forms of capital to provide us with a different way of accounting:

- Living capital – animals, plants, healthy soil, clean water.
- Financial capital – money and financial investments.
- Material capital – tools, buildings, infrastructure.
- Experiential capital – the embodied wisdom from actually organising and carrying out projects and activities.
- Social capital – the connections and influence we have in our communities.
- Intellectual capital – the acquisition of knowledge and ideas.
- Spiritual capital – expressed differently within varying religions, an idea of reaching spiritual attainment through prayer and 'good karma'.
- Cultural capital – only a community of people can hold this capital. It is the shared internal and external processes of the community, including its arts, songs and celebrations.

We can *create* real wealth with our actions. Reforestation and gardening increase nature's abundance. Knowledge, empowerment and connections increase our own wealth. We can also look to *conserve* real wealth by protecting nature and soil, water, forests and species. We can look to halt erosion of communities, sharing stories and preserving skills. We can *use* our real wealth by using our time and exchanging what we have and cycling resources.

Real wealth and abundance in design

Throughout the design process we can give attention to creating abundance. We can use the *pause* anchor point to give attention to developing abundances of rest, relaxation and health. The *helps* anchor point invites us to recognise our internal and external resources. Abundance is a *pattern* of nature we can emulate. In the *integration* anchor point we can focus on meeting our real needs.

We can begin by identifying and valuing what we have. We often place value on something that we do not have. The relationship or the job we want becomes of extreme importance while we forget to be thankful for our family or connection with nature. Fostering contentment and gratitude with what we have will shift our attitude to one of abundance rather than scarcity, and is why the *appreciation* anchor point is important.

Increasing our financial capital

There are two ways of increasing our financial capital: get more money in, or reduce the money going out. Often the focus is on earning more, but we can also make differences to reduce our outgoings that can improve the quality of our lives.

Prepare your own food rather than buying packaged.

 Repair things and buy second hand where possible.

 Change how you look at what you already have – imagine you are shopping in your home, or on holiday in your neighbourhood; what can you see that interests you? Rediscover some of your books, music, hobbies rather than buying new.

 Make use of seasonal produce: this does not necessarily have to be your own; it is still far cheaper to buy local, organic, seasonal fruit and make your year's supply of jam.

 Catch and store energy in the local economy: it is far more likely to come back to you than money spent in chain stores.

 Discover and value free entertainment: sunsets are nature's gifts to us; time with family and friends; walks... there is plenty that money cannot buy.

 Yield is limited only by the imagination. Recognise and discover new yields from whatever systems we are in: work, home, projects, organisations, gardens. There is a wealth of yields to be had.

ACTIVITY: MY WEALTH

In what ways am I wealthy?

Think of all the resources and talents that are available to you.

What areas of my life would I like to be wealthier?

What could help to bring abundance into these areas?

These are areas of your life that could benefit from some design.

Empowerment and self leadership

Empowerment

Permaculture is an empowering process – empowering people to be who they want to be and contribute to life. Most power isn't given to us; other people can help us to tap into our own sources of power, the power that keeps us strong and burns like a fire inside, power that creates and moves us forward.

In physics, power is the ability of a machine to convert energy from one form to another. If we translate this to people we could look at power as the ability to focus our energy into the activities we want.

Power is the strength and ability to go where you want to go, be who you want to be, do what you want to do.

CHRIS JOHNSTONE[9]

ACTIVITY: FEELING MY POWER

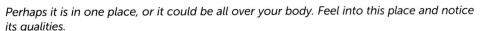

Close your eyes and sense into your body.

Where in my body is my power?

Perhaps it is in one place, or it could be all over your body. Feel into this place and notice its qualities.

Notice the fluidity of its boundaries.

Where could my power take me?

From becoming aware of your power as a physical force within yourself you will begin to notice times when you are using your power.

After doing this visualisation you will begin observing when you are feeling empowered and when you are feeling disempowered. Notice when your power feels muffled. Empowerment is the removal of any obstacles to your power source. What are the circumstances when you feel disempowered? How does that manifest in your body? This is a two-way communication between your body and mind. How is your body reacting and what does that tell you about the situation?

Using our power does not mean being dominating over other people. It is about having the confidence and self-esteem to do what is right for us. We can empower ourselves to be more honest. When we are working from our power we become proactive rather than reactive and work to create rather than consume. We can use our power to find our voice in the world and step up to the mark. If we were all in touch with our own power and all stood up to say we want changes in how the planet is treated, we could experience rapid transformation.

Don't play small – it is a game you have grown out of
Fill every part of your being and stand tall
Stand in your truth and in your beauty
Feel the surges of power through your body
Willing you to make sense of your life
Make the voyage to your destiny
The journey is in the travelling
Each step showing new views of yourself
Reflect and absorb the sights
Appreciate and fully embrace yourself
Your life a celebration of life
Your life a celebration of you
NOW is the time to shine brightly and soar high
Life is anticipating this of you

Self-leadership

What does it look like to be our own leader? How would it feel to wake each morning and to say to yourself "I am my own leader", placing yourself at the heart of everything you do?

When we take leadership of ourselves we accept personal responsibility for all of our thinking and actions. We move away from being the victim and blaming. This includes blaming ourselves. We can trust and follow our inner knowing, there is congruency between our wishes and our actions. We walk our talk. We are proactive in looking for solutions, able to tap into our inner resources and assured that we have answers within ourselves.

Our self-management includes focusing on tasks, and creating and maintaining the boundaries that allow us to achieve the goals we set. We could create a balance of work and play in our lives and be fully present with whatever we are doing.

We could embrace and accept our whole selves in all our brilliance and in all our flaws, able to celebrate our strengths and improve our weaknesses. We could be our own nurturing parent, not overindulging and accepting excuses or criticising our efforts. We could stretch and challenge ourselves looking for growth in our being.

When we are in touch with how we are feeling and able to listen to ourselves we can be more authentic and united with our own visions. We are able to lead ourselves on our own path through life.

ACTIVITY: WHAT I LIKE ABOUT MYSELF[10]

Appreciation of ourselves and recognising our skills and abilities is a vital part of accessing our own power and self-leadership.

Write down as many answers to the question:

What I like about myself is...?

Spend five minutes noting down all the qualities that you like about yourself. Take the whole five minutes (more if you like), you may feel like you have run out of things after a couple of minutes but just sit and dig a bit deeper to find what you appreciate about yourself.

This can be very unfamiliar territory for a lot of us. There are cultural standards of how much we can show appreciation of ourselves, and whether we are taught to be modest and not 'blow our own trumpets'.

Self-appreciation is a valuable tool in our toolkit; it leads to appreciation of others and abundance thinking.

The bright abyss

All that holds you back is fear,
Fear of change,
Of the unknown,
Of you, in all your glory,
Fear of the dizzy space,
The bright abyss of boundless light
Of the starry, starry firmament
And deep unfathomable night.

So leap, leap, leap
Into the bright abyss
Let go, let go
Spread your wings and fly
Coast in the gentle breeze
Soar in the azure sky
For who will remember you as you are
When high above you shoot and flash
A brilliant, brilliant star.

DHAMMADINNA

. . . .

Designing for ourselves

Designing for ourselves is an interesting and invigorating process. It can be very empowering to honour ourselves by giving time and attention to our goals and visions. It demonstrates self-leadership and a pledge to being our best.

We may be inclined to just daydream about it, rather than carry out a methodical design process. However, when we are able to give attention to each anchor point we gain deeper understandings.

Defining some parameters of the design is useful. You may want to work on a holistic vision of yourself or there may be areas of your life that you choose to focus on.

Aranya, one of my co-teachers, started designing for himself as part of his permaculture diploma.[1] In his diploma was an overall design for his life, which included looking at his water, travel and right livelihood. On reflection he sees that each one of these could have been a more detailed design in itself. He found it interesting to work with the concepts of nature and apply them to his life, and continues to use design as a part of on-going development. He has been using design to maintain his effectiveness while writing his book *Permaculture Design – A Step by Step Guide to the Process*.[2]

Overleaf, in Suzi High's design we see how small changes can lead to much bigger outcomes.

Opportunities for design

* Intuitively we know when we are not heading in the right direction. We may have an idea of where we want to get to but can't see how to get there. The design web can break us free of mental loops that we may be caught in.

* Designing builds trust and confidence that the vision is possible.

* It is a chance for 'me' time, experimenting and being creative.

* Our life designs are constantly evolving; using the design web allows us to keep in tune with the changes in our lives. Some of the 'petals' on the design may fall away. We will see in Suzi's design how the zoning was an important feature initially, then had less relevance as those systems started running smoothly. This allowed space for new ideas to come through.

* We can honestly reflect on our life, self and goals.

* The answers are within us already; designing allows them to rise to the surface.

* Small steps can be achievements in themselves, and even beginning a design can be satisfying.

* Observation is key throughout: what is happening within me, my environment and with other people?

* Keeping a written record is a reminder of our progress.

* Reflecting on the process of designing as well as the content of the design improves our skills as designers.

How

One idea for approaching the anchor points is to use methods that stimulate the multiple intelligences. Each of these suggestions and starting points could be used for thinking about one or more of the anchor points. Using many methods has added benefits of activating a healthy mind, and provides different openings for insights to emerge. You can make notes of your experiences in your learning journal.

* *Visual* – create a mindmap. Useful for the *integration* anchor point to see the connections.

* *Linguistic* – write a poem or story to show *appreciation* of yourself and others, or to stimulate *ideas*. Your poem or story could also show the *momentum* of the design.

* *Musical* – what would your *vision* or your *limits* sound like? Make sounds or songs in the bath, garden or car. Music and sound can be part of the *pause* anchor point.

* *People intelligence* – ask a friend to listen to you as you talk through one or more of the anchor points. (see interruption-free listening in Chapter 7, p.118). This can be part of the *reflection* anchor point.

* *Self-intelligence* – ask yourself one or two questions before you go to bed, re-questing that the answers emerge from your dreamtime (not that you lie awake contemplating them!) Write down your thoughts as you wake as a stream of consciousness, without editing or analysing as you go.

* *Naturalistic* – take a walk in nature with questions in mind and see what emerges. Thinking of the *principles* and *patterns* is appropriate.

* *Logical* – write a list, or make a flow chart. The *action* anchor point in particular benefits from some logical thinking.

* *Kinaesthetic* – use physical objects to represent your thoughts on an anchor point. For example use leaves, pebbles, ribbons, buttons or seeds to represent each of your *helps* or *limits*.

Design case study: Suzi High's zone 00

Suzi High is the international co-ordinator for the Permaculture Association Britain and teaches permaculture. Here she shares the story of her last ten years since she first learnt about permaculture and designed her home life to be more effective. (Follow the numbers to see the sequence of the design.)

6 The first thing this did was boost my confidence. I was actually doing a lot of what I wanted to do, and I had learnt a little about looking after myself; I napped most afternoons when the children did so that we could play later. The second realisation was how disorganised I was and the impact of this. I lost hours a week to finding keys, shoes and my purse.

13 Our monthly and yearly plans include time for myself, children and couple time.

10 From doing this I had time to appreciate the opportunity I had in being a parent. I also had the space to think more about my own goals and priorities. I appreciated that I could find a balance between doing my own projects and being a loving supportive parent.

15 From these ideas we set 10 annual priorities. We plan each month's activities with our priorities in mind. These include nurturing important relationships, developing home sustainability and maintaining on-going projects. We have a calendar year wall chart and weekly white board to help us and our children achieve our goals in life.

11 These changes created momentum for part time work, and more design work for the permaculture diploma. I was able to do some community development work focusing on women's health. Later I got the job with the Permaculture Association and was involved in setting up the Leeds permaculture group. This provided a supportive network of like-minded people.

5 I decided to survey my time and spent a week documenting my activities every 30 minutes.

9 Reorganise home.

8 I had identified two important needs; the first to organise my home and place important and frequently used items in easy to find places. The second was to involve the children in tidying the toys away at the end of the day so that I could have a clear living room to do work in the evenings.

PAUSE
REFLECTION
APPRECIATION
MOMENTUM
ACTION
INTEGRATION

16 The design has reached an equilibrium point where the momentum is constantly moving me towards my vision with time to revisit what it means to me to be a world changer. I check how I can be available as a parent, supporting the children in being useful members of society. I see from changing my own world how this can have a ripple effect.

1 My vision was to free up time to get out there and start being active. I want to maintain a balance between world changing that's outside my front door and the world changing work of being a parent and of taking responsibility for my own food and energy use. I wrote a plan for world changing, recognising that I could nurture myself, my children and my community and change the world in the process.

2 Having three children under five meant I was tired and didn't have any time to myself. I felt heavily involved in the minutiae of family life.

3 Having just done my permaculture design course I had some tools for designing and observing. Seeing lots of opportunities for involvement out in the world motivated me.

4 I found the survey of my garden so eye opening (was it really that shape?) that I thought that I might not be aware of my own time use.

7 This led me to think about how I could use the pattern of zoning in relation to my home.

14 We have a folder for parking ideas about doing things around the home and in our lives. The children are invited to add ideas as well.

12 I used *small and slow solutions* and have discovered that little things can add up to make a big difference. The next principle I used was *integrate rather than segregate*: I involved my husband and family in the planning of our yearly priorities.

VISION

LIMITS

HELPS

PATTERNS

IDEAS

PRINCIPLES

Postscript: Since this was written Suzi has continued with the design process and reassessed her goals and visions. This has led to a new direction in her life towards nursing.

PART 3: HEARING EACH OTHER

CHAPTER 7
Communication

HEARING EACH OTHER

CHAPTER 9
Working in groups

CHAPTER 8
One-to-one relationships

Communication

OUR INTERACTIONS
with others influence
everyone's quality of
life. This chapter is probably the most significant in terms of peoplecare, because communication is the key to relationships. It is the bridge between two people, the glue that holds marriages together and allows groups and families to function. Our social well-being relies on good communication. Words can be medicine or poison for our relationships, building rapport or destroying trust.

Central to communication is our ability to listen. This part is called 'hearing each other' because listening is the foundation for healthy interactions; from this we create fruitful, sustainable relationships. Listening shows respect and allows us to be in touch with the other person's feelings and thoughts. Truly listening to people is a gift and deeply nurturing. We can bring our self-knowledge, awareness and development into our relationships to make them more rewarding.

We begin with observation and then think about the limits for communication. Next we think about assertive and compassionate communication. We reflect briefly on distant communication. We move on to giving and receiving feedback, what conflict is and how to restore peace.

Principles are used to bring a permaculture perspective to our interactions. The themes in this chapter are applicable to the next two chapters of one-to-one relationships and groups.

Observation of people

Unless we have some training with our vocation most of us aren't overtly shown how to observe other people. It is something that we learn implicitly throughout our lives. Hence we mostly do it on an intuitive or subconscious level. Perhaps we have an altercation with a friend and later we find out they were feeling unwell, we might think to ourselves, 'they didn't seem quite themselves' or 'I thought something was wrong'. But at the time we might not have been registering those observations and we didn't check in with them or change what we were doing. Improving our observation of people around us will require becoming more conscious and reconnecting with those instinctual processes. This will allow us to interact more with our observations, becoming more mindful of our interrelations.

When we observe other people we can use all of our senses. What words and tone of voice are we hearing? What are we seeing in their body language, their posture, gestures? What are we feeling?

ACTIVITY: BODY SCAN

A scan of our body language can provide us with insights into our own feelings and those of the other person. We can ask these questions first of ourselves and then widen our awareness to the body language of the other person. Listening to your whole body with your whole body.

What are my body language and posture revealing to me?

Is my body open or closed?

Where are my hands and feet positioned?

How is my body listening and responding to what is going on?

Our existing emotional state will impact on what we hear as well as the responses to any feelings as we are talking. If we are tired, angry, worried or afraid we might miss some of the message, or it could get blown out of proportion. Likewise, the other person's emotional state will be influencing what is happening for them as well, so

we can be observant of what their body language is revealing about their emotions.

How people are reacting to us can also be a mirror of ourselves. Does this show me to be the person I want to be?

We will be interpreting the non-verbal communication, the body posture, facial expressions and gestures. Other visual cues such as clothes and hairstyles will also have subtle influences on our filters. Our ears will be tuning in to the tone of voice, pitch and volume as well as the words. We will be continually responding to our internal feelings, although mostly subconsciously.

Any observations are interpreted by our own minds and we make assumptions based on our previous experiences that may not be true. We are guessing what is going on for them internally, based on how we externally express our inner worlds. The words we use express our emotions and our cultural beliefs, but someone else may have a different way of expressing the same things. Likewise the same external behaviours may be used to express entirely different emotions. The most complex challenge of observation is our subjective interpretations.

The phrases people use may indicate self-limiting beliefs about the world or themselves. The use of incisive questions that we used in shifting self-limiting beliefs are appropriate to ask of others, such as 'What do you really want? If we put that limit aside what could happen?' Initially, we may want to just become practised at noticing beliefs as they arise rather than trying to challenge them.

Our observations give us hints about the person's current needs. Perhaps we notice that our friend is rubbing her back while talking; we could suggest that we sit down and continue the conversation. Giving time to observe before jumping in allows time for tact and appropriateness. Maybe we notice that someone is looking exhausted as we are about to ask them to do something, so we could alter our course of action.

We can check with the other person by simple questioning. 'Am I correct in thinking/hearing...?', 'Do you need...?'

The next level is to be able to observe ourselves and someone else simultaneously. We will resonate with their emotional state on some level and we can observe inside ourselves and how we are feeling, to give us clues as to what is going on for them as well as providing insights into our own inner world.

We can build up a long-term picture of our family and friends; how they are in different situations, with other people and at varied times of day. We could use the biotime diary to plot our interactions. For instance we could plot the times we have positive nurturing encounters with our partner and when we have arguments. This might provide enlightening insights into other contributing factors. Another challenge is knowing what is coming from them and what is coming from us, and what is occurring from the alchemy of the two. Recording our observations might be able to shed some light on this.

We can observe any spirals of erosion or abundance; what events precede arguments? What positive spin-offs are there from spending time together?

Look to like

Jodie Tellam teaches permaculture on allotments to young people who have been or are on the edge of being excluded from school. Permaculture has helped her to focus on the positives in life and she has taken this through to her observation of others; it has given her a 'look to like' attitude. This is of particular value in her work where the young people are lacking in self-esteem and are more used to people finding fault with them. With each person she observes them with the aim of finding their positive attributes. From this she is able to home in on strengths and find ways of enhancing them.

The 'look to like' attitude is about where we focus our attention, changing our perceptions and finding the plus points. How we look at people will determine what we see: if we are looking at them wanting to find something we like, or something to connect with, we are likely to find something. It doesn't mean that we have to be blind to someone's faults and weaknesses. It is important to balance 'looking to like' with an awareness of our own first impressions and instincts. We don't need to open ourselves up and trust someone too early if that doesn't feel right. It's also key to take proportional risks and observe over time.

Limits to communication

What are we trying to achieve with our communication? Are we trying to connect, persuade, instruct, inform? Is it for our benefit or theirs? Do we just need to be heard, to think our thoughts out loud? There are countless reasons we communicate with our fellow beings. It is essential in our lives to have social contact, and yet there are times when our communication results in much anguish, upset and misunderstandings.

With effective communication we are clear on what and why we are communicating and so is the receiver. Often though, we are just on automatic pilot when we talk, not really thinking about why we are engaging in conversation, and the receiver misses the point.

A lot of energy is lost in our communications. We spend time communicating and instead of enhancing our relationships it can antagonise the other person. Messages get distorted and misunderstandings lead to arguments, frustration and emotionally shutting off.

Part of the issue lies in how we send the messages and the other is how we receive information. Our messages begin as thoughts and images in our heads, they then have to pass through our perceptual filters to become words. When they reach someone else's filters they get interpreted into thoughts and images in their minds. The filters can distort or trap parts of the message. Our conversations are like waves travelling between two shores: we think the wave arrives the same as it left but often it has either grown or diminished by the time it reaches the other side.

Let's examine what happens with these filters:

- **Words mean different things to different people**.
- **Hearing what we expect to hear**. Our brains try to find similar patterns in our mind for something else we have experienced or heard, rather than hearing it as something new.
- **Expectations, beliefs and stereotypes** interfere with the message.
- **Ignoring information that conflicts with what we already know**. Remember your gremlin trying to maintain your status quo? Here it is standing guard ensuring that nothing new comes in to shift your thinking, or twisting meanings to fit.

- **Evaluating the source**. What we think about someone will greatly determine the weight we give the message. As Emerson said, "Who you are sounds so loudly in my ears I cannot hear what you are saying". The assumptions we have about the other person and their motives colour the message. Do we assume the person to be cooperative or dominant, helpful or bossy?

- **Sweeping statements** such as 'you *always* do this' or 'you *never* lift a finger' are distracting. The listener might get caught up in whether it is always or never true and is busy trying to find exceptions to defend themselves and misses the core of the message.

- **Interference and noise**. Other things going on in the background both in the environment and within the listener's mind can smokescreen the message.

- **Confusion over whether message is opinion, rumour, fact, belief or assumption**. The sender often presents information as fact when actually it is just either their own or someone else's opinion.

- **Filling in the gaps**. As soon as someone starts speaking we will be filling in the gaps with what we think they are about to say. Words are linear but our brains are non-linear. Our brains are taking single words and phrases and forming whole pictures in our minds. It can then be difficult to take out some of the pieces to add the rest of the message.

With all of that going on at any given time it is hardly surprising that what we say may not be received as we meant it. We can get caught in a spiral of erosion where we are not feeling heard so we repeat ourselves louder, which provokes more of the filters in the listener, so less of the message is heard, and so on. How can we tighten up with our communication so that it is of more use in whatever we are trying to achieve?

ACTIVITY: OBSERVE THE FILTERS

1. Listen to someone else's conversation, perhaps on the television, between family members or on a train. Notice when the message appears to be distorted by the listener in some way. Try to guess which filter may have intercepted the meaning.

2. Next time you are in a conversation, tune into your own filters. You may find that this in itself is a distraction and interfering with the conversation, just be aware.

Extending the limits

When we communicate openly and honestly we can move forward in our understanding. Communicating from the heart allows us to express what we wish and to hear what the other person needs to say. Trust and willingness are the foundations to effective communication.

What we want is communication where people take time to understand our opinion and why it matters to us, to bridge the differences and come to mutual understanding, through acknowledgement and positive body language. We can enjoy someone reflecting back what we have said, showing that they have listened and are ensuring clarity by checking their understanding. When there is flow in communication and we can both be fully present there is peace and relaxation and we can be calm and grounded. When we feel received and receiving there is reciprocal appreciation and times of connection.

We learn to communicate from mimicking those around us – our parents, teachers and peers as well as the media – rather than being explicitly instructed. We are conditioned by our cultures in when to talk, how much to say, what to converse about, our body language, how quickly to talk and how much to listen. We haven't necessarily had good examples of communication that is effective and compassionate, that allows us to problem solve together and nurtures our relationships. We could be much more effective in communication if we relearn patterns that facilitate ways of forming meaningful, constructive relationships.

After a while you will begin to see not only when you are listening through filters but also when the person you are talking to is doing the same. It is easier to work with your own filters to begin with and question your own reactions. Becoming more mindful of how we speak as well as how we listen helps with compassionate communication.

We all have some filters to enable us to make sense of the message otherwise it would be like listening to a foreign language on the radio. We could think about replacing these filters with permaculture filters, such as abundance thinking, and looking to like in both the person and the message. We can take self-responsibility for what we say and use 'I statements' to own the message.

Closed questions are ones that only have a limited range of answers; usually they can be answered in one word, 'yes', 'no' or 'maybe'. They tend to be leading – 'do you like this film?' An open-ended question which allows the person to think more for themselves and give an honest, in-depth answer would be – 'what do you think of this film?' The self-enquiry questions in this book are open ended to encourage exploration.

In a sense any and all of the principles could be used as filters and guidance for our listening and the language we use. Here are a few examples:

 Value diversity. Accept that their message may not fit with our map of the world but that doesn't make it any less valid. Just like in the story of the blind men and the elephant, they are presenting a different perspective.

 Observe and interact: Expand our observation and listening skills. Consciously watch body language, and observe our reactions; including observation of our own filters and when they are coming into play.

Find the edge of understanding. Where do we agree?

 Integrate rather than segregate. 'Yes, and' rather than 'yes, but'; 'both and' rather than 'either/or'.

Assertive communication

Let's look a bit deeper into the emotional barriers that may limit our communication. Our emotions very much influence what we say, how we say it and why we say it. This may come across as aggressive, passive or assertive.

The word assertive has negative connotations for some people. They can think of it as synonymous with aggressive behaviour, being pushy and forceful to get what you want. In these pages I will reclaim the word, to see it as the balance point between being aggressive and passive; a place we can be in to meet our own needs without compromising the needs of others.

Aggressive body language can take the form of finger pointing, leaning forward, shouting, trying to look bigger and looking down on the other person. Words can include insults, subtle put downs and inappropriate humour.

Someone may be displaying aggression because they are feeling insecure, wanting to protect someone; they may be overwhelmed, stressed or having a bad day. Fear, pride or anxiety may be underlying their behaviour.

In the short term aggressive people have a chance to vent their anger, feel powerful, and may get the outcome they desire. But they may also experience stress, physical tension and guilt. In the long term they can become alienated and there may be a breakdown in their relationships. There is likely to be a lack of trust. If a solution is reached through one person being aggressive then it is possible that the other person doesn't take ownership of it. If they only agree because of the aggression they may later avoid taking action on the agreement.

Passive people on the other hand may be quiet, shying away from eye contact. They may ignore or run away from the conversation, change the subject or shrink into a corner and appear small and weak.

They may be acting this way from feelings of hopelessness, boredom, lack of respect for themselves or the other person. They may just want an easy life, to avoid conflict and to not upset anyone. Their lack of self-esteem may prevent them from saying what they want to say and they might internalise their thoughts.

In the immediate moment this allows them to feel safe and avoids conflict, but it can set precedents for the future, encouraging the other person to be more dominant. In the longer term the passive person can become resentful, guilty and deeply angry. Squashing the emotions at the time just defers the emotion and can lead to sudden explosions at unexpected moments with unconnected events and people. This is recognisable as the classic 'passive–aggressive' swing. They may just agree for a quiet life and take too much on and then not actually do anything that they were meant to, feeling either guilty and anxious or more resentful and angry.

Aggressive people are looking to get their way regardless of the cost to the other person. They can end up with win/lose arrangements – where they win and the other person loses. Passive people will forsake their needs for the sake of peace and allow the other person to get what they need, resulting in lose/win situations.

The assertive person will take the time to try and find a solution where everyone's needs are met. It is about finding the way to integrate ideas and come to a common understanding. In contrast to the forward approach of the aggressor or the shrinking back of the passive person, we can think of the assertive person as having an upright vertical spine. Communication is much more two way with questioning and listening, accepting feedback and the conscious use of positive language. The body language suggests strength rather than aggression, with open chest and shoulders back.

The assertive person is placing equal value on taking care of themselves and caring about their relationships. They are coming from a place of maturity and perspective with an awareness of the bigger picture.

At the time negotiations may take longer, it may take courage to stand in the fire and stay with the process to find solutions. The solutions that are reached will be more sustainable and develop trusting relationships. This builds assertiveness in others, and increases feelings of acceptance and self worth for both parties.

We can see this pattern of aggressive and passive behaviour in society around issues of injustices and environmental destruction. There are those that get up and fight about it, and those who want to put their head in the sand and pretend it's not happening. When we fight and win an argument, the battle just continues and there is always a new issue to protest against. When we bury our heads, we are giving the message that it's OK for this to happen and more of it goes on. Finding this middle ground of assertiveness is essential to finding long-term solutions to these issues and preventing them from popping up again.

Winning happening

The concept of win/win has been useful to gain an understanding of how to meet the needs of two individuals or organisations. However it has an implicit assumption that needs considering. I win – you win is still thinking in terms of me and you, us and them. It is seeing you and me as separate. It also has the tendency to dissolve into compromise where in fact neither party win and we have lose/lose, or to think of win/win as fine as long as I win a bit more than you. Moving away from personal attachments to winning, Clinton Callahan has conceived the term '*winning happening*', where everyone is happy and benefiting, where winning is an active verb and current for all people.

Permaculture design is a way of engaging with the situation to create winning happening for the whole system.

Compassionate communication

Nonviolent communication

Marshall Rosenberg invented the process of Nonviolent Communication (NVC).[1] While he was growing up he had opposing experiences, one of his uncle caring for his ill grandmother on the one hand and on the other boys picking fights with him on the street. He wondered why some people were able to show deep compassion for their fellow people while others were violent.

His journey to answer this question took him to many places and he realised that language was key. The word non-violence is translated from the Sanskrit word *ahimsa*, its meanings include reverence. Gandhi used *ahimsa* to emphasise his approach to the revolution for independence in India. It is referred to here as compassionate communication because of its benefits in accessing compassion for ourselves as well as others. NVC is a method for creating winning happening without being aggressive or passive.

The giraffe and the jackal

The jackal in me barks and makes a lot of noise, it wants to be heard, it wants to be understood. My jackal's bark is high-pitched, repetitive and forlorn. It stands guard letting me know that there is something going on within. It barks to get through your barriers, to be noticed, "Come and give me the love, acceptance and appreciation that I so want". Instead of coming closer though you run away or bark back at me. "That's not what I want." My disappoint-ment turns to anger. I start to bark at myself "How could I be so stupid to ask for friendship? I should have known better."

The giraffe in me stretches its long neck and views the whole picture. It can see the filters through which you talk, it can see over the filters through which I listen. The giraffe listens and talks with its big heart. When my giraffe talks within me it has kindness and compassion. "I understand that I am trying my best, I can see the need I have for intimacy, I respect my feelings of insecurity. From here I can see where you are coming from, where you would like to go. I can see your need for quiet and time alone."

Rosenberg named the jackal and the giraffe to show the different ways we have of responding. The jackal is really just a giraffe with a communication problem. We can use jackal language to ourselves and to the other person. There can be different parts of us chattering away at any time. While on the surface we remain calm we might be berating ourselves internally.

The giraffe too can speak internally or externally. The giraffe uses its wider perspective to see beyond the thoughts to the feelings and then even one step further to the needs behind this. Compassion with others comes more easily when we have been compassionate with ourselves first. When the giraffe talks to others it can empathise with their feelings, and connect with what their needs might be.

Jackal language	Giraffe language
Demands – making threats so you do as I want	Requests – it's OK to hear a 'no', and connecting with what I am saying 'yes' to
Judgement – what happened is good or bad, right or wrong	Observation – what actually happened or was said, without interpreting it with assumptions
No choice – there is only one way to respond, can't, have to, must	Finding choices and alternatives
Blame – finding fault	Taking responsibility
Imposing my judgement – should, ought to do next	Offering information about how I am feeling and what I am needing
Deserve – rewards and punishment. 'I deserve this...'	Expressing what need or value wasn't met and what you would value.
Labelling – I am, you are, they are	Discussing the behaviour or action (based on the observation) separate from the person

Expressing our needs

With compassionate communication we are making a choice and acting with intention to nurture the communication that we do enjoy, and supporting ourselves to come from this place by acknowledging our own needs. We can hold ourselves and keep our heart open to the other person.

There is a formula for how we express ourselves from a place of compassion, using giraffe language. We come from a place of connection to ourselves and create the space for connection with the other person.

- The first step is to **welcome the judging and blaming**; when we recognise that we are doing this, we can avoid judging the judgement.
- Next we **identify the trigger**, we observe what has happened.
- Then we **fully sense our feelings**.
- We become **fully present with our need**s.
- Lastly we make a **request to the other person or to ourselves**.

The observation of what has happened is like a camera. It is without judgement or assumptions. When a cup of coffee goes over on the rug, the observation is 'there is coffee on the rug'. It would be an assumption to say it was an accident, or the other person was careless. We often jump to conclusions about why something has happened and our thoughts and feelings are based on the assumptions rather than the observation.

The other important thing to do with observations is to take out the 'you did…' This can make the other person immediately defensive, and they can lose the rest of the message. Using 'I' statements allows us to take ownership of what we are saying and acknowledge that it is through our subjective perspective that we are talking. Instead of saying 'you leave the washing up', we say 'when I see the washing up left…'

When something happens our minds immediately fill with thoughts. These thoughts could guide us to our feelings and needs or they could cloud them. If we manage to see beyond our thoughts to our feelings we are then one step closer to our living energy of needs. When we are fully present with our own living energy of needs we can see what is missing – why the jackal is barking.

Instead of acting from the lack of this need, we can change it to positive phrasing, 'I am open to receiving…' The awareness of this need can lead us to then make choices about how to meet the need. Perhaps we can meet the need for ourselves or with someone else. Perhaps your partner is tired when they come home from work and your need is to connect with them, but their need is for quiet and they don't want to talk. If these needs are recognised then it is possible to find another way to connect with each other and have quiet with a back rub or a hug. NVC works towards finding ways of meeting the needs of both parties, never raising one person's needs over another. It is coming from the place of abundance aiming for both/and, rather than either/or.

When this connection is opened and we are connected to the need the options reveal themselves. When presenting the option to the other person we can do so as a request, knowing that it has to be right for them as well as you for it to work. Requests may be for actions to be taken or different strategies to be adopted. Before making the request check in with yourself that it is OK to hear a 'no'. It might be disappointing or even painful to hear a 'no' but if we are unable to accept a 'no' then it is actually a demand we are making.

We can also make requests to ourselves. This might be simply requesting ourselves to just be or to take some time out. We can acknowledge to ourselves that it is challenging.

We are changing the habits of a lifetime as we learn to speak from the heart. Are we able to welcome our own and each other's stuttering, stumbling, and silences as signs that we are replacing automatic pilot with conscious speech?

Lucy Leu[2]

A word of caution: initially this method could be used with jackal undertones or motivations; used to try to get our own ways. People have said they don't like being 'NVC-ed', and feel manipulated by the process. A friend, Kate, was in a discussion group and afterwards another person used this method to give her some uninvited feedback. She had been noting down each time Kate spoke during the discussion. She was trying to use an objective observation but her motives were coming from the place of the jackal not the giraffe, and Kate said that she couldn't take anything else in after she heard this. Before we even start to speak we need to take a moment to connect with ourselves and ensure that we are coming from the heart.

This process can seem quite clunky and formulaic at first, and like anything takes practice to become smooth and flowing. When we first approach NVC we go through the stages of the competence cycle and can feel all of those differing emotions.

Just listen

There is one very key skill at the heart of any successful communication – listening.

Listening can make all the difference between a nurturing, productive, stimulating relationship and one fraught with difficulties. After looking at the filters to communication we can see how challenging it is, when we properly listen we try to dissolve these filters.

Our cultural understanding of conversations is for me to say my bit then you have a chance to say your bit, and then it's my turn again and on we go. In most circumstances this works OK. However, this style of conversation doesn't necessarily give us much scope for either improving listening skills or for exploring the depths of our thoughts.

A wise old owl sat in an oak
The more he heard, the less he spoke,
The less he spoke, the more he heard,
Why aren't we all like that wise old bird?
ANONYMOUS
. . . .

When we are in the flow of our thoughts and someone asks us a question, well meaning as it might be, it can take us off in a different direction. Imagine their words are taking them to a destination unknown to you and your question may be taking them off at a right angle.

Think and listens/interruption-free space

'Think and listens' or interruption-free space is one of the most versatile and useful tools in our peoplecare toolbox. In pairs you take turns for a given period of time to be the listener or the thinker – thinking your thoughts out loud. It is interruption-free space; the listener is active in listening and does not ask any questions, make any comments or prompt at all. The thinker may come to a point of having expressed the immediate surface thoughts and become silent; this is normally the point at which we jump to fill the gap with a question. However, when given the time the thinker can drop down into deeper thoughts without being guided in a particular direction by a question.

The ear says more than any tongue.
W.S. GRAHAM
. . . .

Active listening

This technique encourages us to develop skills that we can bring into our everyday listening style. We develop patience in maintaining connection with the person talking and allowing them to say their all. It can involve putting our own agendas aside and keeping our thoughts as well as our ears with the talker and listening with our whole body. Like when we are meditating, our thoughts may jump around and we need to consciously bring them back to the talker.

It is familiar in meetings or conversations to be so busy rehearsing what to say that we miss that someone has just made the same point. Often people argue and don't hear that they are actually agreeing with each other. In order to be able to keep our thoughts with the other person we need to trust ourselves to be spontaneous with our speech. We can be confident words will flow as they are meant to when we speak from the heart. If we know we are going to be listened to with patience we can pace ourselves and give ourselves time to find the right words as we speak.

Listening is multifaceted, more than just words; the body language, breathing, posture, underlying emotions and context of what is being said can all be attended to. When we open our ears and minds to truly listening we become more observant. We are able to listen between the lines; what words are used and what is not being said? Deep listening involves all of our senses.

Listening is an important way in which we can support and nurture our friends and family. It is within us to find solutions to our problems, and sometimes the best help we can have is the time and space to piece together the answers for ourselves. Within groups listening shows valuing of everyone's contribution and cultivates respect.

We may assume that we are capable of listening, but when we take time to properly listen we may become aware of how little we did it before. It can be like entering stage two of the competence cycle, where we suddenly realise how much more there is to know. This is a positive step in becoming a more active listener. We may also become acutely sensitive to not being listened to ourselves. This is not to be taken personally, we have to remember that most of us are not taught how to listen and we follow cultural norms. Transforming how we listen can start to shift the cultural patterns of listening, initially with those closest to us, and this can ripple out.

There are abundant opportunities for us to practise our listening. It is a gift to hear someone's inner world and an honour that people want to share it with us.

ACTIVITY: INTERRUPTION-FREE LISTENING

Offer a friend or family member some interruption-free time to talk. You may like to ask for an exchange of time and swap over or just offer your listening as a gift. This could be between two and five minutes, even up to ten if you both want. It is good to agree the time beforehand so that if they reach a point of silence you don't jump into the gap but allow them the space to go further. It could be just that you offer them time to talk about the film you have just seen together, their day, or holiday plans, or they may want free range, whatever feels right for the moment.

When you have finished you can ask them how it was for them to be listened to. Some people can find it a challenge to talk in this way at first; they may be surprised at what they say when given the chance. Reflect in your journal how it was to just listen, and if you were listened to what that felt like.

Distant communication

When we are not face to face with someone either professionally or socially we have a different set of challenges and opportunities. We will do a short PMI (Positives, Minuses and Interestings) for emails to start us thinking about their different qualities. This will lead us to a simple tip to ensure that we maintain our peoplecare.

With the PMI there may be some qualities that could be viewed as a positive or a minus depending on your perspective. For example you may think it is positive to be able to receive emails any time of the day, or you may think that there is no escape and this is a disadvantage.

Emails

Positives

- Instant communication at any time of day
- Can send the same message to many people across the globe
- Lower cost
- Can think of responses and reread them before sending
- Written trail of conversations

Minuses

- Don't know if and when it reaches the destination and there can be delays in replies
- Can be bombarded with emails and it's a challenge to keep up with all of them
- Can exclude people who don't have emails or computers
- Can ping pong questions and take longer than just speaking on the phone
- Debates can snowball easily into conflicts

Interestings

- No body language to read
- Can waste as much time as they save
- Diversity of people we can communicate with in one day
- How quickly they've spread to become the dominant form of communication

From the PMI we could then think of a way of bringing more peoplecare into our email communication both for ourselves and other people. This may be around waiting before replying to an email that you find irritating. It could be to do with the time of day that you read and respond to them.

ACTIVITY: PMI ON DISTANT COMMUNICATION

Do your own PMI for whatever forms of communication you use frequently; letters, phone calls, internet social networking, online forums or teleconferences.

From this think of two tips that you could apply to help with peoplecare; one for yourself and one for other people.

For example, you may want to monitor the time you spend on the computer. And for other people you may want to check in with them about whether it is a good time to talk on the phone when you ring.

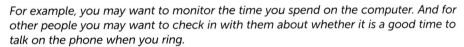

Giving and receiving feedback

Often we are trying to communicate feedback to other people. Feedback can take many different forms from uninvited criticisms to marking of our essays at school, from body language to direct compliments. We are brought up with feedback, both informal remarks from our family and friends to more structured advice from our teachers. The feedback we receive can contribute to our belief systems about ourselves, particularly if the feedback was about us as a person rather than our behaviour. We regularly give feedback and it is important for us to remember that the opinions we give to those around us influence how they feel and think about themselves. Feedback is a big part of our lives whether we are conscious about it or not. Becoming more mindful about it will help to make it valuable.

Feedback in natural systems

In our bodies we have mechanisms of feedback that regulate everything from our temperature and blood sugar levels to the pH of our blood.

There are four main steps to our body's feedback mechanisms:

- The **system** that is being regulated, e.g. body temperature.

- The **receptor** monitors levels, e.g. skin and blood receptors.

- The **processing centre** co-ordinates the incoming information, e.g. the hypothalamus.

- The **effector** brings about change on the system, e.g. sweating, constriction of blood vessels.

There are two types of feedback: self-regulating and self-amplifying.

Self-regulating feedback is when there is a reference point (or a 'normal' or 'baseline') and the receptor monitors deviations from that reference point, the processing centre then sets the effector into action to bring about change to bring the system back to its reference point. This feedback seeks to stabilise the situation, hence it is also known as balancing. Central heating systems in our home work on this basis. We set the thermostat to a certain temperature; when the temperature drops, the boiler is fired up and we get more heat until the thermostat receptor registers that the temperature is reached, then the boiler switches off.

Self-amplifying feedback is used to intensify the situation, and is also known as reinforcing. The more we do something → the more something else happens → the more we do something. You will recognise this as a spiral of erosion or abundance.

How does this relate to giving and receiving feedback to each other? We firstly have the system – the person or action that is being regulated is the receiver. The receptor is the giver of the feedback. Next we have our processing centre – our minds, where the feedback is processed. Finally we can put the feedback into effect and modify our behaviour.

Giving feedback

We often pick up on the behaviour of others and offer them suggestions, advice or criticisms. As givers we can firstly be aware of what the system is that we are giving feedback on. It is then clearer to offer feedback on this and not make generalisations into other areas. For example, if we want to offer our children feedback on their table manners we can stick to that and not bring in their school marks, which just confuses the message. The giver will have their own calibrations for their opinions, based on their filters, experiences, desires and cultural norms. Some of these will be consistent; others can vary with moods and other factors such as time of day. These will influence the behaviour that we notice. Sometimes we will let actions pass us by, other times we mention them.

As a giver we need to examine our motives; why are we giving it and what changes would we like to occur? This will determine what and how to give. Do we want to encourage, correct, show blind spots, express gratitude, motivate or criticise? Self-regulating feedback is trying to stabilise and return the system to the reference point. Everyone has their own subjective reference points. These points are often set by our parents' feedback and hence we find ourselves repeating their phrases when our children deviate from these reference points. We can be trying to return a system to our reference point rather than its own. Therein lies one of the biggest challenges with feedback; that feedback is not acted upon because it does not correspond with the receiver's reference points.

Timing is crucial in giving feedback; what could be taken on board at one time might blow up in your face another time. Trying to assess where the person is at before beginning to give feedback can help determine whether they are open to it or not. We can explicitly ask this with formal feedback: 'Are you open to hearing some feedback?' It is empowering for the receiver to have the choice. Equally though, if we leave it too long after the event, it can feel like we are holding a grudge and the time for intervention may have passed.

Reinforcing feedback aims to increase the activity. If we like something and want more of it, then we give feedback. This feedback is focused on appreciation, approval and gratitude. When we admire the conduct we want, we are implicitly asking to enhance it. Appreciation can be more motivating than criticism. Nancy Kline[3] recommends aiming for a ratio of 10:1 of appreciation to criticism.

A useful phrase for promoting development is 'even better if...' It allows for improvement next time without squashing confidence or denying effort made. "I appreciate ... it would be even better if next time..."

Receiving feedback

When we receive feedback there are three steps: we have to process the information, decide what to do about it, and then we have to put it into action.

The first step of processing the information depends on our own filters and moods at the time; they have the ability to distort or delete parts of the message.

One of our communication filters will be evaluating the source. If we know the person's reference points and are in agreement with them we are more likely to heed the feedback. If we are apprenticing with someone we respect, and aspire to behave more like them, their words will have an impact on us. We are more likely to respond to feedback if we can see there is congruency between what the person is saying and their own actions.

As well as receiving external feedback we have our own receptors that are monitoring proceedings. Our minds co-ordinate all of this incoming information. Before we give feedback we can begin by asking how it went for them. This allows us to gauge their emotional state before launching in, and saves us having to repeat something they already know. As a receiver we can tune into whether we are receptive at the moment.

Feedback sometimes bothers us. It could be because of the process by which it was given or the content or the changes that might have to happen as a result of it. How and when feedback is given can have as much of an impact as what is said. If we feel it was inappropriately timed, in front of other people or said in an offensive tone of voice, it can cause us to not actually hear the message itself. Letting go of the circumstances and focusing on the message can help us to move forward and allows us to self-regulate.

If we want to avoid this information swirling around our heads, we need to move to the next step and find an action or a way to improve and take it forward into something achievable and meaningful. If it is not used in some way or discarded it can become pollution in our minds.

When feedback is given that is wildly different from our own reference points it can be too much for us to process in one go. We can remember to find small and slow solutions and design achievable steps for ourselves.

What can go wrong with giving feedback

It is a well-known phenomenon for children to increase their 'bad' behaviour if they get attention for it. Instead of the attention they get bringing the behaviour back in line, as it would for a balancing feedback loop, the attention actually acts as reinforcing feedback and reinforces the behaviour. You say 'stop doing that', and they think, 'great – I'm getting a reaction; I'll do this more'. To correct this you can shift the system you are regulating from their bad behaviour onto their good behaviour. This also stems back to an understanding of their living energy of needs and tuning into what they may need in the moment. If they need attention and connection with you then they will look to reinforce behaviours that meet this need even if it is in an unhelpful way.

Another issue with giving feedback is when we want to disagree or justify our actions, 'I would have done that but I didn't have time', or such like. Receiving and responding can put us on the defensive. It can lead to ping ponging back and forth and can descend into an argument. It helps to bring in our listening skills and hear the whole message without interrupting. We can do our own processing on the information ourselves later, and remember that what they are presenting is their subjective experience. For the receiver to be allowed to have the last word is empowering. 'Do you have any last thoughts you would like to add?' We can later sort out the wheat from the chaff and find the kernel of truth in the messages.

Feedback is sometimes disguised in anonymous gossip, group emails or broad comments about 'people in general'. Our minds can play with these comments and associate ourselves with them, or blow them out of proportion.

Sometimes we ask for feedback when actually we just want some praise and appreciation for our efforts. Equally frustrating is when we are looking for ways to improve and only get 'it's fine'. We need to be clear and specific about what we want when we ask for feedback.

Benefits of feedback

Feedback enables us to learn more quickly. We can use it to improve our own well-being. Creating a feedback culture can be used to improve our relationships and functioning of groups. It is also part of creating momentum towards the Great Turning. Informal and formal feedbacks are part of the *reflection* anchor point and can keep us on track with our design.

There are four main reasons for giving feedback that we can keep in mind:

- **Improvement** – Highlighting areas to develop and enhance.

- **Effectiveness** – Assessing if actions have desired results.

- **Confidence** – Building confidence by noticing what went well and appreciating all efforts made.

- **Guidance** – Signposting people to extra support and techniques.

Conflict

Conflict can arise from feedback given in the form of insults, criticism and complaining. Conflict ranges from minor discords to long-term battles, from our own inner conflicts to world wars. The harm it causes to all systems is immense and if we are to move to an Earth culture we need to find ways to avoid and deal with it.

With our family and social groups the symptoms of conflict can range from feelings of disquiet and unease, to bickering, to full-blown arguments and violence. Daily niggles, sulking, sarcasm and put-downs all cause tension. Conflict can drain our energy, destroy our relationships, create mistrust in the world, and ultimately wars devastate the life-support systems on the planet.

What function does conflict serve?

A large proportion of the entertainment industry is based on conflict. It is the drama that brings the story to life and makes it interesting and unpredictable. Films and books accentuate these parts of stories, distorting the views we have about the world. We don't get to see the three months of peaceful family dinners, we just get to see the one big blow out. This tendency can then be carried into our own lives where we place disproportionate emphasis on times of conflict rather than times of peace.

Signs of conflict are like the jackal barking at us to let us know that something isn't right. They call for steps to be taken and change to happen. They tell us when our needs aren't being met or our ethics and principles are being compromised. When we ignore these signs they get louder and louder. Conflict can provide a release of tension and allow the unsayable to be said. Clashes can at times provide a deeper understanding of each other and the situation. Conflict can be a catalyst for growth and change, or leave us upset and afraid to talk about something. What other ways are there to fulfil those positive functions without all of the negative impacts that usually accompany arguments? Discord is a natural phenomenon and we need to learn to manage and utilise it so that the ethics of peoplecare, fair shares and earthcare are not compromised.

How do conflicts arise?

Conflicts arise from misunderstandings, greed, fear and jealousy, when we come from a place of ego (I, me, mine) rather than seeing the bigger picture. Competition and the need to protect something can lead to bigger conflicts. The jackal speaks when we have unmet needs. This is especially true when we perceive someone else to be stopping us meeting our needs, or that our needs and theirs are incompatible.

Some conflicts arise from our cultural conditioning; we have inherited a scarcity mindset and its associated beliefs of 'us and them'. We inherit more specific likes and dislikes as well, of people and situations.

Some conflicts arise from us wanting change; we give feedback to provoke people to shift to our own reference points. This sometimes has the opposite effect of entrenching people more in the way they are. We all believe our reference points to be the right ones, but someone else's can be just as valid. We have different maps of the world that guide us in our interpretations of events.

Our brain recognises patterns and will interpret stimulus according to what has happened before in our lives. We were played a piece of classical music on our NVC course, and afterwards we were asked for our feelings. These ranged from joy and freedom by being reminded of trips to the ballet to the other extreme of frustration and anger from memories of being told to mime at the back at a school concert. We were all given the same stimulus but it provoked different emotions and feelings based on previous experiences. Our feelings of previous experiences and associations with different people influence and sometimes predominate our reactions to what is happening in the moment. We are not always upset for the reason we think we are, or from the current experience or stimulus.

When we project the past onto the future we can lose effectiveness in dealing with the present challenge.

Patterns of arguments

There are patterns that are replicated time and again in arguments:

- Not listening to each other
- Voices getting louder
- Interrupting
- Reverting to aggressive or passive behaviour
- Each person only looking at it from one angle
- Confusing the messages
- Agreeing with each other at times but not hearing or acknowledging this
- Focusing on rights and wrongs, 'either/or' rather than 'both/and' and solutions
- Pushing boundaries

Prevention

Preventing conflict saves us time and energy. When we argue we have to deal with the effects of this as well as the issue itself. We can avoid the unpleasant side effects of loss of self-esteem, mistrust and depression that can accompany the conflict by acting in time to deal with arising issues.

Can we spot the warning signs? And if we do see it coming, how can we interact with the observation and deflect it, or move out of its way? Can we observe patterns in when and where the arguments occur? If we often have stressful interactions with our partner when they come home from work can we plan to be out of the house for a while so they have time to unwind before having to speak to us? If our children regularly get into a fight while we are cooking dinner, can we cook earlier in the day, or bring dinnertime forward?

These two examples connect with the needs for space and food. There are other needs that we could look to meet before they build up. Giving people time and space to be heard is important. When thinking of preventative measures we can look for ways to meet people's needs in advance of them having to 'shout' for attention.

There needs to be a balance between nit-picking and letting things go. When we continually pick up on everything that someone does it can be hugely demoralising; conversely when we don't pick up on things in the moment we need to be aware of them not being bottled up in us with the potential to resurface. Passive behaviour is to ignore things we don't like and not comment. However, what often occurs is a swing into sudden aggressive behaviour at an unexpected time when we can no longer hold it all in.

It may be easier in the short term to ignore and turn a blind eye to fraying at the edges, but this could just result in a larger rift. The proverb *a stitch in time* reminds us of putting things right now saving us a bigger job later.

Starhawk[4] looks at how a tree windbreak works as a way of emulating this to deal with strong energy coming towards us. Instead of trying to block the energy with an impermeable edge which can actually create eddies and more energy, or just trying to duck out of the way leaving the energy to blow around indiscriminately, we can seek to bend like the trees absorbing and diffusing the energy.

ACTIVITY: FINDING THE PATTERNS

This is another opportunity for us to use a biotime diary. If there is someone with whom we feel we are regularly in conflict with, we can note the times and circumstances of both conflict and peace. We can also make a note of other factors that we think might be of influence. For example it may be that we are having many arguments with our children: from keeping a record we may observe a pattern of them happening before meal times. Or we may note the amount of sleep we have had each night and observe if this affects the frequency of arguments.

Keeping a biotime diary may also show you the exceptions and the times when you are at peace with others.

Restoring peace

I attended a three day workshop focused on improving group functioning. Ironically a conflict arose in the group, a few minutes of loud voices and disagreement that quickly escalated, leaving feelings of anxiety and irritation in its wake. Despite being given lots of attention over the next two days it was never resolved, it actually gained more momentum. Conflict was spoken about from lots of different angles, and by the end I was thirsty for some positive stories. Different subgroups were formed on the last day, one of which was conflict resolution; this was shortened to the 'conflict' group, and sure enough there was conflict in this group. I heard, in the closing round, one of the main people involved repeating his desire to continue working on conflict, and thought how he appeared to be bringing conflict into his life, even under the guise of wanting to work on conflict resolution.

Reflections on the drive home brought me to a realisation that we were in fact feeding the conflict, in the attempt to try and resolve the few minutes of tension. I thought how different it could have been if instead of 'conflict resolution' we were working on 'restoring peace'. Instead of the word 'conflict' being said hundreds of times over the last three days we could have been repeating 'peace', like a mantra bringing it into being.

'How do we restore peace?' is a very different question from 'how do we resolve the conflict?' When we are focused on the conflict we are still in the past; asking about restoring peace focuses us on the present and the future. It can help us to hold on to the intention to maintain good dialogue and think more positively about the situation.

That doesn't mean to say that events have to be forgotten about or brushed under the carpet; it may be necessary to revisit the incident to move forward, or it may not be. Emphasising restoring peace allows us to consider where we would like to be and the choices we have to consider to get there. We can choose whether to analyse or discuss the incident further or whether to put it to bed and not feed it any more and direct the energy to a different vision.

Ways in which we can restore peace

- Finding the edge between needs
- Interruption-free talking space
- Listening
- Exploring options together
- Making requests not demands of each other
- Owning our reactions
- 'I' statements
- Not taking things personally or misconnecting things
- Having breathing time
- Focusing on the patterns of the argument rather than focusing on the details of what was said can help to create different, more peaceful patterns
- Forgiveness of ourselves and our part in what happened
- Saying sorry
- Speaking of the present

CHAPTER 8

One-to-one relationships

OUR RELATIONSHIPS contribute significantly to our emotional health. We begin this chapter with looking at what happens between people, how we can create nurturing relationships and give and receive support. Throughout our one-to-one relationships we can be mindful of the ways we communicate.

One of the anchor points of the design web is the *principles*; in this chapter we look through the lens of each principle to see how this relates to couples, parenting and friendships.

The edge between ourselves and other people

Humans like to create all sorts of boundaries and this tendency has contributed to our perceived separation from nature. We like to define our 'self' as something distinct and separate from the 'other'. Sharp distinctions can result in alienations: 'us and them'; humans and other species; humans and the Earth. However edges are not impermeable barriers, they are entrance and entry points, passageways between two 'selves'. We live surrounded by air and every time we breathe there is a flow of air from outside to inside the body; where is the edge, the separation? In conversation words flow back and forth. Is it my words or your words or is it the combination that creates a conversation?

The edge between two people is a place in itself. It exists separate from you and me. Communication passes through the edge in the form of conversations, shouting, insults, compliments, music, books and images. How we communicate and the filters we have influence the edge. Emotions are transported through our smiles, laughter and ideas. Touch, intimacy, emotions and of course love all flow from one person to another.

We have filters that determine what we allow to pass between us. Fear, blame, anger and guilt contract the edge and we build barriers, trying to close ourselves off from the other person. When we close ourselves off we can become depressed and this will become a spiral of erosion with us shutting ourselves off further. If we are coming from a scarcity mindset then we will perceive the edge as a place of protection and try and build it up to make it impermeable. This thinking applies on a national level as well. Coming from an abundance mind-set we can actively open up this edge to allow influences from others. Happiness, love and trust expand the edge.

We can support and nurture this edge – the place of relationship – to enhance our own and the other person's well-being.

Life is the gift

Tell me, tell me
Find your way home
Who are you?
Who are you?
In all your brilliance
In all your flaws

Tell me, show me
Your home
I follow your lead
I am my own leader,
We travel together
To distant lands
At home,
Here and there we stand
Together apart
With thanks for life's intensity

Tell me, listen to me
Wonder with me
Gifts wrapped in disguise
To bewilder and amuse
To throw us off course
From life's longing

Who am I?
Who are you?
Who are we?
We share
Pulsating between
The push and the pull,
Who knows where
The current will take us,
Home home
Feel our way home,
For life is the gift
We are all looking for

Nurturing relationships

For most of us our primary experience of being nurtured was from our parents. They hopefully helped us to learn skills, praised us, supported and guided us. They looked after our emotional and physical well-being.

Throughout our childhood the attitudes of parents and significant others such as family members, teachers and doctors can lay down beliefs about the world and ourselves. Comments they made probably related more to their own beliefs, feelings and desires than 'the truth' although we were unaware of this at the time. We continue to be influenced as we grow older, our significant others becoming our partner, boss, guru or friends.

The attitudes of both the critical and the over-indulgent person could have come from a place of wanting to nurture us, but could leave us holding beliefs that do not serve us any more. Our gremlin can use these viewpoints to stand in our way.

A critical person could have been finding fault to try and provoke improvement. This could have left us with self-beliefs such as 'nothing I do is ever right', 'I need to be perfect'. An over-indulgent person could have let us off the hook, allowing us to not push ourselves or continually doing things for us rather than allowing us to learn to do them ourselves. We may now hold beliefs like 'I don't need to try', 'there's always a way out' or 'I can't do it by myself'.

A nurturing person strikes the balance between the two and finds ways to encourage and support without undermining attempts to develop.

When we nurture plants we help them to grow and provide protection; by observing their needs we can provide for them. Their needs will be different at varying stages of growth. We 'harden off' seedlings, getting them used to colder conditions step by step so that they are able to withstand the move from a warm greenhouse to the colder outside.

When nurturing children we support them to gradually make the transition from the warmer, safer home environment to the bigger, outside world. Nurturing other adults can be more of a two-way process, where there is give and take. We can create encouraging environments. We can have physical places that are light, spacious, cosy, warm and quiet, where it is possible to be nourished by just being there. We can create emotional environments that support us in accessing our feelings and working through difficult emotions, by giving people the space to talk and acknowledging that it's OK to share. Social environments can encourage connections, support and feedback with open and willing communication.

Timing is crucial. There are times when we prune a tree and it benefits, and other times of the year when we would do more harm than good. The same applies for our strategies for nurturing people. The effects differ depending on when we do things, again illustrating the key need for observation before intervention or feedback. Imagine you have been trying to experiment in the kitchen with a new recipe and you are unsure what to do next, then someone comes and takes over and you feel disempowered. Imagine the same scenario but you now have people coming over for dinner and a backache – now it feels supportive for someone to come and take over. We need to be mindful of the other person's perspective rather than making assumptions. Awareness and observation encourage us to see individual needs. We can work from the *patterns* of support that we can give to the *details* of what is needed in the moment.

When talking about cultivating a healthy mind I described the importance of being able to learn from our mistakes and how this can provide us with rich information and learning opportunities. In our relationships there will be times when we have to step back and allow someone to take their own course, even if we can see a learning opportunity coming. Sometimes we have to allow someone to make their own decisions which may bring undesirable outcomes in the short term, but will be more beneficial in the long run as they learn for themselves. This is part of *allowing systems to demonstrate their own evolution*. We can provide the conditions to nurture someone but they have to do their own growing.

Leadership of ourselves and others can include the qualities of a nurturing person: guiding but not directing; pushing but not forcing; stimulating rather than being prescriptive; supporting instead of doing it for them.

Giving and receiving support

Support for each other is a necessary part of our human existence; interdependency is the common pattern in nature. We do not live in isolation and are not able to meet all of our own needs by ourselves. There are some basic requirements that by their very definition have to come from other people: our needs for love, affection and connection. Support for each other, from loved ones, work colleagues, friends and even strangers, improves our quality of life, increases our ability to grow into our potential and helps maintain our well-being. Support strengthens and enables people to help themselves.

A nurturing environment allows for passive and active support. Reciprocal relationships create symmetry and balance allowing greater support to travel in both directions. We can create synergetic relationships with mutual benefit; *many hands make light work.*

Giving

Giving support can take many different forms. It may be an extra pair of hands, a listening ear, encouragement, practical assistance with heavy jobs or childcare that is called for. Asking people questions about the continuity of their lives; 'How is your shoulder today; did you find a resolution to your problem last week?' shows care and support.

When we give support to someone it's not essential to do the work for them; this can be disempowering. Our best support is to provide a bridge for them to access their own internal resources. They may need to connect with their stamina, practical skills, decision-making skills, wisdom or intuition. We each have all of these within us but there are times when we lose our way. We can show trust in them being able to do it for themselves. Advice can sometimes be constructive but often it is of most value when we give someone the space to talk and find their own way to the solution.

Just being born is a miracle, to grow and make a difference in this wonderful world, is grace indeed but to live a life that touches others is amazing beyond compare.

TREE OF LIFE INSPIRATIONS[1]

It helps to come from a position of strength; being centred and well in our own zone 00 grants us the space to be able to support others. When we are filled with our own urgent tasks, ill health and emotional upsets it is harder to give to others. Tomas Remiarz and Jed Picksley are permaculture activists and teachers, who travel around projects in the UK volunteering their time. They see themselves as resources for other people. When they first arrive they spend time observing. They look for ways they can direct their energy to apply *minimum effort for maximum effect*. Often they see jobs that need doing that allow for greater flows of energy. They do some of the more unglamorous jobs to release the project owners to do more interesting jobs.

Receiving

Most of us have times when we are feeling low, unwell or overworked. There are times when we might feel we are skating so close to the coping line that we aren't quite sure which side we are on.

Being open to receiving support is crucial in our getting it. This may sound obvious but we live in a culture that fosters independence as opposed to interdependence and hence we may have barriers to asking for help. These might be beliefs based on scarcity: 'People don't have time to help', or personal beliefs: 'I don't deserve help'; 'life is meant to be difficult'. Uprooting these beliefs may be the first shift in accessing the support that we need. Connecting with beliefs of

abundance such as 'there is plenty', 'I have choices' or 'I can trust' allows us to open up to the idea of assistance, creating doorways for support to arrive. When we ask the universe for help support may come from unexpected directions. Likewise being specific with our needs helps support arrive sooner. People generally want to be of help if they can, but may only know how if asked, otherwise your need is out of their sight. Whenever we receive support in big or little ways, expressing sincere gratitude is important.

Vision support

One of the ways we can offer support is to give people the space to talk and be active in our listening. This process is a way of exchanging support. This process can be carried out with families, couples, friends or colleagues.

ACTIVITY: VISION SUPPORT

The process is simple and profound. Each person has an allocated amount of time. During this time they are given interruption-free space to explore their feelings. This time is split between the four questions given below, with twice as much time for the third question. Timings given are based on ten minutes per person, but could be longer if time allows.

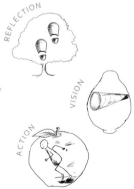

1. *What is going well? (two minutes)*

2. *What is challenging? (two minutes)*

3. *What are my long-term goals and visions? (four minutes)*

4. *What are my next achievable steps? (two minutes)*

The first two questions are reflective. The first question invites us to find the positives in our situation. The second question allows us to think about what is challenging us. The third question allows us to voice our vision; we are invited to have unboundaried dreaming time. We do not need to think about the practicalities or justify how we are going to get there. Expressing where we would actually like to be, can be like opening up our leaves to catch sunlight. Having voiced our goals helps us to be ready to seize any opportunities that come our way, taking us in the direction we want to travel. The last question returns us to the present time and asks us to take action towards our goals.

The questions can be answered generally or more specifically – such as what is going well for me as a parent, at work, at home, as a permaculturist etc. They can also be used as an evaluation tool for designs, projects and work, for example what is going well in my garden?

It is a powerful and nurturing process and can be extremely joyful to reflect back over time and see that one of your long-term goals has become part of your 'what is going well'.

Couples

Healthy relationships

We want healthy connections with our partners based on mutual respect and understanding that promote synergy.

There are four cornerstones to a long-term healthy relationship: love; communication; shared ethics and values; and compatible visions.

Initially we come together with our partners from an emotional connection, and love blossoms. As our relationship evolves we have more interactions based on pragmatic arrangements. We may have to negotiate when we see each other and as logistical arrangements come more to the forefront, compassionate and effective communication is even more vital.

When we have shared values and ethics we are coming from the same centre. We need to understand each other's values even if they are not identical to our own.

The fourth cornerstone of compatible visions illustrates the need for couples to be heading in the same direction, not necessarily to the same place, for we all have our own journey to take and different ways of getting there. Using the *vision* step we can gain clarity of our own dreams and create mutual goals. Taking time regularly to listen to each other and hear each other's aspirations allows connection with the bigger picture.

Friends Caz Phillips and Mike Pattinson use the four questions from the vision support method regularly as a health check on their relationship. They find it helps them to understand and respect one another's paths and where they are upon them. Caz says, "It is an opportunity to listen and feel heard, and gain a deeper understanding of each other in our relationship. Through listening we are more able to accept and appreciate each other. We have found it creates a more loving, caring atmosphere in our home."

Mike observes, "Simply being heard, with problem solving by the other partner being banned, usually leads to a letting go of grievances before they fester. The healing balm of listening miraculously sorts out most problems."

Principles in action

Use and value diversity

As we move into a relationship a new system emerges. 'I' becomes 'we', and at the same time it is important to maintain our own identities and systems. Each person has diverse talents, skills, interests and ways of being; respecting these increases self-esteem and self-worth. We all have strengths and weaknesses and differing approaches to life. The aim of being in a relationship is not to be the same, but to complement each other.

Creatively use and respond to change

Relationships go through different stages of growth. Each phase has its gifts and challenges.

	Pioneer	Growth	Mature	Decay
Gift	Excitement Freshness Spontaneity	Steady expansion Stability Familiarity	Security Comfort Deepening	Relief Freedom Doors open
Challenge	Unfamiliarity Uncertainty about the future	Maintaining spontaneity Giving space to each other to grow	Mundane Complacency Being independent and whole as an individual	Tension Loss Uncertainty about future Comfort zone changes

Recognising these as stages we go through enables us to put strategies in place to see the challenges as opportunities. It can also help to know that they follow a natural cycle.

In a forest garden we try and sustain the most diverse stage of a woodland, where the canopy is not yet closed, by allowing continuous light and maintaining expansive edges. In our relationships we can preserve the mature state without going into decay, we can halt the natural succession through pruning away dead and diseased parts. We may take dates together to invigorate a mature relationship and rekindle the energy and love that was there in the beginning.

Changes occur in the relationship, the people and our circumstances. We need to allow for growth and change in each other and not get attached to our partner being a certain way and boxing them in, or staying the same ourselves so as not to upset the relationship. If we have compatible visions then our relationship can withstand our paths diverging, and this can bring new perspectives.

Produce no waste

We are living in a time in history where waste is all around us. We live in a disposable culture. This thinking has penetrated through to our view on relationships. It is a debatable point as to the cause of the rise in divorce rates over the last few decades. That it is now culturally accepted and hence more people get divorced, could be one explanation, in the past more people might have ridden the storms of the ups and downs.

If we damage the other person with our words or actions we wound ourselves as we are part of the same system now. The maxim *prevention is better than cure* is true in our relationships. We can find ways in which we can provide support, communicate and nurture to prevent conflict and stress. Peace is best restored before the tear becomes too severe, *a stitch in time...* An apology given quickly can save a lot of energy being wasted and the situation spiralling out of control.

 ### Design from patterns to details
For most of us our primary place of learning about relationships was from observation of our parents. When we were young we were probably unaware of the full stories behind what was happening and just picked up on the emotional context. We will have patterns of interaction inherited from our parents deeply embedded within us, without necessarily being able to see, interpret or question these patterns as an adult. Unless we have consciously repatterned our behaviours, what then emerges from our subconscious is played out with our partner who may also be acting from an inherited pattern.

It is not just from our parents that we inherit our patterns, we are also responding to wider cultural beliefs, expectations and patterns. Examples of this are the age at which people get married, gender roles and levels of commitment. There have been cultural shifts relating to the roles of the husband and wife over the last few generations.

As our relationships progress we fall into patterns of interaction with each other. These become our comfort zones and are familiar to us even if some are undesirable. Our patterns of behaviour merge with those of our partners and we can pick up on unhelpful habits as well as useful ones. Our partner becomes messier and we become tidier, for example. Habits that we fall into in the beginning often stick, such as division of labour. Moving from the pioneer stage into the growth stage is a prime time to design helpful patterns into our relationship.

It can take a while to become aware of our own values and feelings about our relationship and to own these together, rather than acting from our inherited scripts. By consciously looking at the patterns of interaction that we would like in our relationship, we can then bring this into action on a day-to-day basis. We can design from our values the relationship we want.

Parenting

Healthy families

Our relationship with our children is lifelong and certainly one of the most significant ones we will have. We keep coming back to the patterns and beliefs that we have inherited from our parents, and we need to be equally aware of those with which we are sending our children out into the world.

As parents the health and happiness of our children has a direct and strong influence on our own health and happiness. You only need to see someone who has been up all night nursing an ill child to realise this.

When parents are warm hearted, peaceful and calm people, generally speaking their children will also develop that attitude and behaviour.

Dalai Lama

The time and energy it takes to raise our children can sometimes be our biggest limiting factors in achieving our own goals. It is likely that some of our energy is not giving direct benefits. For example energy spent nagging and dealing with illnesses, arguments and tantrums drains everyone's emotional resources. We need to find ways to make best use of the time and energy available to improve our relationships. Ultimately this may enable us to put less in without losing any quality and freeing up some resources for ourselves, as we saw in Suzi's zone 00 design.

Keeping our families healthy, building self-esteem and setting up systems of responsibility and training provides payback in the future. Building resilience in the family is important.

As nurturing parents we can show trust in our children and their abilities and support them to access their own resources, while also giving them positive patterns to follow when they are older.

Principles in action

Observe and interact
From the word go we are observing our babies and listening to their cries. We continue this observation of our children, to establish what works well with them and what factors contribute to difficult situations and behaviour. How do they respond to different foods and activities? How can we interact with these observations to prevent, or diminish damaging behaviours or enhance beneficial ones? We can observe where our energy drains are. Can time be spent observing the situations that precipitate the tantrums and illnesses, to help us try and intervene earlier, forestalling them, and using the energy in a more beneficial way?

Catch and store energy
The energy that we put into our family system determines the energy that we get out. If we put energy into family meals, outings and games we are more likely to get fun, laughter, growth and connections out. Remembering the

good times together by sharing family stories with photos and memories enables us to make more use of these positive experiences.

It is of equal importance to allow negative energy not to build up, and to deal with it in time to dissipate it.

The proverb *make hay while the sun shines* reminds us to catch opportunities as they arise. When they are babies, we can sleep when they sleep. With older children and teenagers we can be open to talking when they want to talk.

Apply self-regulation and accept feedback

It is imperative for our children to learn how to self-regulate and establish their own limits rather than these being enforced by the parents. If as parents we are continually saying 'that's enough of that, no more this week' it can become draining for us, and they then might just binge when they have the opportunity, either behind our backs or later in life. If they can agree reasonable amounts like five hours of television a week, and learn to stick to them it can save a lot of tiring debates and provides a useful lesson on self-regulation.

When we give feedback we sometimes attach non-related consequences. We say 'don't jump on the sofa or you can't go to your friend's house'. This makes it difficult for the child to process the actual message, because they are distracted by working out the connection and whether they want the consequences. Faber and Mazlish[2] talk about 'natural consequences', the actual ramifications of the event, what will in fact happen if you jump on the sofa; 'it might break; you will give me a headache; you could knock over the plant next to it'. When shown the natural consequences they are more able to process the information and alter their behaviour appropriately.

Within families feedback can come about very quickly; young children do not store their feelings, they immediately let you know what is happening for them one way or another. We can create a culture where everyone is listened to and constructive feedback can be given and received. This also means being open to receiving feedback from your children about what they would like to be different in your behaviour. Parenting is a two-way process of learning and growth.

Our children unconsciously mirror our behaviour, needs, emotions and past. What is niggling us about their behaviour may well represent something in us. It is therefore important for us to look to our own behaviours and emotions for clues about how to regulate ourselves as a starting point for bringing things back on track within the family.

As detailed earlier, giving feedback in terms of appreciation is a valuable way of creating positive change.

Use small and slow solutions

It takes time to re-establish good rapport with our children if things have been challenging. We cannot just decide overnight to improve the situation and wave a magic wand. Time needs to be taken to build up trust. Spending positive time with your children every day – playing, talking, listening, just being with them – can start to ease the wheels.

Friendships

Healthy friendships

We make friends with people for different reasons. Circumstances bring us together, we are bonded by a common history, spiritual roots or having shared experiences. Friendships can arise in the opposite way from relationships; with interactions based on pragmatic interactions at work for example, that then go on to build emotional connections.

We want friendships that enhance our quality of life, self-image and expand our horizons. Healthy friendships are based on reciprocal support, company, exchange of ideas and advice, sharing of food, fun, laughter, and someone to talk and listen to.

It's easy for a wall to go up in a friendship, and once it starts going up it can be added to brick by brick until you can no longer see each other.

This creates a spiral of erosion:

Misunderstanding → distance yourself → feel more excluded and isolated → unheard → misinterpretations →

Clarity of communication, spending time with our friends and having the bravery to open up honest dialogue are all ways to transform this spiral into one of abundance.

A true friend hears you when no one else can,
Dares you to be yourself when you have lost your way,
Reminds you of the song in your heart when you have forgotten the words,
And above all loves you for who you really are.

TREE OF LIFE INSPIRATIONS[3]

Principles in action

Obtain a yield

There are many yields we can get out of our friendships: learning, laughter, joy, happiness and hugs. We can get different things from different people. What we get out of our friendships depends on what we put in. Some need more work and maintenance than others. Healthy friendships are based on mutual support with a balance of giving and receiving. At times we may be giving more than receiving but overall there is a balance.

All of Max-Neef's nine needs can be met through our friendships; subsistence, protection, affection, understanding, participation, leisure, creation, identity and freedom. We all have different needs from our friendships.

Our friendships can influence and help to build different forms of capital. Our experiential capital expands through organising and carrying out projects together. Our social capital increases with having friends we can call upon for help. Through sharing information, ideas and knowledge our intellectual capital is heightened. Our spiritual capital is enhanced through the creation and acknowledgement of interdependencies and support. Cultural capital is maintained and improved through storytelling and celebrations. We can even use our friendships to improve financial capital by spending our money locally and making friends with local shops and businesses. Our material capital and access to tools and resources increases when we borrow and lend them. Living capital and surpluses of seeds, plants and fresh produce can be distributed.

Use and value renewable resources and services

Our friends are renewable resources in our lives. We can value all they have to offer. As we see with *obtaining a yield* our friendships can enhance all of our capitals.

Within our friendships we can think about whether our entertainments are based on creation rather than consumption. Can our entertainment also be beneficial for our health, such as walking and swimming?

What exchanges can we create with our friends? For example childcare swaps, lift shares, food shares, work exchanges and work days, skill swapping.

Our friendships themselves are renewable – we can put time and energy into them to bring them to life again if they are starting to fizzle out.

Use edge and value the marginal

There are two ways of looking at this principle. One is of having to maintain our positions on the edge and not succumbing to peer pressure and group norms. The other way is that our friendships encourage us to expand our edges.

Friendship groups have group norms and there can be peer pressure to conform. Teenagers especially can get caught up with trying to be like their friends. We can find ways of valuing our own uniqueness and acknowledging the advantages of being 'on the edge'. Demonstrating to our children the value of not being the same as everyone else assists them in holding to their true selves and not getting swept up in the crowd. We can also be affirmative of who our friends are as people, no matter how different they are from us.

The other perspective is how our friendships can help us to increase the edges of our comfort zones. We all have different comfort zones, so we can try activities with them that they are comfortable with but we are in stretch zone with. We can be encouraged to experiment, explore, adapt and respond to new skills, situations and dynamics in our lives.

ACTIVITY: APPLYING THE PRINCIPLE

There is one last principle for you to think about with your own friendships:

Integrate rather than segregate

> *Which of my friends can I introduce to each other?*
>
> *How can I create more connections within my circles of friends?*
>
> *What activities and hobbies can I integrate with my friendships?*
>
> *How else can I apply this principle?*

CHAPTER 9

Working in groups

THERE ARE MANY types of groups that we may be part of. Some groups form through choice, others are brought together through circumstance. Whatever a group's purpose there are common things to consider including the structure, dynamics, roles, meetings, decision-making and facilitation methods. We will look more deeply into how each of these factors can improve the overall functioning and well-being of the group. We can bring our communication skills from Chapter 7 into our group work and take the ideas and methods from group work into our families and relationships.

Synergy and entropy

When we bring people together we create a new system. The system then has emergent properties that can be more productive or at times volatile.

Some groups have synergy; the whole is greater than the sum of the parts – more can happen as a result of people coming together. There is a swell of energy and expectations are exceeded. There are additional yields that emerge from working together, both for the individuals and for the group These could be anything from increased self-confidence, better reputation and more ideas, to laughter and spontaneity. A synergetic group has members that are happy and feel empowered and able to contribute. There are friendships and connections within the group that extend beyond the actual purpose of the group. The group is clear about its aim and is able to be proactive in moving in this direction. Disagreements that arise are dealt with fairly. With a synergetic group a task that would take one person twenty hours to complete takes ten people only one hour. We get more out for what we put in.

However, there are times when it is more like entropy occurring within the group. There is more disorder and chaos happening, interfering with the productivity and effectiveness. Instead of 1+1 = 3, we have 1+1 = 1. The composition of the group does play a part but as Robert Carver said, "A board of governors is composed of an incompetent group of competent individuals".[1] Something can occur within the group that slows down our natural abilities and doesn't make use of our skills.

The group actually achieves less than the sum of its parts because the group dynamics and structure prevent people from being their best. In terms of physics the entropy of a system is the energy unavailable to do work. In groups it is the energy that is subtly withdrawn from the group by members not giving it their all, in whatever capacity that is. Energy is lost within the system by the play of interactions, petty arguments and time-consuming discussions. There are extra costs associated with getting things done, it can take longer to achieve the same outcomes, and it can take effort to motivate ourselves to attend meetings. At worst the group dynamic can result in explosions. There can be emotional distress that takes energy to process. We get less out for what we put in.

Groups as gardens

We could look at each of our groups as a garden: composed of individuals but acting as a whole. Each person could be seen as a different kind of plant. Each plant has its own characteristics and yields and needs different conditions to flourish. Certain people will prefer being in the sun, others the shade, some are hardy, others need shelter from the wind. Some plants nourish the soil and their contribution is underground, others are aesthetically pleasing with colourful blooms. Pioneers are inherently volatile and like to break new ground. Climax trees take time to mature. There are suitable times and positions for each plant, and within the group we can find appropriate niches and create opportunities to fill them.

Weeds in the garden are just plants we haven't found a use for yet. Nettles have a multitude of yields if we know what to do with them. The same is true for people. Each person can contribute in their own unique way when they are given the space. We have to tap into the wealth of skills and experiences and use everyone's input to create a synergetic abundant group.

Different resources are needed at different stages of growth, from a seed to seedling to young plant to a mature tree, likewise for the group and individuals. Groups have varied life cycles, with a succession of people, who inherit existing organising patterns. Groups evolve and demonstrate self-organising qualities with emergent properties.

The group dynamics could be seen as the soil structure. There is a spectrum of soil types and each needs specific treatment to bring it into balance and provide the right conditions. Different plants will prefer different soils. Some people will prefer groups where time is spent on feelings and getting in tune with each other, other people will enjoy groups that are action focused. Whatever the soil, it is always improved by adding organic matter. In the case of groups the organic matter would be listening and respect.

In gardens we can create guilds: associations of plants that provide benefit to each other. This can emerge naturally within a group, and we can actively design it, finding the natural desire lines between people who like to work together.

There are external energies of sun, wind and rain in the garden. In the group there can be external energies of new legislation, funding, red tape, and other groups that will influence growth and development. We are responding to the bigger systems that the group is part of. For example, if we are a charity group, what is happening in the field of charity work that informs our own work?

Group structure

Themes in groups

Whatever the size or purpose of a group, they are all prone to complications. There are common themes that can either challenge the group or provide opportunities for more effective functioning.

- **Why?** Why is each individual part of the group? What are their reasons for being there? What is the overall purpose and aim of the group? Is the bigger picture clear?

- **What?** What is the aim or activity of the group? What are the steps towards achieving the purpose?

- **How?** How is the group operating? What is the group culture? What practical tools are being used? How are the group dynamics?

- **When?** When are the meetings? How long are the meetings? What are the timescales for action?

- **Who?** Who are the individuals within the group? What roles do they fulfil? What are their individual challenges and strengths?

These all interlink with each other, and issues with one area can lead to challenges in another. Let's explore each one of these in turn and the patterns of difficulties that occur.

Why?

Clarity over the purpose in the group is essential. When there is no visible aim and people are unsure of what the group is trying to do, discussions can go round in circles. With no clear group agenda, people's own individual agendas can dominate the group time. People may join the group with an assumption of what the group is about that may not be accurate, or people that might have been interested stay away.

Everyone will have their own individual reasons for being part of the group; these may be fringe benefits that they are hoping to get alongside the main function of the group, for example improving their skills or meeting friends. Being open about these can help to meet them without interfering with the main aim. They can be added yields.

When the group is aligned to shared values and vision there is a common bond and heart connection that will nurture the relationships and enhance the group's effectiveness.

What?

Obviously, if the aim is not clear then the steps towards it will also be undefined. Even knowing where the destination is, groups can be overambitious with what they are trying to do. Individuals and the group can over commit, and action points can get left undone, leaving the same items revisited repeatedly. When people take on jobs and don't do them this can lead to conflict.

Groups can find themselves being reactive to what is coming their way rather than proactively seeking actions to move them towards their aim. Meetings can get filled with business with no room for creativity and visioning.

Clarity is needed with the overall functions of the group. Creating achievable and meaningful action plans in line with the function – for both individuals and groups – creates a pattern of success.

How?

A group becomes a system in its own right, having a life of its own. Dynamics evolve in the group and the group develops norms and patterns. Having group agreements and protocols in place from the beginning can provide a solid foundation. Finding a pace and style of working that suits everyone is a challenge.

A group needs to have tools and processes that serve its values, and find a balance between structured organisation and flexible adaptability. Poor meeting facilitation and woolly decision-making processes can waste time and be disheartening. Ineffective meetings can lead to a lack of cohesion and planning.

It is important that there is a clear focus to the meeting, which is aligned to the group's aim. Allowing everyone to contribute to the agenda creates ownership; this can be done either by sending the agenda round prior to the meeting or by making it together at the beginning of the meeting. Timings can be given for each point to ensure that all points are covered; the timings need to be stuck to, or else everyone agrees to extend them.

Changes in organisation may be necessary as group numbers grow or decline. What worked with 10 people may not work with 20. A local permaculture group that has been running well for nearly 10 years is now having challenges as its numbers swell. The informal decision-making processes previously used are now cumbersome with so many people. Just like moving from a garden to a smallholding, different processes and structures are needed.

When?

When a group meets is an important factor affecting who can attend, people's energy levels and the structure of the meeting. The frequency of meetings will also influence the productivity. Too close together they become a burden to attend; if they are too far apart momentum is lost in between or there can be too much to cover in one meeting.

The container is the size and shape of the meeting. Lengthy meetings can bore and irritate people; too short and important things can get dropped off the agenda, decisions are rushed and people may not get the chance they need to speak. The whole group needs awareness of the leaks in the container; time and energy that is wasted within the meeting.

Realistic timescales for action are needed. It is important for the group's morale to feel that progress is being made. At the same time it's important not to overwhelm people and create an overbearing sense of urgency and need for commitment and action.

Who?

The size of the group will affect its functioning. If a group is too small, people may feel over-burdened; if it's too large it is difficult to come to decisions.

Groups with rolling membership have their own particular challenges. Hierarchies between new and long-standing members can cause issues. In order to move forward new members need to have trust in previous work and decisions and long-standing members need to have tolerance and understanding for having to repeat things. Often within groups there is an imbalance of effort with a few people working hard to keep things moving. This is often accompanied with an uneven taking of responsibility. Sometimes one or two people hold great responsibility, become indispensable, feel they can't leave and are prone to burnout. Groups need to have succession of different roles or opportunities within the group and clear entry and exit strategies, as a part of the natural life cycle.

If people are attending because they feel duty bound they can be cut off from their imagination, creativity and intuition and the group's energy can become stale and caught in the mundane. The key to a successful group lies in people's abilities to connect with their own inner resources, where people feel empowered and confident to contribute.

Roles within groups

Does the group stimulate our best or worst self to show up? Our best self contributes, listens, connects and is able to see the bigger picture of the group. Our worst self over- or under-participates, hiding in the corner or dominating, bringing baggage into the group.

How we show up as individuals in a group depends largely on where we are in our own personal journeys as well as how we fit into the group.

Each person brings their past, their beliefs, assumptions, conclusions, habits, opinions and anxieties as well as their enthusiasm, skills and experiences. All of these influence how we express ourselves within the group, and how we perceive the individuals and the interactions in the group. In group situations it is all too easy to be triggered by someone else's words or actions.

While we all have different facets of our personality, we show up in a habitual way within groups. We each take on a role within a group. Different roles are necessary otherwise we have a monocultural group with no diversity. We need diversity in the group to help us to have different perspectives and broaden our skill base. We don't all need to be and do everything, but together we need to have a range of skills and perspectives – that is the whole rationale for working in groups. We have patterns of how we interact in groups. We have our comfort zones of how we behave in groups. This can link in with our self-identity, the part of ourselves we show to others and how we perceive ourselves to be within a group.

A group becomes a team when we use all our skills to maximum advantage. Roles allow us to play to our strengths, to use our skills and to work on our weaknesses. Our roles can enable the group to work towards the overall aim.

There are explicit roles within groups such as chairperson, treasurer, secretary and minute taker. There are also hidden, unspoken roles that people take. People are given archetypal labels; the wise one or the risk taker. There may be a role that seems to have positive characteristics around it: the do-er; or there may be roles that have negative connotations: the critic. Roles can be defined by one quality that is picked up on: the confident one or the optimist. How we see ourselves and how others see us may not necessarily be the same. The questioner may think they are providing a useful service by probing deeper into issues, other people may perceive them as wasting the group's time. Or perhaps we don't value our own contributions as much as other people do.

Within each role there are benefits and drawbacks and becoming aware of these helps us to consciously choose the appropriate way to be. It may be helpful to be a good facilitator, but if we always do it then we inhibit other people gaining experience and expanding into the role.

Answer the following questions before reading on, to open up awareness of the roles we habitually take.

ACTIVITY: MY ROLE IN GROUPS[2]

Answer the following questions:

1. *In a group I mainly...*
2. *What about this role is helpful?*
3. *What about it is unhelpful?*
4. *Are there any changes I would like to make?*
5. *Any other insights?*

If you do this activity in a group you can cluster together people who have similar answers in question 1, and then answer the following questions together.

Helpful and unhelpful aspects of some roles

Name of role	Helpful	Unhelpful	Changes we could make
Leaders/ Facilitators	Provide focus, inspiration, drive Use time efficiently	Hierarchical Too hasty Isolating Domineering	Train up others Be transparent about when we are facilitating or not
Connectors	Flexible roles Balance Mitigating of personality clashes	Not contributing as an individual Hesitate with their own ideas	See their own place in the whole
Ideas people	Generate ideas Creativity Expansion	Can interfere with thought process Can throw a spanner in the works	Help others to 'think outside of the box' See what's happening 'in the box'
Observers	Flexible and no rush Allow others to speak Insightful Provide the crucial piece of the jigsaw	Sit back and chill out 'Hot heads' charge ahead Over-contemplation	Balance observing with speaking
Joker	Keeps things light and entertaining	Sometimes inappropriate humour for the situation and/or the person	Think before making a joke Use the jokes for the benefit of the whole group
Peacemaker	Able to bring harmony to the group	Sometimes their own needs get overlooked	Whole group could look more at prevention so the role isn't needed

There are times within a group when someone seems to be in a subversive role, which can take different forms from criticising, blocking or withdrawing to dominating, bullying, arguing or undermining. This may be coming from some discomfort in the group; perhaps they are responding to another individual, or not in alignment with the group's aim. We all have a shadow side, and there are times when we slip into a way of being that might not express ourselves in our best light. This can become an issue when people have built up expectations of this behaviour and label us; 'Oh here goes John again finding fault in what we want to do'. People can get stuck in their role, or other group members can associate them with the role or label they are given, and this will be the filter for their perception of that person.

It is part of the succession process to move to different roles and train other people. Moving away from our habitual role can be disconcerting and take some focused effort. It doesn't need to be all or nothing, we can expand our edges. I have a friend who was comfortable taking the role of leader, however when she wanted to step back and allow others to take this role she then moved into a non-participatory role, taking too many steps back. If a group is used to you responding in a certain way and you suddenly decide to shift into a new role, this creates a gap, provokes questions and may unsettle people. It may feel appropriate to let people know that this is what you are intending to do. It is a good policy to have back-ups and *multiple elements for important roles/functions.*

The roles we take could be seen as our primary identity rather than sole identity. Each is multi faceted, with many edges and interlinks with other roles. We can work to get *many yields from each person.* By expanding our roles we can tap into the abundances of skills and experiences within the group and create gateways for new abundances to enter.

Group life

Group cultures

The differing energies at play create dynamics within a group. However, it is more than just the personalities, the group has emergent properties that determine whether it is a well-functioning group or not.

A group culture will evolve, including traditions of how meetings are run, the patterns of interactions and decision-making, as well as habits for how people are treated. The group develops a collective voice and consciousness that can be healthy or not at ease (diseased). The ways of working, the patterns of communication and language used, of hierarchies and dominance, the levels of commitment to action and the underlying beliefs, are all held in the collective consciousness. This may be inherited from past group members, especially when there is rolling membership. We all bring to the table our own consciousness filled with these things from our own experiences, our cultural upbringing and our past. What we express of that is dependent in part on how the group operates and what is stimulated.

Looking at behavioural patterns in nature can give us some ideas as designers. It may be appropriate to have a hierarchical structure with a clear chain of command, or we may want to organise ourselves more co-operatively. If we are thinking of the flocking behaviour then we may be trying to draw more people in.

There are people who are focused on the 'task' and those who are focused on the 'process' and those focused on the building of relationships. Task-oriented people are keen to get things done and have a 'product' from the meeting. They have a strong goal and are often good at giving information, concluding and calling for decisions to be made. Process-oriented people are more concerned with how the group operates than the outcome. They will want to ensure participation by everyone and keep the energy going. For some it is the relationships within the group that is most important. There can be a clash between the task, the process and the relationship people, with each thinking that their focus is more important, while in fact all are necessary for the smooth running of a group. A group that is just focused on the task may neglect group members, sweep different points of view under the carpet and rush headlong into things. A group that pays too much attention to the process can avoid coming to decisions and actually having to act.

There are times and places for all of these to come to the fore and it is the skill and maturity of the group and/or the facilitator to know when each is necessary.

Different types of meetings can be called. I know of several intentional communities that have two distinct types of meeting: one for business and decisions and one for feelings. This gives the feelings time without them spilling over into the business and decisions being made on the basis of personal dynamics.

Suzy Erskine lives in an intentional community that pays significant attention to how they communicate. One of their key joining criteria is the ability and willingness to communicate honestly. They put people first and it is more important for them how things are done than what gets done. Suzy says, "Through being heard the situation itself may not change but people's attitudes towards it can shift." One of their guidelines is using 'I statements' and owning what they are saying. A core ethic they share is of responsibility, for the land, for each other and for themselves as individuals.

Designing the culture

Instead of just falling into a group culture we can be proactive and create or design it at the offset. Spending time initially aligning to the group's values can set the groundwork for future interactions. It can also make it easier to integrate new people into the process, as they know what they are coming into.

Stephanie Futcher trains groups of patients, carers and volunteers for Macmillan cancer support. She uses the four 'Gs' as a way of creating a group culture, and giving everyone a sense of group ownership.

> **Gains** – What are we hoping to *gain* from the group? We can voice our aspirations of how we would like to be as a group, to steer us in the right direction. If everyone is facing the same direction and pulling together this creates a harmony of movement.

> **Gives** – What are we ready to *give*? This creates a transparency for individuals' motivations and deepens everyone's understanding of how people would like to contribute. It sets the scene for valuing everyone's contributions.

> **Groans** – What *groans (anxieties or concerns)* do we have about the group or groups in general? Giving people the time to express this can be liberating, almost as if once they have said them out loud they can let go of them. This isn't always the case, some concerns linger longer, but knowing of these personal backdrops enables compassion.

> **Guidelines** – The group as a whole can create a set of *guidelines* for how we would like to operate together to take into account all of the above.

Even on a one-day workshop she will go through this process in a brief form. She says, "Whenever I skip or shorten this process because I think people are too sophisticated to need it, something goes wrong."

Guidelines

These may be called group agreements, ground rules, or group culture. Just the process of coming to group agreements can be informative in itself: it can show how people are starting to interact with each other, how decisions might be made, who is eager to contribute and who wants to spend more time considering. It is not just the end product of having an agreement that is important, honouring each other in taking time to listen and share ideas has benefits in itself.

The group agreements can include functional items such as whether to turn off mobile phones or not, whether to allow food and drinks in the meeting, and timings – do you wait for any latecomers or start without them? It can also focus on the qualities to hold in our interactions: respect, honesty and empathy. Some of these may sound obvious – we need to respect each other, but that means different things to different people and this is an opportunity for clarity. Group agreements can bring together individuals' hopes for the group, ways of working, and weave in the values and purpose of the group.

Examples of group guidelines:

- Accept personal responsibility for meeting own needs
- Not labelling or boxing people
- Not making assumptions or putting words in people's mouths
- Willingness to stretch ourselves
- Equal opportunity to speak
- Look at people's strengths
- Listen to each speaker
- Acknowledge and value everyone's opinions
- Smiling is good, laughing is better
- Don't judge
- Keep to topic
- Confidentiality when asked for

It is obviously easiest to do this at the formation of a group. It can still be done at any stage, although it can be more of a challenge to get people to feel its importance later on. Actually becoming conscious of the culture and naming it is the first step to bringing about changes.

Meeting methods

A lot of us have unfavourable experiences of meetings. They can be dull, boring, tiresome, energy draining, controversial, argumentative and bring out the worst in us. Some meetings can be inclusive and productive, harvesting the best from everyone and a coming together of kindred spirits. Obviously the latter are able to gain more from the individuals and the group as a whole.

The following processes can be used to engage people, allow them to contribute their thoughts, skills and experiences, are time efficient and harvest the best thinking from the group.

Chris Dixon developed a pattern for meetings in his local permaculture group. This provides a template to follow in which to use the following tools and techniques. There are three phases, the first sets the scene, the second deals with the business of the meeting and the last phase is to close the meeting and move forwards into the next one.

Each meeting begins with an opening circle. This is followed by a reporting back circle, where everyone can hear progress and new ideas; this can be accompanied by a round of comments if appropriate. From this the agenda for the meeting can be agreed. The agenda can be in part prepared beforehand and just amended and agreed here as necessary.

There is then an edge before moving on to the next phase and each agenda item. This has clear stages of presenting the item, then the treatment of it, then the decision. The treatment is the way in which the agenda item is dealt with. Different tools can be used to ensure that everyone's voice is being heard and the item is being examined from a variety of perspectives. Over time the group and facilitator will increase the repertoire of tools that enable agenda items to be dealt with effectively. Between each agenda item there can be a short 'edge'.

The third phase of the meeting involves a reminder of the action points, choosing the next meeting time and place and carrying over unfinished agenda items. If there is a revolving facilitator the next person can be chosen here. The meeting evaluation can include appreciation of the facilitator, people's

(1)

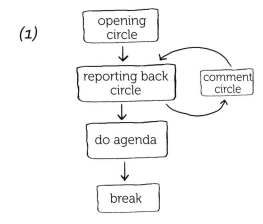

(2)

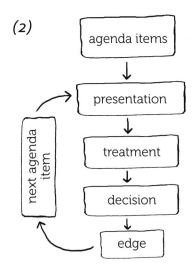

(3)

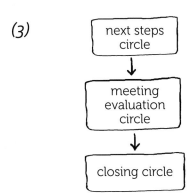

participation and progress made. Ending with a closing circle provides symmetry to the meeting.

The following tools can be used for opening and closing circles and treatments of agenda items.

Discussions

A lot of the time treatment of agenda items is based purely around discussions; this is receiving information in auditory form, which only works for some of us. There are people who prefer visual stimulus or to learn by doing, or to move while listening. With discussions generally only one person is talking at a time, and although other people are listening, it doesn't necessarily make the best use of the time or everyone's skills and thinking.

With discussions there is a tendency for some people to over-participate and others to under-participate. When one or two people dominate discussions the collective voice of the group gets squashed. The group misses out and does not get the best out of the people that participate less. We need to move away from the 'loudest voice wins' and ensure that everyone has an equal voice and is valued within the group.

Giving voices to everyone

Check–ins at the beginnings of meetings are good opportunities to hear from each person and set the tone for the meeting. The facilitator invites everyone to say something; this could be how they are feeling at the moment, something significant that happened to them since they last met, what they hope to get out of the meeting or something that made them happy recently. If time is a big constraint or the group is large, people could be asked to say it in one word, three words, a phrase or one minute.

Other gauges, such as the thumb dial, can be used at the beginning and throughout to quickly read how the group is doing.

Closing circles – at the end of meetings it is favourable to spend a few minutes to complete the process. However, many people want to rush off at this time so choosing a quick process usually works best. You can ask people for three words about what they enjoyed, how they feel, what they learnt or something they are looking forward to.

Go-rounds – can be used at any time to hear from each person in turn about a specific topic. This can be a useful way of intercepting a debate between two people.

No one speaks twice[3] – until everyone has spoken once, people are able to pass if they want, but they are given the opportunity.

Think and listens – breaking into pairs, and giving each other interruption-free space, is a useful way of allowing people the time to clarify their thoughts. When reconvening in the main group it could be followed by a go-round to allow everyone a chance to report back.

Matchsticks[4] – everyone is given a certain number of matchsticks (say five). Each time they speak they have to put one in the middle; when they have run out, they have to wait until everyone else has used theirs. This is a useful exercise to use to bring awareness to everyone who is speaking more than others.

Small group work – having small break-out groups working on particular aspects of a topic can make it easier for people to contribute and increases productivity.

Talking stick – this is a Native American tradition, where a talking stick is held by the person talking; everyone else gives the person talking their full attention and does not interrupt. This has benefits when the group is tending to talk over one another.

Debate circle – this is a fabulous way of getting people moving and seeing where the land lies, particularly if something is controversial. A proposal is made, or a statement about something, an object is placed in the middle of the room (an open space is needed for this), you move close to the object if you agree and further away if you disagree, and can stand anywhere in between. You can then talk to anyone else in the room, either close by or far away in order to understand their position. You can move around as your thoughts on the subject change.

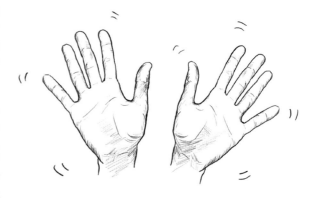

Hand signals[5] – wavy hands for agreement comes from deaf culture, and is often used in consensus decision-making. This is sometimes called 'silent clapping' and is a great way of instantly seeing how people feel about a proposal. Groups can develop their own set of hand signals.

Mind maps – help the group to map out issues and find connections, representing something visually. It can help avoid repetition in discussion as people can see that their points have been recorded.

Creating edges

Creating edges in meetings is useful to refresh the energy.

Breaks – informal opportunities to connect with each other and meet the need for a drink or fresh air.

Silence – the simplest of tools that isn't used nearly enough. A call for a moment's silence can change the atmosphere profoundly; it gives everyone the chance to connect with themselves. Silence can be used as a break between agenda items, rather than one flowing into another, and to defuse heated situations.

Games and energisers – games are useful for breaking the ice, team building, using both sides of the brain, increasing oxygen to the brain, reducing stress and just for pure fun. They can create a more playful, light-hearted mood in the group.

Movements and shakeouts – sitting for hours can be draining in itself; getting people to stand and shake out their bodies can re-energise a group. Getting everyone to swap seats can shift the energy dramatically.

Decision-making

The challenges of decision-making

Decision-making can bring up unhelpful patterns, our limiting beliefs about ourselves and the group, and activate our filters depending on where the idea is coming from. We can become possessive about an idea, not allowing the group to develop and adapt it.

The group can go round in circles, with polarising of ideas and people taking sides. Everyone gets bored, frustrated and more entrenched in their own point of view, or no decisions are made because there are either too few or too many options, or no one wants to commit.

Making decisions can be a source of conflict within the group, and the process by which decisions are made can be as important as the decision itself for the feelings of the group.

It can take a long time, we can feel like our ideas have been compromised, we can dwell in limbo between decisions, and when decisions have been reached, actions are often not followed through.

These challenges can be turned into opportunities: to feel heard, to make decisions owned by everyone, and we can come to a better arrangement than we could have arrived at by ourselves.

Decision-making tools

These processes below aim to enable us to think about the whole of the issue, allow further ideas to emerge and are inclusive. Firstly it is important to get all the ideas out, then there needs to be some impartial way of evaluating the ideas. These tools have as much value within our one-to-one relationships as in our groups.

Contemplanda[6] – this is actually the opposite of making a decision. Andy Langford coined the word 'contemplanda', when you are asking someone to have a think about an idea. It may be a seed idea that you have had and would just like to hear first impressions, or for people to mull over the idea for a while. You want to share it but are not expecting or wanting a decision at this stage. This is a helpful first stage in the process that can then be followed up with another process.

'Yes, and' rather than 'yes, but' – a simple shift in phrasing that shifts our thinking to that of abundance instead of scarcity. Using the phrase 'yes, but' suggests that you don't agree with the person or that you have something better. Rather than approaching it as my idea or yours, 'yes, and' phrasing opens up the possibility of these ideas co-existing.

This method works well in a visioning session. After one person presents their idea, the next person begins 'yes, and...' then adds their idea, and we can continue adding ideas, building up a more complex plan for the future. The strength of this process is to bring forth ideas. We will then need to take this to a further process to make final decisions.

Hopes and concerns – every person has an opportunity to express their hopes – what they would like to happen; and their concerns – what they think might happen but wouldn't want. Just being able to voice the concerns is often enough to allow the conversation to move on. This gives the opportunity to design towards the hopes and avoid and minimise the concerns. The journey can be designed together.

Sunset[7] – with this method the group acts as if an option has been decided upon for a set amount of time. Then the group changes to another option and acts as if this one has been agreed, for the same time. During these time periods discussions continue as if this decision has been made, and time can be given for individual reflection. Time spent on each option could be anything from five minutes to one week. After time has been given to all options, everyone is given time to talk about their feelings for each choice. The process takes you out of the decision-making frame of mind and allows more immersion in the idea itself and to see what things present themselves as part of each alternative.

Six Thinking Hats – devised by Edward de Bono,[8] this is a method that harnesses more thinking from each person. I have found this to be one of the most useful and versatile tools in my toolbox. Any proposal gets put on the table and everyone has to examine it objectively, no one can hold the idea as their own.

Everyone puts on the same hat at the same time, so everyone is thinking the same way (making it another method for parallel thinking like PMIs). This method moves us away from habitual roles; we all get to be the optimist or the critic together. Each hat has a significant colour relating to the purpose of the hat; this is represented by something that reminds us of its function, such as the black cloud for critical thinking.

The *red hat* is the hat of the emotions and feelings. We can give our gut reactions, our intuitive responses and first impressions. Intuition can be based on experience. We do not need to justify our feelings. I have found it useful to do this as a go-round and allow everyone their turn to speak without being interrupted. The red is represented by fire, illustrating the emotions.

The *black hat* is used for critical thinking. We can find the faults and weaknesses, the ways in which we think it won't work. We can think of all of the limiting factors. The person who proposed the idea has probably already thought of some of these but in usual discussions where they are trying to persuade people they wouldn't necessarily state them. Here they are encouraged to share this as well. Does this fit our values, abilities, resources, strategies and objectives? The point of this hat is to work towards mitigating limiting factors and think of contingency plans if any of these scenarios occur. Critical thinking is represented by a black cloud.

With the *yellow hat* we explore the positives, the possible benefits and values it might give. How it fits with the values and aims of the group. The yields we could gain if it worked. Every thinker is 'challenged' to find positive value. The benefits are illustrated by yellow sunshine.

The *white hat* is the hat of the facts and figures. What facts do we know? What do we need to know? What information is missing? What questions could we ask? How might we get the information that we need? What are the logistics? This is the hat of factual information and represented by paper.

The *green hat* is the productive and creative hat. The green hat asks for ideas, alternatives and possibilities. There is no screening or analysing of the ideas as they come; they can be wild and wacky. Green is for growth and energy.

The *blue hat* sees the overview. This hat is different from the others, in that it is held by one person throughout: a facilitator who defines the focus, uses other meeting tools within the discussion, and ensures people keep within the current hat until it feels appropriate to move hats. They then instigate the change, explaining the new hat to everyone. While one person wears this hat throughout, there are times when it may be appropriate for everyone to wear it and think like a facilitator, examining the process and suggesting tools to use. We can think of the blue sky as the overview.

Consensus decision-making

C.T. Butler[9] first introduced consensus decision-making. The central idea around it is that everyone agrees to make decisions that are best for the group. The common misconception is that everyone has to be in full agreement for every decision. In fact people may not agree totally but are willing to *stand aside*. *Blocking* or *vetoing* the decision happens only when there is a concern for the well-being of the group or when it is felt to be against the core values of the group. In order to work with consensus everyone needs to agree to work in this way, and the group has to have clear aims and/or values.

The process starts with a proposal; there is then a brief discussion centred on questions, for clarity. The next stage is where people can state their concerns. At this point they are not discussed, only noted. Once everyone has had a chance to voice their concerns, they can be discussed, drilling down to find what's behind them and attempting to resolve them. This may well lead to a revision of the original proposal. When it feels like all of these have been addressed, there can be a vote on the proposal. People can fully support, not fully support but go along with, stand aside or veto/block.

If there are any blocks then the proposal cannot go ahead and amendments need to be made. The next steps need to be agreed by everyone, whether that is to go ahead, abandon the proposal or reconvene with it at the next meeting.

Consensus decision-making doesn't replace inclusive meeting techniques or skilled facilitation; these are still very much key to its success. Consensus provides a framework that can include any of the other techniques presented here.

Facilitation

The word facilitation comes from the French, meaning 'to make easy'. The role of the facilitator is to smooth the path for the group, to encourage the group to be synergetic and build on its strengths.

The facilitator is ideally aware of the personal environment (what motivates and demotivates us), the social environment (what integrates the group and creates connections; what segregates us), and the physical environment, as well as how these all overlap.

Ideally the facilitator needs to remain neutral. There are times within a small group where it may be necessary to step out of the facilitator role for a moment; this can be done in a transparent manner.

Observation is key, with the need to increase awareness of the periphery, who is trying to speak and who is dominating the discussion. Equalising participation meets both the fair shares and peoplecare ethics. The facilitator needs to be conscious of the content of the discussion, the energy of the group and the dynamics, encouraging inclusivity, time, and the process or techniques to use. The facilitator has to balance between structure and free flow, and judge when to speak and when to let the group speak, and how long to let discussions run for. They need to gently guide and maintain the focus without crushing creativity and visioning.

It is a lot to be aware of so some of these tasks can be distributed amongst the group in roles such as time keeping and mood watcher. Facilitation is also easier when a healthy group culture has been agreed and established.

When the group is stuck for whatever reason, the facilitator can use the different tools to 'unstick' the group, either giving voice to everyone or creating an edge.

They need to be aware of when the group is getting caught on details or when the details are being avoided. It may be of use to restate the question, summarise the discussion so far or to split the issue apart or put ideas together. Sometimes when a proposal contains different aspects it is practical to discuss it in parts and come to agreements in sequence. For example if you are debating whether to charge a membership fee of £5, it may be useful to first discuss whether to charge a fee at all, and then secondly to discuss how much that could be.

The facilitator needs to maintain boundaries of time, topic and ways of interacting with each other. There are times when conflict emerges and needs to be managed in a fair and open manner. The conflict may be based on differing points of view or not feeling able to come to a decision. This is the biggest challenge of the facilitator; using some of the different tools given can help to move groups through. Conflict is not something that needs to be feared, it can have a purpose in the group; exposing flaws in the proposal or allowing for synthesis of ideas leading to sparks of creativity and more comprehensive plans. However when conflict is personal between people it can lead to a lack of trust and feelings of disempowerment.

Rod Cunningham of Philosophy for Communities[10] introduced a technique of *self-facilitation,* where the group moves towards being able to organise itself and is less reliant on one facilitator. When a person wants to speak they hold their hand out, rather than up, which can get tiring and feel like school. The person that has just spoken then chooses the next person to speak. It helps the group as a whole to become more aware of who has and who hasn't spoken.

Facilitation is a skill and like all skills it improves with practice. As with other skills it is tempting to let the most experienced people do the job. This leads us into a catch 22 where only the experienced people get more experience. We are not allowing for succession of roles if we have an imbalance of only one or two people regularly facilitating. Poor facilitation however can be disastrous in a meeting.

The role can be rotated around the whole group with everyone receiving the job training. First the apprentice shadows and supports an experienced facilitator. Next they take the lead and the experienced person provides the support. The next time they facilitate they are now the experienced person and can have the next apprentice shadow and support them. Eventually everyone in the group has had the opportunity to facilitate, so no one is stuck in that role.

Gaining experience within small groups is also valuable. We can practise facilitation around the dining room table, noting who is trying to speak and who is dominating the conversation. There are many opportunities to practise opening up your awareness to the peripheral.

Facilitation is one of the ways we can lead groups, but leadership can come from any of the group members. With a non-hierarchical structure and no one person leading the group, the group does not need to be leaderless, it can be leaderful in that each person is able to step up in the way appropriate for them. We will look more at the different styles of leadership in the next part.

Designing with other people

In the previous part we were just designing for ourselves, when we come to design with other people we are presented with a different set of opportunities.

When it is ourselves and other people as clients we have the added dimensions of being both client and designer, and in relationship with the other clients.

Opportunities

- It can be a unifying process in itself to give time and space to design together, and for everyone to see the importance, relevance and benefits of design.

- We can make group agreements before we start about how we are going to be with each other in the design process.

- We can involve others in planning, organising and facilitating the process to create a sense of group ownership.

- We can have a plan ready but be prepared to ditch it and go with the energy and flow of the group.

- The design process can be fun and creative. Making it seem more like a game works well if we are designing with children.

- This is a great opportunity for us to observe the dynamics and flow within a group. We may observe desire lines to particular anchor points.

- There are many different approaches for guiding people through the process, and it is only limited by your imagination and skills as designer and facilitator. As rules of thumb, the more creative approaches you use the more you are likely to get creative designs, and the more participation, the more ownership over the designs.

How

One way is to have all of the anchor points out on pieces of paper, and allow people to move freely between them, writing their thoughts. You can use visual props and cards to help people to navigate their way through the process. These separate experiences can then be collated at the end and brought together, identifying themes and actions.

You could also deal with each anchor point together using tools from the previous chapters. For example, think and listens are powerful ways to hear people's reflections.

It is unlikely to all be covered in one session, and the papers could be left accessible to everyone to add to whenever they want. It is good policy to end each session with an agreement over when the next session is.

There are movements for each anchor point, which help to embody the learning. These are useful and effective for introducing the design web to a group quickly. They also help to convey the idea of the design process as travelling along a pathway.

Movements

Vision – rise up on to tiptoes as you bring your arms up above your head, and spread them out with palms upwards, look up to the sky. Feel expansive and growing. What is the bigger picture you see?

Helps – jump up, like you have springs on your feet. What is going to help on your journey?

Limits – crouch down small. What is blocking your growth? What needs to be moved out of the way?

Patterns – walk around in a spiral. What patterns can inform your design?

Ideas – imagine you are plucking ideas and inspiration from the air. What ideas can you bring?

Principles – hold up an imaginary magnifying glass, and look through the lens of the principles. What do the problem and the solution look like through this?

Integration – Wave your hands around as if drawing in strands, gradually bring your hands together. Imagine you are holding all of your observations, ideas, vision and resources, and can see the needs of the design and different ways of fulfilling them.

Action – run fast. What can you do to get moving? What are the steps to make?

Momentum – rock back and forth as if on a swing. How can you keep going?

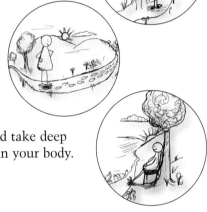

Appreciation – place one hand on your heart and the other on your belly, maybe rub your belly! What yields can you appreciate?

Reflection – walk forwards and then look back at your footsteps. What has the journey been like?

Pause – sit quietly for a moment and take deep breaths, feeling the energy flowing in your body.

Design case study:
Permaculture Association Britain's staff

This design (reproduced overleaf) focuses on how in Britain the Permaculture Association[1] staff work together as a team. The parameters for this design are just within the staff group, although it also links in with other designs for the overall strategies of the organisation, trustees and working groups.

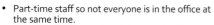

The aim is to have an effective, communicating, functioning team which can be efficient with its time. The team also wants to be supportive and caring towards its members.

The group is working towards a wider vision of being able to serve the network and make positive change in the world. This bigger vision is displayed in the office to keep everyone focused on the aims of the Association, and stop tangents and dead ends being followed. It helps to keep the daily tasks linked with the bigger picture.

The team has the following resources:
- Permaculture skills and continuing research and development of permaculture both personally and collectively.
- Volunteers.
- Everyone has a shared understanding and strong commitment to permaculture and the Association.
- Transferable skills, such as administration, facilitation, event organising.

- Part-time staff so not everyone is in the office at the same time.
- Even 45 minute meetings take up valuable work time if only working seven hours a week.
- Office space.
- Time to design.
- Changes in staff.
- Busyness and general workload of staff.

- Sharing patterns of being effective with the book, *Eat That Frog*.[2]
- Sharing patterns for organising events.
- Some of the meeting patterns can be shared with the board of trustees and working groups of the Association and vice versa.

There is a large white board in the main office where all staff write down when they plan to be in the office in the next four weeks. This enables meetings to be arranged, helps tell enquirers when they can phone back, and keeps everyone in touch with others.

Stand-up meetings were introduced once the staff team had expanded to eight members. These take place on Tuesday afternoons. Everyone has to stand up (which makes the meeting much shorter than if sitting down) and follows the format of everyone who is there saying briefly what they will be doing during the forthcoming week. This keeps everyone in touch with others, enables co-operative working, and can often eliminate duplication of tasks. For example, the LAND[3] team has organised a number of events, and can therefore assist in organising a Diploma event.

What we have learned: two members of staff only work seven hours a week – if 45 minutes is spent in a meeting, their working day is reduced. It has recently been agreed that the Stand-ups will happen on the first Tuesday of the month. On other Tuesdays there will be a five+ rule: if five or more members of staff are in the office, there will be a very quick go-round.

Every quarter, all the staff come in for a planning meeting (staff who work one day/week are paid extra for this). There is a timeline on the wall where each quarter everyone's tasks are written down. At the meetings, everyone has time to say what they have done, and what they plan to do for the following quarter. This is useful in prioritising tasks. It also aids co-operative working and patterns of work emerge.

All staff have a regular one-to-one meeting which is a mix of their reflections on their own self-guided management, supervision and action planning. Targets are set for the forthcoming period, and previous tasks reviewed. This is also a chance to voice any feelings.

We appreciate being part of a genuine, diverse team which has a shared understanding of permaculture and a long-term commitment to each other, the work and making things function smoothly. We like the challenges that give opportunities for personal growth and reflection, and the pragmatic way of working. We enjoy the fun and friendly banter and the sharing of skills on a daily basis especially with gardening, and that people give time to answer questions. We like the fluidity of roles and the openness for asking and receiving help from other members of staff. We feel it's a safe space to be expressive and enjoy the balance of fun and professionalism.

We like working with people who bring lots of stimulating ideas into their lives. We appreciate the opportunity to serve such an exciting and inspiring network and working with people committed to bringing about positive change in the world.

Some of the ideas that we could take forward are to involve more people in the design, spending dedicated time on how we function as a group. Peer reviews, team and trust-building activities. We could share non-permaculture related skills to give a sense of our wider selves. Create a forum for people to share how we feel as a whole group.

Move office to somewhere more accessible and with separate areas for quiet work space, creative and social space, meeting and training room, outdoor demonstration space and volunteer accommodation.

Have more time for reflection, training and group communication. To share with the whole group lessons learnt on courses. Have time to work more effectively with a slightly bigger team and be better paid. We could have more biscuits and flowers in the office.

The needs for the design that have emerged are:

1. Communication with each other
2. Communication with public
3. Meetings
4. Training
5. Skill-shares
6. Co-operative working
7. Improving effectiveness

These are currently met with the following systems:

1. Meetings: weekly and quarterly. Message board and white board for timetable 4 weeks ahead
2. Message board
3. Stand up check-ins, quarterly business meetings and one-to-one meetings
4. Training budget for staff members
5. Out of office collaboration and skill sharing and drawing upon the skills within the group as required
6. Sharing ideas and experience for running events
7. Sharing techniques from *Eat That Frog*. Spending time and money on improving the computer systems and making the space more ergonomic.

Every Tuesday we bring lunch to share. We also have a social secretary, who arranges a trip to the cinema, curry, or outing every few months. The team has a lot in common (as well as a love of permaculture) and very different, very busy lives. We feel it is important for us to keep in touch with each other.

The Association does not employ anyone for more than four days a week.

Apply self-regulation and accept feedback
Before the one-to-one meetings each person takes time to reflect on their own work and what they would like to spend time talking through; the emphasis is on taking personal responsibility and adapting work plans accordingly rather than them being imposed from top-down.

Creatively use and respond to change
The Permaculture Association staff has expanded from four part-time workers to ten part-time workers in the space of less than three years, and grown from one office to two. During this time it has been appropriate to review how the team functions and to keep responding and adapting.

Use edge and value the marginal
There are connections with outside work, such as gardening help, local permaculture groups, teaching together and working on a local community-supported agriculture scheme.

Obtain a yield
Amongst the many yields we gain from working with the Association are friendship, purpose, skill development and participation in working for a positive change in the world.

PART 4: LIVING IN SOCIETY

CHAPTER 10

Where are we?

Observation of cultures

Problems in society

The Integral Model

Cultural conditioning

Cultural identities

Social systems

LIVING IN SOCIETY

CHAPTER 12

How do we get there?

Circles of concern and influence

Transition movement

Governance

Facilitating cultural shifts

Leadership

CHAPTER 11

Where do we want to be?

Abundances in society

Education systems

Healthcare systems

Integration of different generations

CHAPTER 10

Where are we?

WE ALL LIVE within a
society and are intimately
affected by our cultural
surroundings. It is therefore
appropriate when thinking about peoplecare to look beyond our own
direct interactions and explore the wider context of society and the
bigger systems we are part of.

This part follows the three basic steps of design. This chapter takes a
wide perspective on *where we are*, to gain an understanding of some of
the cultural forces at play.

The next chapter focuses on *where we want to be* with more
peoplecare integrated into the infrastructure of our education,
healthcare systems and intergenerational activities.

The following chapter asks *how we get there.* We again take a broad
view of the mechanisms that can be utilised to create change, and the
steps we could take individually and collectively.

Observation of cultures

How can we get an accurate picture of what is happening regionally and nationally around us? Can we obtain reliable information that we can use to assess the health and happiness of the systems we are part of and read the signs of what is to come?

Our regular sources of information are the media, internet, scientists, anthropologists and sociologists. Gossip and discussions with people also provide us with informal material. Almost all of this information is second hand; it has come from someone else and has already been edited and interpreted. It may be translated with filters of stereotypes, generalisations and other biases. We can observe what is going on in ourselves and what we feel and sense about the world as a mirror for what is happening in the wider picture. This gives us one avenue into the bigger picture but it is still only part of it, and we are likely to be looking at this through the filters of our own circumstances.

Reality is multifaceted and each of these sources of information tends to be looking in one direction predominately. Let's think of the information we get in terms of which of the *Six Thinking Hats* are used.

The statistics that we are presented with come from a *white* thinking hat. We have measurements that can be used as indicators. While they are presented as facts and truths, they are still only a part of the picture; statistics can be manipulated depending on the standpoint and what you want to show. Sometimes statistics are hidden behind, or used to avoid the real issues; time is spent debating when the 'peak' of peak oil actually is. This is akin to finding a leaking tap and spending time discussing how much water is being lost before working out how to fix it. We will see in the next part how statistics have been used to give us a representation of the global picture and provide motivations for change.

As the saying goes, 'bad news sells newspapers'. The daily news focuses almost solely on the *black* hat. It reports what has gone wrong in the world today. What the traumas are, the disasters waiting to happen, how bad things are and how bad they could get.

To get a sense of the *red* hat and how people feel and what emotions are present in our communities, we can observe the people directly around us: our friends and strangers in shops or on the streets. What emotions are being expressed, what is their body language saying to us? The news is often watched from an intellectual perspective focusing on policies and strategies rather than the feelings and the people. There is a disconnection with the red hat. The Great Turning will involve reawakening the feelings of pain and anguish about the pains of the world, as well as the pleasure and enjoyment for the delights the Earth offers us.

Positive News[1] is a newspaper that intentionally gives a voice to the *yellow* hat, to show how much good there is happening, and be evidence for the constructive actions that are taking place across the globe. It now includes pages dedicated to permaculture and the Transition movement. It is easy to get caught up with what we haven't done and where the problems are, both personally and as a society. Using the yellow hat we can celebrate our achievements and restore our faith in humanity. There are inspirational magazines, books and websites that provide the seeds of hope and optimism for the future. *Permaculture* magazine[2] gives practical solutions for earthcare, peoplecare and fair shares, and it unites people working together for positive change. Through sharing of our real-life experiences we are able to focus our attention on bringing the changes we would like to see in the world.

Spending time with like-minded people can kindle our confidence in a bright future, and help us to see the benefits of the present. Using the yellow hat we can be appreciative of the small, personal things around us in our communities, the kindness and smiles of strangers and local shops. We can start to see the resources and capacity we have to change. Even observing that many people are becoming angry and disillusioned is a positive and necessary step towards change.

If we think about how the voice of women has grown around the world over the last couple of centuries, and the many choices we have today with more women coming into leadership, then there is hope for the gender gap to diminish further.

The *green* hat encourages us to use our creativity to see where the alternatives to the mainstream are, to look at edges and other cultures. Humans are incredibly innovative and resourceful and this hat encourages us to open up to creative solutions.

The *blue* hat wants to gain an overview and be able to look in all directions and see the picture as a whole. The blue hat would ask who is part of the discussion and who is under-represented, ensuring that information is gathered from all directions and that there is a flow of the observations into decisions and action. Blue hat thinking would verify our conclusions and check they are not based on assumptions.

The view we have of the world depends on where we are standing and in which direction we are looking. For example, we might think that most people get their food from supermarkets these days, but in fact the supermarket 'food chain' feeds only 30% of the world. Seventy per cent of the humans on the planet are still fed by the peasant food web.[3]

When we move to the edge we can turn our attention to a new reality and see there is another culture that can exist, other ways of being in the world.

Problems in society

There are many problems around us today. Each ethic has been compromised in a myriad of ways by the actions of humans. Debt, crime, violence and unemployment are rising. The feelings of isolation from ourselves, others and nature lead to further health and social problems. Prejudices and drink and drug abuse are prevalent, and there are massive inequalities of wealth, opportunity and health. These are to name but a few.

The problems at large in society are a mirror of personal problems. In addition to this scaling up of personal problems we have emergent properties and the problems themselves lead to larger-scale side effects. With a global system the reactions and effects of our actions are often out of sight.

We could see these as symptoms, showing us that there is an illness in society. These problems can be so deeply woven into the fabric of society with such a cyclical, complex web of interconnections, that it can be difficult to trace the causes. These might be actions of individuals but they are showing the voice of the collective. Somehow our cultures are failing to meet our needs. There are deep needs in society for belonging and trust amongst others that are widely unmet.

Points of intervention and transformation

Instead of spending too much time describing where we are, we can ask the questions of how and why we are here, and what the symptoms and causes are. The question could evolve into 'what one thing could we change that would have the most positive ripple effect on the problems of society?' In effect we are looking for points of intervention[4] and transformation, the place of *minimum effort and maximum effect*. The following are suggestions of possible transformation activities.

- *Increasing ecological literacy,* to fully understand natural processes.
- *Reconnection with the Earth,* as something we are part of.
- *Holistic thinking,* to move us away from dualistic thinking and alienation from one another.
- *Valuing parenting more.* When greater significance is placed upon parenting, there will be less distancing of children from their parents. This will impact on the value children place on themselves.
- *Increasing the feminine voice in the world.* Many of the problems arise from patriarchal structures of dominance; by giving more voice to the feminine we start to redress the balance.
- *Recognising the greater costs of our actions.* Having too easy a life does not give us incentive to change. It is easier to ignore the need to change when we are comfortable with where we are, even if changes could take us to a better place for ourselves and the planet. When we recognise the wider costs and implications of our actions we are more likely to seek change.
- *Appreciation.* By increasing our appreciation of what we do have and fostering 'enoughism' we move away from the greed of the 'too muchness' or 'never enough' world.
- *Accessing our hope for a bright future* will help us to move in that direction. Rather than thinking, 'We're all doomed anyway; what I do won't count', we shift to asking ourselves 'What can I do to help this become reality?'

What I like about these is that we are all able to start them immediately, as individuals. We don't need to wait for others or for the right time, and as more and more people become involved there will be faster transformation and wider impacts.

Limiting factors

Focusing on the *limits* anchor point enables us to find ways to release their hold and move forward. What are the limiting factors for achieving a socially just and sustainable future? What's taking us off in the wrong direction? Is it lack of information, imagination, education or resources?

Perhaps we do not have a clear vision of what we would actually like as a society, and share the ambition of wanting to get there. If we knew where we wanted to get to, and were all aligned to the values of co-operation and sustainability we would be able to prioritise actions that took us in this direction. The overemphasis on creating material and financial capital is pulling us away from creating living, social and cultural capital.

People need access to attractive alternative ways of living. It is not encouraging people to live sustainably when we are given beliefs like 'It's not easy being green'. This was the title of an otherwise excellent British television series. Again the television and media are feeding on the drama and the challenges rather than the joys, benefits and the ease. Another television programme focused on the negative responses when a family is faced with an abrupt, shocking change to a low impact lifestyle for two weeks. On return to their home lives they did however go on to make several significant changes. Successful small steps lead us to bigger changes.

With more people stepping forth into their own power and brilliance we can create a groundswell of movement into a positive future. We need to change the current trajectory as well as create forward motion.

We currently have on the planet enough skills and resources to feed, clothe and provide shelter for every single person, as well as begin to address the issues of climate change, deforestation and loss of habitat. Paradigms of fear and greed are controlling the distribution systems. There are grossly unfair skews of poverty and wealth on the planet and the gap is growing. We need co-operation, vision, joined up long-term thinking and a shift of paradigm to one of connection, peace and abundance.

The Integral Model

The four quadrants of the Integral Model

For the vast majority of people there is a gap between how we would like our lives to be and how they are. While we can certainly take action for ourselves to improve our own lives, and expand into our own radiance, there are times when the culture we live in does not support us in this. It is appropriate to ask the question of how can we facilitate cultural shifts to sustainable behaviours that will lead us towards an Earth culture?

Cultures are composed of more than just external behaviours. In order to shift cultures we have to work on the underlying beliefs as well.

The *Integral Model* from Ken Wilbur[5] provides us with a useful framework for understanding the connections between the individual and collective and the inner and outer. These are the two axes that cross to provide us with four quadrants.

We are looking here at the wider collective in society but it could be as small as two people. This model applies equally well to our groups and one to one relationships.

The left quadrants are the internal landscapes, the hidden processes, individually and collectively. The right quadrants are the physical aspects that are visible, the behaviours and social structures we have in place.

	Individual		
Inner	WHY I DO Intentions and beliefs Assumptions Emotions	WHAT I DO Behaviours Biological functions Physical states	Outer
	WHY WE DO Cultural beliefs Norms, worldviews Organisational culture Collective wisdom Visions and dreams	WHAT WE DO Social, political, economic, organisational structures, processes and systems, including health, food and education systems	
	Collective		

Every problem has corresponding issues in each of the four quadrants. There are resistances and limiting factors in every one, and each quadrant influences every other. For instance we may want to change our eating habits, but the social networks for buying seasonal, local food are not present.

There is often a focus on the outer changes and trying to establish new systems and behaviours. But if people have no internal awareness about peak oil then a new public transport system won't necessarily be used.

Another example of outer actions being carried out without the necessary shifts in the inner quadrant, was a carbon neutral fund cutting down an ancient woodland to make way for planting new trees to offset the carbon footprint of big companies. This emphasises how the inner thinking needs to be in line with the outer actions or you can get nonsensical actions.

Solutions can also arise in the four quadrants. The lower right quadrant contains our collective wisdom as well as our cultural theories, dreams and visions. Our cultural capital is held here, and we can tap into this to create a sense of 'we'. Through the stories we tell about ourselves and our culture we can strengthen our sense of unity, diversity and resilience.

We will look at the cultural conditioning, beliefs and identities within the internal collective quadrant before moving on to some of the systems in place in the outer collective quadrant.

Cultural conditioning

Conditioning is a way of patterning our brains to certain ways of thinking and behaving. Conditioning has its uses; we are able to communicate quicker with each other when we have mutual understandings of the parameters in which we operate.

Our cultural conditioning predominantly comes from the media, religious structures, parenting and schooling. We are subtly given messages about how we should be and what to believe. Music is also a way in which we receive messages about the world. All of these messages are drip-fed into our consciousness and we are often not even aware of their effect. Often the images we are shown give us a false sense of family, life and how we can be as humans. Advertising is constantly telling us that what we have is not enough and that we need more to be happy and successful.

The consequences of these messages are far-reaching. People are unaware of their own capabilities when they buy into the messages about what they should be doing. Conditioning inhibits systems to demonstrate their own evolution, to find their own path in life, whether as an individual or collectively. Towns are losing their local identity as they are swallowed up by chain stores. Conditioning leads us away from a diversity of thinking and behaving into a monoculture of being, where we have less creativity and choices.

Many of the messages encourage a competitive outlook on life. The overriding behavioural pattern is a hierarchical branching pattern. Patterns of co-operation and the lobe pattern are given much less attention.

The types of abundance we focus on depend on the values that our society gives to them. Is it our education, community, family ties or is it material possessions and money that are valued and invested in?

Our family upbringing and peer groups also provide us with a set of rules, habits and ways of being. We have cultural norms, which we want to follow even though they are not rules. When asked 'how are you?' it is a cultural norm to reply 'I'm fine'. This isn't a rule of language, but it is accepted as a reply. We have cultural norms about whether we can talk about the problems of the world and how they affect us. Are we heard or does it make people feel uncomfortable? One of the benefits of the Transition movement is that it has opened up a forum for people to talk about these issues. By engaging in dialogue we open up to solutions emerging.

We have cultural norms about how we look, sound and even smell. Can we smell of wood smoke? There are cultural levels of complaining, judging, criticising, complimenting, self-appreciation and happiness.

We can get swept up in the currents, like in rush hour coming off the train. Which rivers do you want to step into? The river of permaculture can take us to unexpected places. When enough of us look towards an Earth culture the impetus will create the Great Turning.

Cultural beliefs

Here are just a few of the common cultural beliefs that can hold us back:

- Individuals cannot make a difference
- Change will be painful
- New technologies are improvements
- People want an easy life

Let's take the last one and look at the consequences of this belief. If people are looking for an easy way out then they won't see challenges as exciting, inspiring and opportunities for growth, but something to avoid. If alongside this we are told that living sustainably is hard work, we are going to shy away from these changes.

In contrast permaculture has cultural beliefs of abundance; we can make a difference; there are solutions; interconnectedness; valuing every contribution.

Paying attention to our cultural patterns, beliefs and conditioning is key to designing a positive future.

ACTIVITY: DAY OFF FROM THE MEDIA

For one day remove yourself from the messages of the media. For this day avoid newspapers and television. More of a challenge perhaps will be to avoid reading the adverts that surround us in towns and cities. You could choose to read only positive magazines and newspapers for the day.

Notice your reactions that day and also the following day when you re-engage.

Cultural identities

We all have cultural groups we associate with, based on our gender, race or religion. We are connected to large numbers of people by having some commonality, without even knowing most of them. Other groups may form out of bioregions, skills and interests. For some of us these associations are strong and meaningful. We may flow in and out of some groups and others we stay with for life. Cultural groups have common beliefs, assumptions, goals and values comprising their own unique collective internal quadrant.

The groups we belong to form sub-cultures of their own. These may be very distinct from others. Cultural identities can be a blessing or a curse.

The advantages of group identity:

- Unity
- Co-operation
- Familiarity
- Shared language and assumptions lead to faster communication
- Strength
- Recognition
- Sense of belonging
- Connections
- Cohesive aim

The disadvantages of group identities:

- Can create cliques
- Separation
- Competition between groups
- Segregation
- Can create barriers
- You may become attached to attitudes and beliefs that aren't necessarily your own
- The need to protect identity can lead to aggression
- Can lead to feelings of superiority and oppression, when 'different' comes to mean 'wrong'
- Can perpetuate cultural limiting beliefs

When a group of people come together there are many benefits to creating a strong identity, though it can seem like a closed clique from the outside. The identity can create an 'us and them' perception from both the inside and the outside of the group. With identity being an important need for the group and not something we want to do away with, the question becomes *how to create an 'us' without creating a 'them'?* This question is relevant for many different scales, from small groups to whole countries. Identity and belonging are deep needs. However, identity can foster feelings of exclusion and alienation from those on the 'outside'. By being aware, celebrating diversity and seeing edges as fuzzy, fluid boundaries we are more able to remain open and tolerant.

If we want to engage more people in working towards regeneration and social change we need to ensure that such work is not seen as impenetrable. New people need to be able to get involved and feel welcome.

Oppression

Throughout history and all over the globe groups have tried to dominate over one another. People have used their group identity to divide and rule. They have tried to protect and maintain the boundaries of their group. They come from a place of 'we are right, they are wrong'. One group acts from a perceived hierarchy and wants power over other groups. This perception of being better or above is also instrumental in our actions towards the planet.

The dualistic thinking that separates you from me continues to whole groups of people, and allows us to distance ourselves from feeling the effects of any harm that is caused. In fact, we are just hiding from the effects; they still enter our lives under our radar.

The oppression of people on the basis of their gender, race, age, even looks and size, is deep-rooted in our culture. Even while overt discrimination has been tackled to some degree in the law there are many residues left in our societal behaviour and cultural psyche. These have ripples into our own internal landscape and the external quadrants. We need to look deeper at the underlying messages that are being transferred, particularly in the media, looking out for the subtle messages of superiority, inferiority and oppression. The first step is to recognise and name them, not allowing them to go on unsaid.

Groups oppress others because they want to control things, protect themselves and acquire resources. They prevent the flow of information to the oppressed group to keep it in a place of disempowerment so it is subservient. The effects of oppression are frustration, helplessness, anger, fear and poverty of resources as well as financial poverty.

Cultures, like people and trees, have varying rates of growth and development. Oppression is working against the nature of the person or the group and not allowing systems to demonstrate their own evolution.

Often the oppressed become oppressors, as an outlet for their frustration, and because they see no alternative way of escaping. The bullied become the bullies. This is seen in the caste system in India where castes are oppressed by the castes above them, and they in turn continue to oppress the ones below. Often people at the 'bottom of the pile', like disempowered children, abuse animals or vandalise property as a way of expressing their anger.

To deal with oppression, education of the oppressors is needed, otherwise conflict will ensue as the oppressed try and break free.

Privilege

How much are we heard and listened to within our communities? We can have earned and unearned influence. Tribal elders have earned their influence by having a proven track record for making decisions and learning from their mistakes. In our groups and communities we can allow people to earn influence by giving them responsibilities and supporting them to carry them out.

Privilege is when we have unearned influence from our group identity rather than earned from things we have done ourselves. This could be from our gender, nationality, race, class or parents. A university degree will give you influence and in some respect you have earned this by studying, but there is also perhaps an element of being able to go to university because you or your parents had the money to send you, and better opportunities during your schooling.

Privilege can come from owning land, going to expensive schools, having money, being healthy, speaking English, being able to read and write, where we live, our looks or having access to information via books and the internet. People who are on low incomes, in debt, parents without childcare, homeless people, refugees and asylum seekers all have less privilege, with the latter even being oppressed by the law. We may be in the middle somewhere with more privilege than most in the world (you are able to read this book) and less than others. Privilege is sometimes confused with value; we misguidedly place value on ourselves or others according to how much privilege we have.

The privileges we have in society may well be invisible to us, our ability to read for example taken for granted. When we are working as change agents in society we need to be aware of the unconscious barriers that may be present for people with less privilege than ourselves. Rather than pushing our own agenda on to them we can spend time listening to find out what their needs are, approaching people with respect and integrity and making alliances by going to them rather than wanting them to come to us. If we are trying to work in subcultures other than our own, we can take time observing what the group norms are, rather than making assumptions that things will operate in the same way we are used to.

Acknowledgement of privilege is the first step to gaining a more level playing field and addressing some of the issues needed in order to achieve fair shares.

Social systems

We move now to the outer quadrants of the Integral Model. The running of our society is based on bigger systems. Systems embedded into our societal framework are healthcare, education, social care, food distribution, transport, sewage and financial systems. All of these systems could benefit from a permaculture design to enhance overall peoplecare. The next chapter will focus on improvements that could be made to our education and healthcare systems, as these represent two major aspects of peoplecare.

These systems all have various elements in common. They are mostly based on top-down hierarchies of governance and management. The development of these systems is often based on input from select workers and users. There is so much these days that is being taken out of our control, centralisation leaving the people on the ground powerless for everyday decisions. Teachers in schools can no longer make decisions over what to teach and find unique pathways for their students. Paperwork is taking over hospitals. Meanwhile the people at the top are only able to deal in patterns and are mostly unaware of the details of the schools, hospitals and towns. While it is good to begin a design looking at the patterns, we need to work from these to the details, so that the design fits the unique situation. By trying to avoid looking at the details and assuming all towns are the same, we are getting ever pushed in the direction of a monocultural society.

A lot of the thoughts behind the running of these systems are short term. Ideas to invest in long-term solutions or equipment get swallowed up by the constraints of 'this year's budget'.

We are lucky to have free schooling and healthcare for all in the UK. The overall idea of everyone paying something to pay for bigger systems to meet everyone's needs is a valid one. It has enabled the systems to advance and develop and be much more resourceful than could otherwise have happened. However, one of the consequences of collective systems is that they can allow us to become lazy and not take self-responsibility for our own needs. With our health there is a reliance on doctors to 'make us better'. Having schools to teach our children means we don't need to maintain and continue our own education. With mass food distribution systems there is less incentive to grow our own food.

Upgrading our social systems could include people becoming more responsible and self-reliant. The advances are not about dismantling the existing systems, which would be throwing the baby out with the bath water. They are about allowing the systems to be adaptive and improve with our changing times, and having the resources to be able to cope with a shifting world and needs.

Currently we see	**What we want is**
Problems are linked	Integration of systems
↓	↓
Symptoms are treated	Identification of root causes
↓	↓
The further downstream the more difficult and expensive it is to treat	Timely action and intervention
↓	↓
Decision-making is distant and solutions are out of sight	Local decision-making
↓	↓
Increase scale = increase in problem	Appropriate human scale
↓	↓
Resulting in degradation, dependency and disempowerment	Resulting in regenerative, productive, self reliant and empowering systems

CHAPTER 11

Where do we want to be?

IN THIS CHAPTER we bring our design skills to take a fresh look at education and healthcare systems. This is intended to illustrate how we can bring permaculture design into much larger social systems. Healthcare and education systems are focused upon as these represent two major aspects of peoplecare. The last section looks at how we can integrate different generations to bring many benefits.

Abundances in society

What would regenerative, productive, self reliant and empowering systems in our society look and feel like? We don't necessarily know all the details at this stage but with observation and design we could be responsive to what emerges and able to act from an understanding of ethical behaviour and living within limits. Some of the qualities may be:

- A supportive community
- Many links between different generations, races and subcultures
- Safety and trust
- Confidence in strangers
- A thriving local economy
- Good health
- Nurturing education

Motivations

We need to be motivated in order to make changes. If changes are imposed from the top down, people lose the opportunity to find their own motivations for making changes. When more people are involved solutions are owned and there is less resistance.

The benefits of creating more sustainable settlements are widespread for individuals, the settlement itself and extend beyond. Currently a lot of problems created with the current systems leave people on the other side of the planet unable to meet their basic needs because they are being exploited for Western gain.

Our motivations for change can include both the moving away from the problems we currently face or see on the horizon, and the moving towards a culture that is more fulfilling.

Resources

We have many resources available to help us make changes. There is a growing awareness of the need for alternatives. People are inherently creative and resourceful. Having infrastructure already in place that could be utilised to bring about widespread regeneration is a huge resource. We also have many permaculture skills to draw upon: design skills, ability to think in systems and awareness of the four quadrants.

Education systems

Reflection

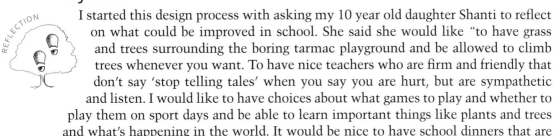

I started this design process with asking my 10 year old daughter Shanti to reflect on what could be improved in school. She said she would like "to have grass and trees surrounding the boring tarmac playground and be allowed to climb trees whenever you want. To have nice teachers who are firm and friendly that don't say 'stop telling tales' when you say you are hurt, but are sympathetic and listen. I would like to have choices about what games to play and whether to play them on sport days and be able to learn important things like plants and trees and what's happening in the world. It would be nice to have school dinners that are fair trade and organic with no harmful pesticides."

The basic idea of children learning together in groups with trained teachers and spending time socially together is sound. However, I think that the needs of many children aren't being met and schools could be improved to get more out for the same or less in.

I then thought about one of my most satisfying learning experiences; my permaculture design course. During the course the creative teaching processes captured my attention. They were engaging, thought provoking, empowering and fun. Everyone's opinions were sought and we were encouraged to seek out-of-the-box solutions. The methods used arise from 'accelerated learning'.

Our most precious natural resource – the minds and hearts of our children and young people. It is their curiosity, their eagerness to learn, their ability to make difficult and complex choices that will decide the future of our world.

CARL ROGERS

. . . .

Patterns of accelerated learning

We can look at the patterns of accelerated learning for ideas to bring into a design for schools. Permaculture is informed by cyclical and non-linear natural processes, so it follows that permaculture is also taught in this way. The pattern of permaculture has parallels in accelerated learning. Accelerated learning is a reinforcing spiral of learning based on reviews and connections in a diverse, fun, integrative, cyclical manner.

Like permaculture, accelerated learning is more than just a set of techniques, it requires a way of thinking that enables us to get more out of the learning experience, just as permaculture design aims to get more outputs for less inputs.

Whenever and whatever we teach, the content, process, relationships, aims and progression are important.

- What we teach – is the content relevant to the learner?
- How it's taught – is the process engaging and interactive?
- What relationships does this information make with our existing knowledge; does it connect with previous learning?
- Why it's taught – how does it fit into the bigger picture?
- How does it lead us forward – what can we do with this new knowledge?

Accelerated learning works equally as well for children and adults. In a nutshell it aims to inspire and motivate students to learn, enabling a high retention, integration and progression. Central to accelerated learning is the creation of a positive learning environment; this is the physical space and the emotional and social environments.

Our emotional environment deals with our motivations. Conventional education promotes extrinsic motivation, where we are encouraged to learn something to get a qualification, or to do our homework so we don't get told off. Intrinsic motivation is where we find the reasons for learning internally. Teachers have positive expectations of their students and they are encouraged to find their own intrinsic motivation and relevance for the work.

The social environment is developed through making connections between the students through collaborative learning, and outside of the learning context. Students are stimulated to ask questions of the teacher and their fellow students.

Subjects are taught with an awareness of the different multiple intelligences to cater for different learning styles and for fun, diversity and maintaining interest.

Some of the accelerated learning principles[1] Dave Meier talks about are:

- *Learning involves the whole body and mind* – head, hands and heart learning.
- *Learning is creation not consumption* – learning is not just the passive storage of knowledge. We literally have to create connections with our existing knowledge and skills, in our minds.
- *Collaboration aids learning* – co-operation between learners speeds up learning, we are all able to learn more when we help each other. Even those understanding the material easily will learn more by having to explain it to others.
- *Learning comes from doing the work itself with feedback* – trying skills out and hearing constructive advice.
- *Positive emotions greatly improve learning* – when we are relaxed and happy we can learn more.

The activities in this book are designed on these principles to help you get more out of your reading.

Integration

We can use the *integration* anchor point to assemble the information we have so far and distil it into the needs of the design. We can then look at systems that could fulfil these needs and move us to our vision. The focus of this design is for schools, but it could easily be extended into other parts of the education system.

These do not include the predominant activities already in school of learning with our head and the building of intellectual capital. The assumption here is to leave existing subjects in place, although in reality these would adapt as well. Maths and physics, for example, would still be key skills for the engineers of the future but their emphasis might shift to designing renewable energy systems.

Many of these activities are already happening in various schools and a future part of the design would be to do a comprehensive stocktake: share stories and reflect on the outcomes, to take them into a more detailed design tailored for individual schools and areas.

It is also helpful to reflect more on the 'why' we do these things. Then we can see the needs our activities are meeting, and if there are other ways of meeting the same need. We can also identify extra yields for the same activity.

Functions/needs

We can draw functions from the previous chapters and then look for common themes. A good starting point for this is some of the points of intervention and transformation for the problems in society. If we can embed a different way of thinking in the young this can have a big impact in years to come.

- *Increasing ecological literacy and reconnection with the Earth.*
- *Teaching self and collective responsibility and giving and receiving feedback* so that we can recognise the greater costs of our actions.
- *Appreciation* of ourselves, each other and the planet.
- Accessing our hope for a bright future by *visioning and designing the future.*
- *Accelerated learning* would be a fundamental need.
- Accelerated learning would include *creating positive social, personal and physical learning environments.*
- *Learning with our heart, hands and body.*
- In the creation of real wealth we would be looking to *build experiential, spiritual, social, cultural and living capital.*
- Children would need *mentoring and coaching* to find right livelihoods.
- In order to break the spiral of erosion of poor education leading to poor educators we would need *teacher training in peoplecare skills and in accelerated learning.*

Systems and elements

With permaculture design each of the functions would have backups and be met in at least three ways – *multiple elements for every important function.*

We would also want every system or element to do more than one thing, so we wouldn't actually need so many things to be in place – *many yields for every element.*

Function	System/element
Increasing ecological literacy and reconnection with the Earth	Time outside in nature Forest schools School gardens
Teaching self responsibility and collective responsibility – giving and receiving feedback	School gardens Allow some risk-taking and mistake-making Co-operative learning Peace restoration skills Peer feedback
Appreciation	Valuing of education by adults and children Focusing on and appreciation of children's abilities Celebrations Valuing of practical and peoplecare skills and all the multiple intelligences as much as academic subjects
Visioning and redesigning the future	Positive visualisations to access hope for the future Design skills Avenues for ideas and designs to be seen and heard Problem-solving skills
Building experiential capital – learning through doing	Real-life projects Practical skills Natural building School gardens
Building spiritual capital	Meditation Yoga, tai chi Time in nature Peace restoration skills
Building social capital	Collaborative learning Integration of different classes Integration with wider community Peace restoration skills Taking skills back into their homes
Building living capital	School garden Encouragement of children to garden at home
Building cultural capital	Celebrations Storytelling Songs
Accelerated learning techniques	Multiple intelligences Thinking tools Collaborative learning Questioning skills
Positive social learning environment	Collaborative learning Peace restoration skills Storytelling Songs Communication skills Decision-making

Emotional learning environment	Intrinsic motivation Choice in what and when children learn Awareness of the emotions of learning – competence cycle Relevance of learning to person's life
Mentoring and coaching	Choices Listening Appreciation of individual's talents Questioning skills Peer mentoring
Learning with hands and body	Outdoor activities including gardening Yoga Forest school Practical activities Natural building Crafts Movement within classes
Learning with our hearts	Awareness of the emotions of learning – competence cycle Attitudes Intrinsic motivation Peer support Emotional literacy
Teacher training in peoplecare skills	Negotiation Listening Mentoring and coaching Shifting patterns from their own education experiences Accelerated learning techniques

Ideas

These systems could be composed of a huge variety of elements. After getting to this point we could visit the *ideas* anchor point and generate many creative imaginative elements. For example, crafts that meet the function of learning with our hands and body could include green woodworking, cooking and repairing clothes.

These functions could all be met without having to do any deep restructuring of the current educational systems. We could think further outside the box and suggest that to encourage collective responsibility and collaborative learning, no one passes a class until everyone passes. We could also redefine 'pass'.

A school in Sweden has taken the idea of choice and intrinsic motivation to a high level where children have the choice to attend every lesson. When this was first introduced the children didn't quite believe it and still went to every lesson. Then it swung the other way and no one went to anything. Finally it settled down and the children had to find their own motivation to attend lessons and learn. It also meant that the teachers had to put more effort in to make their lessons interesting.

ACTIVITY: ASK CHILDREN

For each of the systems above ask children for their ideas about how to meet the needs above and also the different elements that could comprise the systems. We might be surprised with the creative and out-of-the-box ideas they come up with.

Action

As one of the limiting factors in schools is time, when it comes to deciding what could be done first we would choose anything that frees-up time. In this case practising accelerated learning techniques during existing classes could ease the pressure and provide a springboard for other systems as well as giving yields in its own right.

Philosophy for communities

Rod Cunningham, a secondary school teacher, uses a method called 'Philosophy for Communities'[2] or P4C for short. It started in the US in the 1960s by Professor Matthew Lipman, and is now in over 60 countries. P4C engages children in developing their own questions in response to a given stimulus. They then choose one question and enquire thoughtfully and collaboratively, guided by the facilitator. It aims to build 'communities of enquiry' where participants develop the 'four Cs': creative, critical, caring and collaborative thinking skills. P4C puts great emphasis on open questions where there is no single right or wrong answer.

The stimuli used can be related to the three ethics of permaculture and may lead us to conceptual or value questions such as 'is it important to save species?' Rod often uses a photo from South Africa showing very expensive homes with people living in shacks and squalor right outside the fence; this leads to questions about fairness and distribution of wealth and resources.

A school in London uses this method and has 18 students trained up as facilitators, further enhancing opportunities for collaborative learning. Behaviour shows improvement as a result of P4C as students become more open-minded and are more willing to talk than resort to violence. Students' exam results also show improvement.

It is also used in community groups, prisons and youth custody centres. It is very successful in prison environments as it gives people an outlet other than violence.

P4C fulfils many of the functions above including visioning the future, collaborative learning, creating a positive social environment, learning with our hearts, emotional literacy, building cultural capital and self and collective responsibility.

Healthcare systems

When we think of healthcare systems our thoughts immediately turn to nurses and hospitals, doctors and specialists. If we want a nation of healthy people we must broaden this understanding to include all aspects of life that impact on our health. Again the assumption here is not to replace existing systems; we do need our surgeons and hospitals. The idea would be to create spirals of health that increase the overall well-being of society.

Hippocrates is often cited to be the father of modern medicine. Practising in Greece in 460BC he viewed illnesses as imbalances in the body, responsive to medicines, rather than as expressions of supernatural forces. One of the biggest themes of his practice was to facilitate the body's capacity to heal itself, by properly supporting it with clean air, good food and adequate exercise. In his vision the role of medical practitioners was to work with and assist the natural healing forces that bring the body back into balance. Although the focus of their practice might have changed, medical practioners today still have to take the Hippocratic oath.

Transformation points

We can begin to better comprehend our health care service through a whole-systems perspective. Quite simply, a system that enables profit to be made from illness will establish feedback loops over time, which will increase rather than reduce illness, creating an illness industry. In creating systems that sustain health, profit cannot be a prime motive and must be removed from any health care system.

Changing the goals of the system from one of treating illnesses to one of maintaining health will kick-start a huge transformation of our healthcare services and lifestyles. We will be creating a system that supports people in staying well. There will be two main focuses – one on health and one on care.

Cuba has a high level of health in comparison to other majority world countries. They have an integrated approach to their health care with herbal medicine and acupuncture available. There are a high percentage of family practitioners and small clinics in relation to specialist doctors and bigger health centres, with one doctor to every 200 people, compared with one doctor to every 400 people in the US.[3] The family doctors are very much part of the community and know the family and social context of their patients. The focus on preventative and primary health care has resulted in a high life expectancy of 76 years for men and 80 for women.[4] They have rationalised the pharmaceutical medicines available to a limited number manufactured not-for-profit by the government. Where profit of the pharmaceutical industry reigns, we see the reinvention and reconfiguration of these basic medicines to produce a confusing array of pharmaceuticals, and growing health care bills.

In Germany doctors will prescribe the plant St John's Wort for depression, in preference to a course of anti-depressant drugs. This both moves medicine away from multinational corporation profit, and results in less extreme side effects than refined pills and medicines.

Spirals of health

We can create spirals of health within our societies.

Spiral of awareness and self-responsibility

Self responsibility for maintaining own health → more awareness → receive and interpret feedback from our own bodies → trusting the wisdom of our bodies → diagnosing problems earlier → treating problems sooner → more self responsibility →

With this spiral we are more likely to be treating causes rather than symptoms that have had time to develop.

Spiral of empowerment

Integration of complementary practices → Choices available → Empowerment of patients → healthier and happier patients → training in basic first aid and herbal back-yard treatments → more integration of complementary practices →

Complementary practices are also helpful in maintaining health through relaxation and reducing stress.

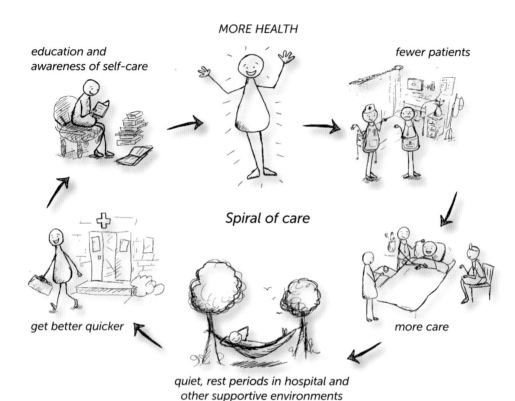

Spiral of care

MORE HEALTH

education and awareness of self-care

fewer patients

more care

quiet, rest periods in hospital and other supportive environments

get better quicker

Key to the success of this spiral is the shift of goal to one of focusing on care so that a drop in the number of patients doesn't mean fewer staff.

Spiral of communication and learning

System-wide learning → communication loops between doctors and nurses → feedback between different medical professionals → skill sharing → system wide learning →

We can maximise the existing knowledge and systems and improve quality with perhaps only small *minimum effort* actions.

Spiral of healthy living

Training medical professionals in health → education → prevention → influencing other systems to address issues of health → healthy diet and living → training in health →

Currently most training is centred around treating illnesses and not on how to maintain health. This spiral starts to introduce a more holistic understanding of health and illness; the causes and the other social systems that are related, in particular nutrition, exercise and socio-psychological well-being.

Health in the four quadrants

Our bodies are integrative systems. They are part of the physical and social environment and will reveal the imbalances of the bigger systems they are part of. Disease in our collective psyche appears as external individual illnesses.

Most diseases of 'modern' industrial societies are chronic and degenerative, arising as a consequence of poor nutrition, lack of exercise, stress and social dislocation. Doctors rarely have the opportunity to address the source of the imbalance and affect the disease process itself. Instead they have drugs available that may alleviate symptoms, but may be needed to be taken for life and which themselves cause further imbalances.

The current paradigm is to look at things in parts not wholes. Connections have been broken and we need to weave them back. There is a striking parallel in how we treat the natural world and how we treat our own bodies. The relationship between the health system and food system is key in tackling the root causes of many of the chronic diseases. Thus a health system could start to influence other systems in the outer collective quadrant such as agriculture and food processing. The advertising industry is highly influential in our cultural conditioning and the inner collective quadrant. Advertising of alcohol and unhealthy food could be banned or taxed to pay for the treatment associated with them. If the burden of these chronic diseases could be lessened, it would release resources for keeping people well and happy. It is significant to note the number of people who do recover from life-threatening diseases through changes to their lifestyles and diet.

Schools play an important part in education and in laying down patterns for later life. The increase in childhood obesity, sitting in classrooms all day and tuck shops in schools would be seen as linked.

The current emphasis is on individual rather than collective health. Our emotional health is directly influenced by our sense of community or lack thereof. If we are lacking in community we feel the effects of not having support around us. There could be a sense of 'we' as a healthy community evolving through food-growing projects in council estates, community clinics and health centres. There could be peer-to-peer learning in the community, where people who have had a particular illness and become 'experts' in it could share their experiences and support and advise other people, helping others to find solutions for themselves.

The design of our hospitals is an outer expression of the thinking of the collective inner quadrant. The collective intentions of health, care and system-wide learning could be reflected in hospitals. It would be beneficial to design opportunities to exercise and to connect with other patients as both of these can help speed recovery. Studies show that patients who are next to the window in hospitals recover more quickly than those who aren't. Hospitals could be designed with more input from all the users, everyone from the surgeons to the cleaners and especially the patients.

The four quadrants can support each other in the spirals of health above. Health becomes a strong cultural pattern.

Action

Nicole Freris works as a GP in London, and also teaches permaculture. She has brought her knowledge of systems into her practice and is taking action to initiate the *spiral of awareness and self-responsibility*. When she speaks to her patients she makes small steps towards this vision of health by handing back responsibility to her patients. She listens and then reflects back an understanding of everything that they bring in terms of systems. She opens up for them a new way of understanding their bodies as a natural system that is affected by the things put in to it, and their illnesses as a state of imbalance. Even within the constraints of 10 minute appointments Nicole has an appreciation of the whole and opens up a different way of seeing the problem. She says, "because this makes sense to most people it reassures them and it's amazing how easy it makes the consultations". She describes the options they have available to them, while illustrating the limitations, benefits and issues of the current medical system, and what the system does and doesn't do. She empowers them to take responsibility for their choices.

Creating change in systems as big as our national healthcare systems can be daunting, but we can all make individual actions to improve our own health and well-being. We can begin the *spiral of empowerment* with the simple step of growing herbs that can be used in teas as simple remedies in the home and could reduce our reliance on allopathic medicines and ease the strain on GPs. There are also the added benefits of connecting with nature and the feelings of empowerment that accompany the growing and using of herbs.

- Sage tea – good for coughs and menopause
- Mint tea – eases digestion and heartburn
- Chamomile tea – relieves insomnia and aids relaxation
- Raspberry leaf tea – useful for strengthening the uterus in the last trimester of pregnancy
- Nettle tea – rich in iron

ACTIVITY: HEALTHY SOCIETY

What is my vision of a healthy society?

What would that look and feel like in all of its expressions?

Integration of different generations

Every person follows different phases of development. Within our cultures we have different generations of people at the same phase.

Child → apprentice → adult → elder

Each phase has different approaches to learning about the self and the world, as well as different perspectives. These phases relate to the design web, where the child phase is about growth, the apprentice one about searching and experimenting, the adult phase about doing, being decisive and productive, and the elder phase is reflective.

In the past there was, and within current indigenous cultures there still is, a web of connections[5] between the different generations embedded into everyday life. Each generation would have connections between all of the others as well as peer support. Now, along with so many other connections, these have been broken and people are segregated. Children are isolated within their age groups at schools, elderly people are alone in homes, the apprentice stage is being eroded and adults are lacking in support. The consequences of this are probably much deeper than realised. We are unable to learn from the other generations and expend energy making the same mistakes or reinventing the proverbial wheel.

We are falsely insulated from the need to connect with each other by the reliance on fossil fuels and material goods. The broken web means our communities – and we as individuals – are less resilient. Our emotional health suffers from the lack of connections, as does our on-going education.

When we lived in extended families we would have had natural connections with different generations, but now there is greater distance between families, both physically and metaphorically. We have grown up in a culture of 'stranger danger' where we are actively discouraged from talking to people we don't know. These broken pathways in our culture mean it is difficult for us to respond on a person-to-person level with each other.

This isn't to say that we need to take integration to extremes; there are times when children and work don't mix, for example.

Mending the web

The connections are not just linear from one stage of life to the next, or within each generation, they are woven between all of the generations. There can be flows of energy, wisdom, learning and support in all directions. We can recognise our inter-dependence.

Increasing tolerance by having a 'look to like' attitude, valuing diversity and examining our own beliefs creates flows of respect in all directions. Personal connections help to break down the media caricatures of grumpy old man/woman, bossy adult, young hooligan and troublesome child. When we know individuals we can move beyond these stereotypes and prejudices. We can see the wise elder, active adult, enthusiastic teenager and playful child.

Each generation has different strengths and characteristics. By respecting the value of each, people will start to have more time and incentive to connect. Combining these strengths will compensate for weaknesses. We can try to find ways to harvest the gifts of each stage. Focusing on the strengths will start to shift some of the negative language and attitudes that we have about the different stages. Every human (unless their life is cut short) will go through each of these stages. By not honouring them in other people we are actually pushing away part of ourselves, whether past or future. It is important to know about the stage of life that is coming next.

There is a natural succession from one phase to the next. As well as acknowledging birth and death, the movement from one generation to another would be recognised with people clearly knowing which stage they are at. Indigenous cultures honour the progression with rites of passage, acknowledging the loss of the previous phase and welcoming the gifts of the new stage. In the West youths might create their own, possibly destructive, rites of passage such as stealing a car, or getting drunk.

By listening we will build a better picture of how to meet everyone's needs. We can find out what they think life is about, ask them what they want and what they know. Elders and teenagers are both marginalised groups in our culture; together though they represent a significant proportion. They have things in common and similar needs; when they speak together their voices are louder. There has been a push for more buses and public meeting places when these groups have connected.

Each of the generations has its own gifts and abundances, as well as challenges; these could be matched up to share both to create beneficial connections.

Children bring joy, enthusiasm, curiosity, creativity, humour, wonder, lightness, playfulness, imagination and observation. They need entertaining, teaching and care.

The apprentice can be the role model for children. Playing with children allows apprentices to stay connected with this aspect of themselves.

Apprentices have willingness, new ideas, ability to think outside the box, and energy. They need teaching, self-esteem and a channel for their energy.

Adults bring stability, knowledge and responsibility, taking care of hearth and home. They need support with their work and home life. They are able to share their responsibilities with apprentices who are thirsty for real life experiences.

Elders are the wisdom keepers holding a wider perspective; they have time, patience, introspection and reflections. They need to be honoured, have dignity and respect, and be listened to. As elders slow down they are in tune with the pace of children and able to walk together, hopefully having time and patience to spend with children too. Traditionally elders have had the role of passing down ancestral wisdom and tribal knowledge through storytelling to children and apprentices.

If we remember from looking at inputs and outputs, when there are unmet needs in the system there is work, and when there are unused outputs there is waste or pollution. This is exactly what is happening. If you imagine elders who have no one to share their stories with, this then becomes a waste and they can feel depressed. Meanwhile there are children and apprentices who want entertainment and guidance, and this becomes extra work for adults. Age UK has schemes where the elders help young people with their reading and provide mentoring roles.[6] Connecting these generations makes use of the skills and wisdom of the elders so that they feel useful and valued, and gives children and apprentices the attention they need.

There are many other ways we can connect up the inputs and outputs of the different generations, saving energy and avoiding waste. This will ultimately mean that education will improve by us having a more complete understanding and different perspectives to draw upon, and all aspects of health will be enhanced. Our emotional health will be increased through being valued and the feeling of belonging.

It can become a web of kinship, love, learning, health, reciprocity and support.

Apprenticeships

My colleagues and I run teacher training courses. We are all permaculture teachers and it could be seen as strange that we are training up our competition. If thinking in the scarcity model of the world then it wouldn't make sense to do this. However we are thinking from an abundance mentality and have the belief that there is enough for everyone. Training up other teachers, and having them apprentice with us, has allowed us to pass on our skills to the next generation. We have improved and developed our skills in the process of transferring them. If we did not pass on our knowledge and skills to the next generation they would have to take the same learning curve as we have. Instead the energy saved has allowed everyone to advance their skills. The overall body of knowledge of permaculture teaching has increased through sharing. Our sense of 'we' and being a community is also enhanced.

Contrary to the thought of competition, having more permaculture teachers has actually enhanced our work opportunities. We have expanded the centre, the core of teachers, which has also expanded the edges and links with interested people. The more edge the more links and the more people come on everyone's courses.

Knowing that there are other people to run introduction and design courses we are also able to move away from this centre and into different niches, extending our skills to more advanced and specialised courses.

The formal passing on of knowledge to apprentices is just one of the ways in which we can value and use this stage.

Outcomes of bringing the generations together

Bringing these generations together on a person-to-person and group-to-group level will enhance our understanding of the whole human experience. Building these connections will start to heal the fragmentation and separation and create a friendlier, more balanced, sustainable society. Connecting the different generations is a way of using *renewable resources* to increase health and education in society.

ACTIVITY: WHO DO I KNOW?

What generation am I in?

What strengths do I hold?

Identify three people that you know from each of the different generations. Perhaps you can't personally name three people from each generation outside of your own family; it wouldn't be too surprising if you can't. Now you have some awareness of this perhaps an opportunity will present itself to you to connect with someone from another generation. This could be something simple like initiating a conversation at the bus stop or in a shop. Perhaps you might even choose to go looking for an opportunity, volunteering or offering your services.

CHAPTER 12

How do we get there?

FOR THE FORTHCOMING challenges we face it will be survival of the most co-operative and adaptable. We can't live by ourselves, so 'survival of the fittest' will be the survival of those who can be most interdependent. We will have to learn to give and receive, to share what we have and to ask for what we need. It is the people who can think as a community and consider others, who are in the best position to do this and will give humanity the best chance of survival.

The third step of design is finding the steps that would take us to a positive future. This links with the *action* and *momentum* anchor points. In this chapter we are going to look at some of the overall patterns of change, individually and collectively rather than directly focusing on any particular system.

Circles of concern and influence

We all recognise things in the world that are disturbing and we would like to be different. Perhaps it is social injustices in faraway countries, habitat destruction in the rainforest or gangs roaming the streets in your town. There could even be things closer to home in your own family that you would like to amend, like sibling rivalry. A lot of energy could be spent worrying about these things and wanting them to be different without actually achieving any change. Our abilities to transform these situations can be small because we cannot or choose not to force changes in people's behaviours; it is more effective if they decide to do this themselves. We can however create conditions for change.

Stephen Covey[1] introduced the concept of circles of concern and influence as a thinking tool for where to focus our energies. Within our circle of concern are issues such as social or ecological problems as well as those involving other people. Within our circle of influence are things that we have a much greater ability to manoeuvre and direct.

For the vast majority of us our circle of influence lies inside our circle of concern, and we cannot influence all the things we are concerned about.

When we spend our time acting in the wider circle of concern, worrying, generating fear and playing out disaster scenarios of what could happen, we use up available energy that could be spent in our circle of influence. Our circle of influence shrinks as a result of lack of attention and energy and also because the energy spent in worrying disempowers us.

In contrast, when our energy is spent in our circle of influence it expands and we become able to tackle some of the issues that were previously out of reach.

Many people come to permaculture after spending time campaigning for change. Graham Burnett was an activist who came to realise that he was spending his time being 'anti this' and 'anti that' and wanted to discover what he was 'pro'. Permaculture offered him a way of finding solutions and bringing positive change into his life. He described finding permaculture as turning a mental switch from a blame and 'us and them' paradigm to a proactive way of thinking about how we can create workable solutions together. His circle of influence has grown and he is now a permaculture author and teacher. Permaculture encourages us to find actions that are within our capacity for where we are at this moment with our lives, taking steps from the here and now.

How to widen our circle of influence

The primary action is to focus our attention and energy on the things we can change. This brings us back in to zone 00, ultimately the place of most influence. Our own self is the place of *minimum effort for maximum effect*. Any activity that we can do to centre ourselves, align with our aspirations, increase our well-being, improve our communication skills and expand our knowledge is within our circle of influence. Just by demonstrating these things our words will start to have more weight with the people around us. When we have more presence and focus and keep the commitments we make, others are more likely to listen. When we are awake to our own leadership we are able to move forward. Teaching, modelling, designing, being strategic and effective come more easily. As Gandhi said, we can "be the change we want to see in the world".

Within our families we may worry about our children's future, their behaviour, the dynamic between them... these are all in our circle of concern. What is within our capacity to change is our own behaviour, the time we put into family activities or our home environment. Shifting these things can have ripple effects into the other concerns. For example a nurturing environment may help them to play together more.

Within our professional lives we can develop our skills, make contacts and be polite and honest with our colleagues. When we become good at what we do, provide a service and supply a demand, people will come to us.

In our communities we may desire change in our health, education systems or more integration between the generations. It is in our circle of influence to maintain our own health and research different tools for education. We can act to develop a sense of community by talking to our neighbours, offering support, smiling at strangers, using our local shops and walking around our towns.

Developing our observation and design skills increases our capacity for finding points of intervention and transforming systems. There may be something that was previously outside of our influence that now orbits close by as our circle expands, and perhaps there are stages within a spiral of erosion that come within our circle of influence. For example there are some phases of an electoral cycle that are more effective for petitioning politicians to influence policies than others. This brings us to a traditional poem with an addition from a friend.

God grant me the serenity to accept the things I cannot change,
The courage to change the things I can
And the wisdom to know the difference

TRADITIONAL

• • • • • • • • • • • •

And the observational powers to notice when something that was unchangeable becomes changeable
And to notice when something that was changeable becomes unchangeable.

JED PICKSLEY

• • • • • • • • • • • •

The first line highlights the acceptance of problems in our circle of concern but outside of our circle of influence. The next bit emphasises the need for courage to act within our circle of influence, and the wisdom to see the edge.

The addition underlines the shifting nature of situations and the need to be able to respond to changes of size of our circle of influence; things that were outside of our influence may now fall within it. We can imagine the world orbiting around us. There are times when something is out of our reach, but rules change, people move, new contacts are made, and suddenly it comes within our grasp, within our sphere of influence; but we need to be observant enough to notice this and make the necessary actions. There may also be times when something we have been working on moves out of our reach, and we could waste our time and energy by continuing to work on it.

The edge of our circle of influence is dynamic and fuzzy; there are many factors affecting it at any given time. We have all noticed that we are able to convince some people and not others. This can vary with many factors, perhaps just the time of day can determine whether our words are heard or not. It can decrease as well as increase with a change of job or other circumstances.

The growth of permaculture illustrates how a circle of influence can expand. In the early days of permaculture in Britain it was a fringe activity, most people would say 'perma what?' During that time we have tried and tested ideas, developed resources and built up our infrastructure. Nowadays permaculture is receiving more national and international coverage and we have more scope for influencing policy, action and opinion.

When something is outside of our circle of influence there is a limiting factor that could be addressed to bring it within our circle. For example Bill Mollison was concerned about monocultures taking over the fields in Australia, and the use of chemicals on the land. He identified a limiting factor for changing this was lack of knowledge of alternative ways of farming. He spent his time working within his circle of influence observing nature, developing permaculture and writing books independently and with David Holmgren to provide alternatives to the conventional way. From his writing and teaching and the knock-on effects he has been able to influence thousands of people globally.

Most limiting factors are issues that stop the solution from being within your circle of influence. By identifying the ones that are within our circle of influence and therefore ones we have the ability to change we can find ways to expand our influence.

We can look to create pathways of influence that take us to a specific concern. We could become a school governor or the trustee of a charity. We could undertake research or initiate contacts. We will find our own desire lines of where we want to act, what we would like to focus on. This can lead us to our right livelihood.

ACTIVITY: ACTING WITHIN OUR CIRCLE OF INFLUENCE

Think of one issue in your work, family or community that is bothering you at the moment. Now break this problem down into component parts.

For each component on your list find at least one action that may help to mitigate either the problem as a whole or the component. These actions need to come within your circle of influence.

Next, you can weigh up which of these actions would a) be most do-able and b) likely to have the greatest effects.

This exercise is intended to be empowering for us to find our own choices even for problems that can seem big and overwhelming. We always have choices available to us, in how we feel as well as how we act.

What can I do?

*I've seen the vast plains of destruction
Eyes devoid of joy,
Chaos and mayhem when our uncertain future arrives.
Our egos fighting for air clinging to what we once knew.
The fog of fear descending as we seek to protect our own
Paralysis in the face of the challenges ahead.*

*And yet,
And yet,
Do we really know the fate that lies before us?
Is there no turning from this path?
Is there nothing I can answer to the question*

What can I do?
What can I do to turn towards the light?
What can I do to put a smile on a stranger's face?
What can I do to build bridges?
What can I do to strengthen the web of connections in my community?
What can I do to deepen my love of nature?
What can I do?

I see I have a part to play
Lines to say on this great stage of life
I extend the invitation
To you and you and you
To join the party
And dance and sing and garden and play and create
And bring a joyful, abundant, magical future into being,
Together we can grace the skies
Shimmering as the dance of starlings

There are no certainties.
We have choice.
We have power.
We have community.
WE
Can do it.

Transition movement

There are many ways in which we can engage with people in our communities: community allotments, orchards and woodland projects, time banks, LETS (Local Exchange Trading Schemes)... Whenever we come together we create connections that build our resilience, as well as meeting more of our needs locally. Through these connections we make friends and find support.

A particular big and popular method of community mobilisation at the moment is the Transition movement. In this section I explore it in more detail to understand its patterns of popularity, growth and effectiveness.

The idea behind these initiatives is that we need to move to a new culture that is more life-sustaining. The age of cheap fossil fuel is drawing to a close and that will mean big changes to how we currently live. Instead of waiting for energy descent to happen and then trying to think about what to do and dealing with crises as they occur, the model of Transition calls us to put plans into place now so that the pathways are there for when we need them. It invites us to get involved and plan steps towards a more local, resilient culture based on sharing and interconnectedness.

The key message is 'together we can build the future we want to see'. It is not based on fear and guilt but tries to entice us into a future with abundant connections and benefits that nurture us on all levels.

It looks to integrate the solutions to many of the diverse problems we are tackling. When thinking about big issues such as climate change we have in the past looked either at individual actions, such as changing to energy efficient light bulbs, or living in hope and expectation of governments taking action. The Transition movement bridges the gap between individual and government action and covers the ground of community action. Transition groups combine practical grassroots action with engagement in wider debates and involvement with local councils, and they provide a framework for cohesive solutions to emerge.

Kinsale in Ireland was the first town to adopt an energy descent plan and to really look at how the town might work in a post-oil world. Rob Hopkins then took the idea to Totnes and from there started the Transition movement.[2] The idea has rapidly spread across Britain and has extended across the globe, with over 800 initiatives in 2011. Activities include skill-sharing workshops, showing informative and inspiring films, courses, allotments, repairing workshops, local currencies, community orchards, community composting schemes and wood recycling.

Transition initiatives start to put pathways in place for local interaction that could then play a crucial part in a world trying to transition from a fossil-based economy to a thriving local economy.

The model is still in its infancy and there is plenty of potential for growth and evolution of the idea. This SWOC (strengths, weaknesses, opportunities and constraints) analysis is part of the *reflection* anchor point, where people working within the Transition movement have offered their insights.

SWOC analysis of the Transition movement

Strengths
- Overall concept of making world a better place by working together.
- Permaculture background – integrated approach.
- Can be based on the needs of the community.
- Recognises that people need other people.
- Self defining – people and groups can find their own path and fit in.
- Sense of ownership.
- Diverse in what they do and who's in them.
- Can share and learn from experiences from other towns.
- Focuses on both the inner and outer work.
- Values everyone's contribution – everything you bring is right.
- Inclusive of age, gender, skill, occupation, interest.
- Actively getting things happening, not just ideas and meetings.
- Umbrella for other groups, a uniting discourse.
- Spanning grassroots and council involvement.
- Focuses on the positives while keeping the bigger picture in mind.

Weaknesses
- Focuses on the three problems of peak oil, climate change and financial instability – but the problems are much wider than just these three.

- Deliberately non-political.
- Many initiatives are having the same challenges and repeating similar mistakes.
- Initiatives currently aren't fully representative of the diversity in our culture.
- Some people see them as too cuddly, fluffy, egalitarian. Those that think in this way see it as the only way, and those that don't are alienated and switch off and don't get involved.
- People don't know how to grasp the opportunity.
- Some people excluding others.
- Groups can get stuck in meetings.
- Competitive egos brought together.
- The challenges of people working together.
- People burning out.
- Some people pushing their own agendas.
- Polarising of the thinkers and the doers.

Opportunities
- Bringing people together to learn from each other.
- Solving local problems at a local level.
- To make significant difference to carbon footprints.
- To be vibrant and fun.
- To be interconnected.
- To spread globally.
- Continuous invitation to do things – this change is down to us.
- Inner transition – for sustainability on all levels (physical, mental, emotional, spiritual).
- Bringing people together who wouldn't normally be engaged.
- Creating the imaginative space for new and different ways of interacting with each other.
- Creating bioregional networks.
- Creating a culture of living in place.
- Whole-settlement approach.
- Organic framework for bringing together thousands of different groups which are of a narrower focus.
- Stretching the boundaries of people's imagination.
- Pushing edges so other change organisations seem more mainstream and socially acceptable.

Constraints
- Cultural aspects of the cultures and countries they are in.
- In the West there is a tendency to talk too much.
- Time: community self-reliance is not a quick fix; do we have the time before big problems hit?
- Hard to bring people in and motivate them.

- Far from the realities of some communities
- Need resilience to build resilience
- Many people are disempowered to take responsibility and make change in their lives and communities
- Not seen as relevant to people, the oil is still flowing, the party is still happening
- Ahead of the curve, the rest of society isn't there yet. Trying to plan for a future that hasn't arrived, in a soil that isn't yet fertile.

These reflections lead us on to further designing and improving the effectiveness of the Transition movement. It is clear that one of the biggest challenges individual projects face is how groups function. Maintaining momentum and involvement is a limit of their success, so this maintenance becomes one of the building blocks of further design work. The meeting methods, decision-making tools and group structure work mentioned in this book are all vital to the overall capacity of the Transition initiatives to make wider changes in their communities. The weakness of people working together reflects one of the major limitations in our society and hence tackling this is one of the biggest opportunities for growth and transformation.

Another theme is the connection the group has to the outside. How is it perceived? How to bring new people in? How to acknowledge the outside influences on the group?

The strengths of diversity, inclusiveness, self-evolving and action can be utilised to support and navigate the way through the constraints and weaknesses towards the opportunities.

Transforming the four quadrants

We can look back at the four quadrants to think about how we can address another theme that emerged from the balancing of the inner and outer. When we think of the problems faced in the world today they don't just lie with the individuals or with collective systems. They aren't just problems with our actions but also with the thinking that creates the actions. Problems arising in one quadrant shape and are shaped by the other quadrants.

If the problems occur in this way, it also makes sense for the solutions to as well. What happens in one quadrant will have knock-on effects in the other ones, but in order to have a complete transformation all of the quadrants need to shift. Changes will be quicker, longer lasting and more effective if all of the quadrants are attended to. For example laws might get us to change our behaviours but if we haven't changed our beliefs we may keep looking for ways to avoid changing behaviours.

Nick Osborne from *Response-Ability*[3] ran a workshop at the Transition conference illustrating how we can use the four quadrants to increase the viability of our work. Many change movements only focus on one or two quadrants and so limit their effectiveness. When other quadrants aren't being stimulated it can slow or stall projects. By attending to all four quadrants we can make the ground more fertile, accelerate change and make a more complete transformation. Nick gave the example of how an energy group wanting to set up a community renewable energy project could be encouraged to create changes in all four quadrants.

In the outer collective quadrant there would be actions around business plans, finding investors, publicity, getting quotes and suchlike.

In the inner collective there would be an awakening shared value of community reliance. From this mutual understanding greater connections would form. It would start to shake the assumptions around how the community can meet its needs.

In the inner individual world our relationship to our own energy use could evolve. We may start to appreciate finite resources and feel more responsible for the energy we use.

In the outer individual quadrant we may start to use less electricity. There may be ripples into reducing our car use and where we buy our food. We may start to talk to people about other possibilities.

Each of these could stimulate further changes in any or all of the quadrants, helping the overall growth of the project.

These shifts can be prompted and facilitated, even just by naming and acknowledging they are occurring. By focusing on them we are able to see the resistance that there might be in each one and thereby work through it, so that it cannot limit the possibility of change in another.

Another example of where we might find resistance would be in setting up a garden share scheme, where anyone with land they are not using can connect with someone who needs space to grow food. Initially we would focus on setting up the infrastructures for people to connect and the functionality of the scheme. In our publicity if we are able to recognise and speak to the concerns people have around trust and privacy, we start to overcome some of the limiting factors of the inner quadrants. This scheme might have knock-on effects in how we view our parks and public spaces, and it may lead to them being planted up with edible and useful plants.

Desired outcomes of the Transition movement

Transition initiatives aim to build bridges in the community and find common ground for people to interact. Ideally there is more community involvement for everyone and people are brought together in gatherings and celebrations as well as work and planning. The outcome of this would be people naturally knowing and caring for other people of other generations. There would be a rich social capital of friendships and reciprocity.

Living capital would be shared, with food and trees growing on community land. Experiential capital will have evolved through the familiarity of working together, decision-making and organising events and projects. Cultural capital will be stored in our tales of transition.

By having these capitals in our locality we are less vulnerable to global fluctuations in the financial climate and less reliant on oil to meet our needs from afar. By using more renewable resources we have less impact on climate change.

It is clear from the rapid spread and huge involvement in the Transition initiatives across the globe that they have opened up a desire line. People want to act to strengthen their local communities.

Governance

Our current government model follows a branching pattern. The branching pattern has the characteristics of spreading, covering a large surface area, gathering, exchanging and transporting information in both directions. We can use these properties in thinking about how to use governance to help create the Great Turning.

To improve our governance we could think of where there might be blockages in the system. One of the significant characteristics of this pattern is the ability for travel in both directions. Dialogue and consultations are part of this two-way flow. How can we create more flows of communication?

In the UK, the national government feeds into the county councils and then into community and town councils. This pattern is mirrored around the globe with slight variations. What is missing is the next level of flow between town councils and individuals. Transition initiatives are trying to fill this gap. It is a crucial hole in the effectiveness of the system. Without some mechanism in place there is a lost opportunity for the gathering and distributing of information and ideas. Using an analogy from nature where there is the same pattern we can see its importance: as individuals we are just a small stream; if we have to flow into a huge, fast-running river such as local councils, it is daunting and our voice feels lost in the current. However, if we are able to join with other streams we have a greater impact as we join the main river. Having formal intermediate steps increases the feeling of being heard and empowers us to speak up. These intermediate nodes could be representative of the diversity of members and generations in society, creating channels for the minority voices and encouraging more leadership.

Community councillors have more influence than individuals and can be effective in initiating actions at the county council level, although their presence, routes of communication and powers are not widely known or used.

Opening up communication can allow for the gathering of positive visions. How do we want our world to look? Can we put together petitions based on what we do want, as well as what we are opposed to? Having more of a flow allows greater feedback and responsiveness. As individuals we are more able to see where our ideas have landed, which will encourage more contribution, and our governments are more able to interpret the response to policies and laws.

What we are leading to here is a way in which people and government can work together to create the world we want. When people are involved in the decisions there is a sense of ownership and commitment to making them work. Governments can assist in creating a current to move people more quickly in the direction they are already going. With a greater communication system it is easier to see where the resistance lies before putting policies in place and work with this to find the edge of agreements and create whole-system wins. Our governments can be supportive of grassroots movements as they are part of the same direction of change.

The principle of *designing from patterns to details* is of great significance here. Policies are inevitably based on patterns; trends, averages, targets, budgets and standardisation. What is then needed is the opportunity and the ability to focus on the details: specifics, individual cases and towns, differences and exceptions. There needs to be a definition of the parameters from a national level, while allowing for regional divergences. Trying to micromanage from the top takes the energy away from the more strategic directional tasks. This is true at an organisational level as well, where a board of trustees needs to determine the overall aims and direction rather than trying to micromanage the staff.

This will increase local capacity to respond to situations as they emerge. We cannot always predict all the effects. More regionalisation will allow for shorter feedback loops, enabling the ability to respond and adjust accordingly. Our communities will increase in *adaptive capacity*, the ability to adapt to change as it happens. With a changing world ahead it is going to be increasingly important for us to be able to respond in the moment, rather than having a time delay while decisions are made by a centralised body. The regional levels need to be able to be more responsive to the social and physical uncertainties that will emerge in the next few decades. They will need to be able to make sense of complex situations and be able to think beyond the straight lines of cause and effect.

Alongside this responsiveness is the ability to take a more long-term viewpoint. This is thinking beyond the term of office, and even the current generation into the lives of future generations and the legacy we leave for them. We need to expand our parameters of cause and effect into the consequences for the planet. A Ministry of Integration would be useful to connect the policies across disciplines, from local to national levels, from now to the future and from people to land.

There are many skills that will be advantageous to politicians as individuals and as groups. Decision-making, thinking tools, problem-solving, ecological literacy and co-operative learning will all play a critical role in their ability to navigate the changing seas ahead. Coincidentally this skillset is the same as that of the education systems. While we may not be able to directly influence the politicians' skills we can work within our circle of influence and expand our experiences of using these within our own groups. We can also pass these on to our children. From becoming practised at these our circle of influence expands and we might be surprised at the edges it touches.

It is easy to think of governments as impersonal entities but they are composed of people. We can get caught up in 'us and them' thinking or the blame game; thinking it's all the politician's fault and they should do something about the state of the world. This doesn't help us to move forward. We can respect their skills and willingness to do tasks of administration and finance that some of us would shy away from.

It is true that there could be a fuller representation of the diversity of our cultures. This would be achieved by more of us being willing to be one of these people. Danny Alderslowe is an activist turned city councillor in Glasgow. He has the courage and confidence to work within these systems to create change. When he first started he realised it was key not to barge in and try and make his points too quickly. He took time and used his permaculture observation skills to understand the system and learn what was already in place. He uses the ideas of Nonviolent Communication to pause when one of his colleagues interrupts him, and think about what their need might be rather than getting worked up. He believes that "we need courage to put permaculture on the table, and see how many times we can get it minuted in meetings. We can create healthy debate and find integrated solutions. Thinking just right or left narrows the magic we can hold."

Facilitating cultural shifts

The Great Turning

To move us to an Earth culture we have to make the Great Turning. We have to move from our current trajectory on to a new path.

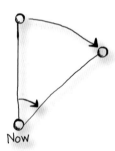

Now

This brings us on to the question: how can we facilitate cultural shifts in behaviour and attitudes in a direction that enhances the ethics? How can we move in the direction of regeneration at a speed and volume that dramatically halts the global spirals of erosion that we are currently swept up in? How can we align cultural values to the ethics so that our patterns of interaction and resource use follow suit?

This can seem like a big task but a small shift in our trajectory can lead to a big difference in destination.

Initially it may seem like not much is happening, but even a shift from automatic pilot and a subtle turn of the head changes the direction we are looking in. It is a source for hope to notice an increase in awareness and public debate, even if it can seem like we are still far away from solutions.

Raising awareness

Awareness is fundamental to cultural shifts; firstly we need to become aware of the need to change; why something isn't working. We can become desensitised to the problems around us, and low quality of life can be an acceptable baseline. Next we need to know about the alternatives and choices we have. Thirdly comes understanding of the steps to change, pathways to follow and empowerment to make changes. This is a mirror of the design process.

The catalyst for change can take different forms. If we think about it in terms of the *six thinking hats* again, people may be more open to persuasion from a particular hat. For some the facts and figures of the white hat inspire action, for others it is the desire to move away from the doom of the black hat. For some people it is the red hat of emotional connection that provides the motivation. For others it is the optimism of the yellow hat, and for others it could be the call to think creatively and try alternatives of the green hat. Some people may be looking at the overview of the blue hat, the bigger picture and seeing the connections.

Raising awareness in all of these different ways is important to try and motivate as many people as possible. There is a caution though that while some people will be persuaded by one of these hats more than the others, there are also going to be ways of thinking that turn people off and shut them down to the possibilities of change. It is therefore useful to use more than one method of communication to engage people, and to balance the different viewpoints, admitting it's complicated.

The film 'The Age of Stupid' painted a very bleak picture of the future in the effort to move people away from this fate and incite change. For many this dose of black hat thinking was just too much and it was too uncomfortable to face. When this film has been screened by Transition initiatives, it was often accompanied by speakers afterwards who could expand upon the alternatives we have at the moment and engage people in what they could do.

Appealing to the heart and being genuine are more likely to build trust and confidence in the alternatives. Transition initiatives aim to attract people with a positive vision rather than making them feel guilty or fearful.

Facilitating the ground

If people are able to slow down they can observe what is happening around them. We can perceive the need for change for ourselves. When we encourage people to think for themselves, the choices they have open up and change can come from within.

We need to facilitate the ground to allow for communication and development to occur and individuals to make their own choices, rather than being too prescriptive. What are the right 'soil' conditions for change? Observation and feedback are essential parts of the change process. When we allow ourselves to receive feedback about our actions and make the connections between actions and reactions we can make conscious decisions. Creating a culture of observation and feedback will start to shift other behaviours. If we see someone dropping litter on the street is it culturally acceptable to tell them we don't like it?

We can encourage people to think and question for themselves and make connections between individual actions and bigger-scale problems, such as their buying habits and ugly, smelly landfills.

Permaculture centres

In 1988 Chris Evans started a permaculture network of model farms in Nepal. Their overall philosophy is to attract, engage and support. The project aimed to encourage change in the practices of surrounding farmers and did this in four basic ways: demonstration, training, producing resources and conducting research. This model has been taken up by the Permaculture Association in Britain with the LAND (Learning And Network Demonstration) project to link permaculture sites in England. We'll focus on each one of these in turn and see how they make up a holistic, achievable way of facilitating change.

- *Demonstration* – Capturing people's attention and showing them that there are alternatives can be the first spark. When people have direct experience of the beauty and a share in the abundance, such as a walk through a forest garden, they are inspired. If visitors can see for themselves that people can live attractive, radiant lifestyles they will be interested to know more.

- *Training* – Moving people from seeing to doing for themselves. Building people's skills and providing them with the practical know-how supports them on their journey. Giving people the information they need; a map of the territory and map-reading skills.

- *Resource production* – Seeds, plants, trees, films and books are instrumental in continuing the journey. Sometimes it is a tool or resource that is needed to enable a shift in patterns. Having the right resources enables self-responsibility.

- *Research* – It is of ongoing value to be continually refining and improving based on research. Research can reveal the benefits, costs, disadvantages, and short-, medium- and long-term effects. A centre can afford to make mistakes they can learn from, more than farmers in Nepal who are dependent on results for their livelihood.

We can do these things as individuals as well, inspiring others by transforming ourselves, widening our own capacity and modelling the values we believe in and thereby promoting the benefits.

Communicating messages of sustainability

We can get messages top-down, bottom-up, sideways – from our peers, and internally from our own feedback mechanisms. If we get messages from more than one direction we are more likely to sit up and take notice.

We need to strike the balance between shying away from challenging people and speaking for what we believe in, and barking at people or being evangelistic.

There is an ongoing debate about whether to use existing terminology or to introduce new terms and phrases. The use of everyday language can make it more accessible. However using new words to describe original concepts can help us to expand our perception of reality.

Opening up conversations and debate creates waves of messages. There needs to be a degree of resonance in the message for it to sink in. We can practise our listening skills and understand where people are at in their lives. We are then more able to help them see the best next step for them to take.

When people are struggling to meet their basic needs they are less able to think about change. Naomi Saville was trying to encourage some Nepali women to attend a workshop on health; they told her they couldn't because they needed to weed their potatoes otherwise their families wouldn't eat for the next year. The same is true in the West when people are preoccupied with basic needs.

We need to meet people close to where they are. Not exactly where they are, but close so they have to make a step and expand their edges. We can also look to our edges: who is close to us that would be easiest to influence and inspire? If we imagine 'the world being sung and danced into existence' as the Aborigines say, we can look for people who are already swaying and tapping their feet. It is said we are all only seven steps away from being connected to everyone on the planet, so if we can influence seven people around us, and they can each influence seven others and so on, then soon enough we become the vast majority.

Creating new patterns

New paradigms can be created by providing a tool from which new knowledge can emerge. The tool can be a physical tool that allows a whole new branch of science to develop, such as the microscope. It could be an invisible tool – a process that facilitates further research and discovery. Permaculture design has been the tool that has enabled many people to bring sustainability into their lives. The design web is a new tool that will enable more people-based design thinking to emerge and push the edges of permaculture. Nonviolent Communication and Neuro-Linguistic Programming are methods that have provided frameworks for new tools to shift thinking. Ecofootprinting is a tool developed to assess actions and ecological impact to enable people and countries to take more self-responsibility.

There are some actions that we can take as individuals to make changes in our lives, and there are some things that need to happen on a wider scale. Sometimes what we are encouraged to do as individuals is not acted out in our towns. Take for example the heating of buildings. We are encouraged to turn the thermostats down in our homes to save on fossil fuels. However, public buildings are not following suit. People would need to make the connection between lower temperatures and a necessary move towards sustainability, and there would also need to be behaviour changes, so that it becomes the cultural norm to wear more clothing. I have visited Canada and the Ukraine in mid winter, both with outside temperatures of minus 30–50°C. In Canada all of the public buildings were exceptionally warm and toasty, in the Ukraine they were barely heated. In the Ukraine, this was handled by people wearing plenty of clothing, even indoors. There is probably a happy medium to be struck here with the use of appropriate technologies to increase comfort without using fossil fuels. Passive solar design for our buildings would be a first step. Becoming more active increases our circulation and keeps us warm. My friend who cycles and walks everywhere complains of buildings being too hot in the winter.

There are cultural shifts all the time; we could collectively be more reflective of the changes that have occurred and the benefits we have gained. Expanding what is working and celebrating our successes provides motivation for more change.

There are many 'if everyone did that...' arguments; if we all went vegan what would happen to the animals? If we all stopped buying food from Kenya there would be many people out of work. When change is in incremental stages that allow the build-up of alternative systems it is more manageable and sustainable. There is also the rationale for us all making small achievable adjustments rather than just a few of us overhauling our lives. For example, compost toilets use no water and save 30% of household water, however there are perhaps only 1–5% of the population in the

UK who are willing and able to have one. Low-flush toilets can save up to 20% of household water but almost every household could have one.[4] We would save more water overall by installing low-flush toilets in 50% of houses than having compost toilets in 5% of houses. Of course, we could have both.

Helps and limits

The *helps* anchor point in our design web focuses on internal and external resources and the motivations we have to change. Connecting people up with their hopes of a satisfying life, in a meaningful way for them and their internal resources of confidence, stamina, courage and creativity, can push people in the right direction. Making the alternatives fun and appealing motivates people, as does seeing that small steps can make a significant difference. When we work with like-minded people to create community and support, we can make changes in our own lives more easily.

The *limits*, the things that hold people back and prevent change, are limiting beliefs, both self and cultural, emotional ties and peer pressure. Naming the fears we may have – fear of change, of letting go, fear of the unknown – allows us to move through them. If people feel threatened they are more likely to cling to the comfort they have. This is going to become an increasing challenge in the uncertain times ahead.

Change is a process we can invite people to participate in. How can we make change easy for people, for it to feel like something they want to do?

ACTIVITY: APPLYING THE PRINCIPLES

If we were to look at the principles to facilitate cultural shifts, what guidance would we get?

Think of a particular change you would like to see happen in your locality. This may be a shift relating to the meeting cultures of your Transition group, or it could be a decrease in the amount of litter thrown on the streets of your town.

We are particularly focusing on the process of making the shift and encouraging people around us to do so.

For example, the principle observe and interact *would lead us to notice when people are dropping litter and to interact and bring their awareness to it, or perhaps to pick up the litter ourselves.*

Leadership

There are many scales of leadership, from our home to community groups, from political movements to global organisations. At whatever scale, it is our leaders who facilitate the breaking of new ground and forge new ways of being. It is not enough for us to sit back and wait for someone else to take the lead, we need more leaders who are capable of taking us in the right direction towards a sustainable and just future.

Characteristics of leaders

Leaders are charismatic, having a steadying presence that shows resilience. They are empowering, giving direction and enabling others to reach beyond their own expectations. Their humility, inclusivity and ability to listen and respond ensure they are able to compromise when appropriate. They are able to think on behalf of the group and guide it towards the bigger vision. Their patience and support facilitates everyone to give their best. They are inspirational and visionary.

This is the picture of the leaders of history that have kindled respect and admiration in their followers. However, there is also a different picture of leaders who have led through control and domination.

They have been imposing and use fear and violence as a means of 'power over', rather than finding 'power with'. They are often corrupt, using their place of leadership as a way of feeding their ego. They can be blinkered in their vision, cajoling people to do things their way and obstructive to anything else.

Obviously these are two extremes and there is a continuum between them. However the latter image builds unhelpful beliefs in our minds about leaders.

Beliefs about leaders

Unhelpful beliefs we may hold:

- Leaders are bossy
- Leaders are not allowed to make mistakes
- Leaders are targets for the media
- Leaders have to be there 100%
- Power will go to leaders' heads
- Leaders are not able to have fun
- Leadership is unpleasant, because other people will resent you
- Leaders are responsible for everything
- Leadership is an isolated and vulnerable position

If we hold these beliefs in our consciousness, they are going to keep us back; stop us from stepping forth. We are likely to feel self-conscious, to think that if we do stand for what we believe in and initiate projects that we may become bossy, a target or unable to have fun.

There are other beliefs that we may hold that may not be so immediately obviously negative, they are subtler, and could be holding us back none the less. 'People are born leaders; leaders are on pedestals; leaders are superhuman; leaders need to be competent at everything; leaders are exceptional.' Or we could hold an egalitarian philosophy and believe that we don't need leaders.

Roles of leaders

Leadership can take many different forms. We can lead from the front or from behind, connecting and ensuring things happen. There isn't one correct style, there is appropriateness for the group and time. We can take leadership for key moments, making critical interventions, for example to get the ball rolling and instigate a project. Leaders don't have to be one person standing in the front alone, we can have rolling leadership, such as a revolving facilitator. We can observe what is needed in the moment, and ask ourselves if we are able to fulfil that role. Leadership can be a role that is taken to achieve a specific task, then set down when that task is completed. When the followers are closely aligned it becomes one movement, a unified dance, with a flow of leadership through the group.

Six ways of displaying leadership are described in *Primal Leadership*:[5]

- *Visionary* – holding the vision and sharing what the bigger picture is with the group. They may also be able to give texture and detail to the group's aim.

- *Affiliate* – affiliate leaders help to get everyone working together. They can be the peacemaker keeping an eye on everyone's needs and helping people to contribute their best.

- *Coaching* – the coaching leader can provide mentoring and help people to step up to challenges.

- *Democratic* – the democratic leader ensures everyone's voices are heard and makes suggestions of how to make decisions together.

- *Pace-setting* – the pace-setting leader can work hard and provide the driving energy for the group. Other people can get left in the wake trying to catch up.

- *Command* – the command leader is in charge and tells people what to do.

The last two types are more of what we might traditionally think of as a leader, and people may have negative associations with them. There are times when each of these is appropriate though: in an emergency situation it can be reassuring and vital for someone to take charge. Historically pirate ships contrasted with the merchant navy, in that there was non-hierarchical control during trade and sailing, but a leader was always chosen for battle. When deadlines are looming a pace-setting leader is important. The first four types of leadership help to create a sense of connection and trust within the group.

Women and men as nurturing leaders

Women often know how to nurture but often don't recognise or step into leadership roles. Men are more familiar with leadership, but are less in tune with their nurturing skills. These are of course just generalisations, but provide us with a springboard for thinking about what is needed.

Women and men have different things to offer and distinctive perspectives on the world. Each gender has strengths, gifts and abilities to bring to our leadership. We also have faults, weaknesses and challenges. Transparency in our leadership and in our vulnerabilities will help us to strengthen our weaknesses, whatever they are.

Women tend to have strengths of co-creativity, nurturing and interdependence. Men tend to have strengths of focus and drive. A nurturing leader combines these strengths and is able to hear others, able to make and admit mistakes, acknowledge interdependence and give support as well as being purposeful and determined.

There are deep assumptions buried within our patriarchal culture that men are better at being leaders. There is a tendency for women to take leadership roles by 'playing a man'. At this point in history we need to turn up the volume on the feminine voice in the world. We need to support women to find their path to leadership.

Jules Heavens works for the empowerment of the feminine on an individual and collective level, by offering a place and space for women to explore their femininity through sacred ritual and creativity. There is a literal process of women finding their voices and singing from their hearts and a deeper metaphorical message for them finding their voice in the world. Jules says, "Through the wisdom of heart and the strength in their belly women can find their way to leadership."[6]

Ourselves as leaders

Some people are looking to our nation's leaders to get us out of the mess we are in, waiting for them to take action and show us what we need to do. Maybe they will, maybe they won't. Either way we can't wait for them and avoid the responsibility of taking action for ourselves, for changing our own attitudes and behaviours. We need to redefine leadership. What do we want from leaders? What do we want from ourselves?

Leadership can take many different forms. In our homes and work places we can stand strong. We can start our own organisations and projects, writing and speaking in public, or take on responsibilities in our groups. We can be pioneering, breaking new ground. We can expand our circle of influence into our circle of concern. We can look for opportunities, align ourselves with others who share our concerns and take the initiative. We can forge new pathways of influence.

When we take time to look we can see leaders all around us, people who are stepping into their power, people who are willing to speak out against injustices, people taking charge of their own lives; movers and shakers, activists, writers, campaigners, spokespersons, organisers and the people who keep track of the administration that enables things to happen.

By standing for what we believe in, and being willing to push edges and boundaries, we are taking leadership in our own lives. We don't need to wait until we know everything or even know the right thing to do. We can act now to speak our truth and step into our power, we can shine our light as brightly as possible and attract followers. We can know that we will meet challenges along the way and trust that support and our own inner resources will come through when we are ready and in need. Leaders are ordinary people who become exceptional through their leadership.

ACTIVITY: MYSELF AS LEADER

VISION

Look around you at what role models there are in your own workplace, extended family, and community.

> *What qualities do they bring?*

> *What qualities can I bring to a leadership role?*

If we were to accept the fact that no-one is going to lead us away from the gathering storm but that we have to all of us, each single one, become the leader and walk towards the storm, trusting that others will follow...

If we can do this – and we can if we choose – then this period of human history will be the time that humanity chooses to honour the gift of life and come of age and it will be a time of great celebration.

TIM MACARTNEY[7]

• • • • • • • • • • • • • • • • •

Designing for larger systems

When we are designing larger systems in society, we move into another way of designing. We become facilitators and designers for other people. We can shake off our perception of ourselves as clients. Although we may still be users of the system, we are just one of many and we don't need to think of our individual needs in the same way as before. This allows us to be more present to whatever else is arising and to put personal agendas aside.

Opportunities

- With bigger systems there will most likely be a large number of people involved and different user groups.
- There may be someone at the top, such as the headteacher of a school, who just wants a design to be done and may need convincing of the relevance of involving and consulting different user groups.
- It may initially seem like the variety of clients are pulling in different directions. This is the opportunity to create a design that accommodates these different perspectives.
- The people using the system at the moment will change and it will evolve, so we need to design for future users as well. There will be a natural succession and flow of people that needs to be taken into account.
- It may be impractical to involve everyone in design, especially in the decision-making. We can get representatives from the different user groups together. For example the permaculture diploma development group consists of tutors, students and staff members.
- The presentation of the design needs to be coherent. While the web allows us to move smoothly between the steps and we can revisit any point more than once, it may be useful to write it up in a more linear format.
- We can design ourselves out of the role of designer and hand over responsibility, tools and methods for maintaining the design as it evolves.

> *By designing ... flexibility into the process we can make it infinitely more powerful, and give the community a far stronger sense of ownership and involvement.*
>
> ROB HOPKINS[1]
> ....

How

There are two methods that are particularly useful for working with large groups. They can be used at the beginning of the design process to allow people's voices to be heard. The information from these can then be taken and worked on to bring it into a design. These methods are both for generating ideas and debate rather than coming to decisions. They are useful as a first round; a smaller group can then be formed to take things further.

Open Space Technology[2]

In brief, Open Space Technology starts with one overriding question that sets the parameters for the design. For example, how can we make our town more resilient? How can we improve care in this hospital?

Participants are then given the opportunity to bring the questions they have concerning this bigger question. Each question becomes a discussion topic for a smaller group of people. Everyone is free to choose which discussions they attend and move between them as and when they like. This technique helps to raise issues, gather ideas and information. Processing of the material will be necessary to bring it into the design. Some questions and discussions will be more relevant to one or more of the anchor points, some may show additional concerns that hadn't yet been considered.

Running open space technologies is a simple, fun and often unexpectedly productive process.

World Café[3]

With the World Café method the questions or topics for discussion are preformed; this is the key difference between this and Open Space. This allows us to work more within the design web and formulate relevant questions for each of the anchor points. Each question is written in the centre of a flipchart page and each one is put on a table like a tablecloth. The idea is that interesting chats occur when people feel relaxed as if at a café or kitchen table. People split up into groups around the different tables. For each table you need a host who will stay throughout and scribe the discussion. Every 10–20 minutes you ring a bell and people (other than the table hosts) move to another table of their choice. The host shares the previous discussion and other people can share the discussions they have been having. This method works well in creating connections between the anchor points as well as seeing the overlap of perspectives from different people. At the end each host shares the discussion from their table with the whole group; from this patterns, connections, overlaps and ideas emerge.

The seven principles of World Café[4] are:

1. Set the context
2. Create a hospitable space
3. Explore questions that matter
4. Encourage everyone's contribution
5. Connect diverse perspectives
6. Listen together and notice patterns
7. Share collective discoveries

Design case study:
Sustainable communities conference

Ed Tyler shares his design for a two-day event for 150 people, gathered to discuss how to make their bioregion in Scotland more sustainable with renewable energy. The event is part of a bigger vision for the whole bioregion.

The vision for the whole project is to create a sustainable bioregion in Argyll based on a permaculture understanding of integrated, regenerative systems; including food, energy and housing with good building design.

The vision for the event was to have cross-sector working; with farmers, council representatives, landowners and community organisations. We wanted to partner people up and move beyond just networking to getting things happening. We wanted it to be an educational event as well with speakers and themed workshops.

The size of the venue was a potential limiting factor although in fact it could have held a few more people. In terms of organisation we were at the limit of what we could handle without getting overly stressed.

There was a limit in terms of what kind of event landowners and farmers would attend. It was important to frame the event in terms they would understand. This was the main reason for calling the conference 'sustainable communities' as sustainable is a familiar term, rather than using the words permaculture or transition.

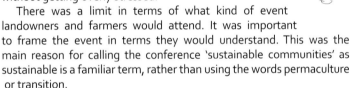

We had one person on the team who had organised a conference before; the rest were all new to it.

We managed to get funding from the Sustainable Development Commission (SDC), who also provided books to sell and resources to give away at the event.

We had lots of intellectual resources and expertise. We invited specialist speakers and had a live video link with Michelle Colussi from the Canadian Centre for Community Renewal.[5]

During the event there was connecting up of resources. For example, community organisations are more able to get funding, but they need extra help with legalities.

Functions	Systems
Show bigger picture	First day speakers
Focused discussion	Second day workshops
Education	Speakers
Talking into action	Second day workshops
Follow up	Report, email exchange
Collaboration	In planning of event as well as at the event
Exploration of a big topic	First day open space
Engaging	Use of open space
Participation	Use of open space

During the two days there was plenty of time scheduled in for networking and chilling out. The food was provided by a local farmer and fitted with the theme of the event.

Instead of trying to organise a social event for the Saturday night, we decided that it would be more beneficial to the organisers to be able to go home and rest, ready for the second day.

We observed a similar pattern with the thinking of many delegates. They mostly came frustrated, knowing that there was a good idea floating around government concerning renewable energy projects, but they were getting caught in red tape, disincentives and hurdles. They came hoping to make progress and break free of these limits.

In designing the event we used these principles:

Integrate rather than segregate – cross sector in the attendance and also in the planning of the event.

Catch and store energy – a comprehensive 90 page report was made and is publically available on the web.[6]

Small and slow solutions – the idea had a two year gestation and then nine months to plan.

1. Decide venue, visit and choose from different options
2. Book venue
3. Funding
4. Planning meetings with representatives from farmers, landowners and community organisations
5. Identify and invite speakers
6. Merge different ideas to create a cohesive programme
7. Name of event with strap line and synopsis
8. Publicity using blog and database provided by one of the organisers
9. Bookings
10. Book caterer
11. Run event
12. Write report

Some of these action points overlapped each other. There was a team of six people; five volunteers and one paid. These action points spanned nine months.

The key idea that people went home with was that these projects are do-able and can have substantial rewards. Michelle Colussi talked about 'jumping off the cliff', letting go of set ways and preconceptions, this idea really took off over the two days with many people talking about how they could do this (not literally!).

People appreciated the practical benefits and the potential partnerships for wind turbines and hydro electric projects that were seeded.

There was genuine appreciation expressed by one community activist upon hearing the head of economic development from the council, that they were talking the same language. This was echoed by other delegates.

If I were to organise the event again I would look to bring it together into a cohesive event sooner. Because we were late doing this we didn't have time to do any pre publicity and get the event in people's diaries.

One of the speakers at the event was a community organiser who has a formal agreement with a landowner for the community to buy shares for a wind turbine on his land. The revenue from this then goes directly to the community. The landowner was also at the event and together they provided a positive example and inspiration to the other delegates.

This event has provided momentum for me as an organiser and kept my faith in the bigger vision. This has led me to develop a food growing project which has received two years funding, and is the first example in the area of a regional partnership project involving four different communities.

PART 5: FEELING CONNECTED GLOBALLY

CHAPTER 13

The bigger picture

Observation
Similarities and differences
Global problems
Global systems
Regenerative development

FEELING CONNECTED GLOBALLY

CHAPTER 15

Connecting with nature

The Work that Reconnects
Deep ecology
Learning from nature
Gardening

CHAPTER 14

Learning from others

Learning from other cultures
Learning from our ancestors
Caring for future generations

The bigger picture

ALL TOO OFTEN we get caught up in our day-to-day lives and forget what is happening for our fellow world citizens. Out of sight is out of mind, but we are still interconnected with everyone and all life on the planet. This part aims to open us up to feeling those interconnections.

This is the beginning of an approach to a global permaculture perspective. It is continually developing as more and more people start to think and act like a global family.

This chapter begins with observation, we then think about similarities and differences and how these can be used to promote understanding. We look at global problems from the point of view of the permaculture ethics. This leads us into thinking about the global systems crisscrossing the planet. The last section takes a permaculture approach to development.

Observation

As with the other parts we start with observation. Much of what is going on in the world is beyond our sight and we receive information through other sources, the media being the primary one.

We need to be able to observe the effects of our actions, and we want to know how and where to direct help. We want to observe what is happening elsewhere in the world that will affect us immediately or in the long term, indirectly or directly. We need to observe to deepen our understanding, to feel gratitude and increase awareness of the problems. Informed by our observations we can ask for change, be provocative, and alter our own behaviours, attitudes and priorities.

Global indicators are used to determine where we can focus international efforts, look at global trends, forecast and hopefully avert future problems.

Media

We have a prolific global media system, but the news we receive through our newspapers and television is subject to the biases and filters of the culture through which we are viewing it. We are rarely given the whole story from all the different perspectives.

Our access to varied perceptions has increased manyfold now with the internet. It provides us with unprecedented insight into the world, from the perspectives of individuals, charities and businesses right up to governments; it is all available at our fingertips (for those of us with access to computers and internet). We can use these perspectives to widen our vision and connect more strongly with what is happening in the world.

Gross domestic product

The global indicator of the wealth of nations has been the gross domestic product (GDP) or gross national product (GNP)[1]. Since 1948 it has been used to measure the money generated per capita. It is used to compare the financial flows of different countries. However, as Robert Kennedy so eloquently shared in 1968, the GNP (and GDP) are not accurate measurements for what is truly happening in any nation, and these measures ignore important issues:

> "Too much and for too long, we seem to have surrendered personal excellence and community values for the mere accumulation of material things ... GNP counts air pollution and cigarette advertising, and ambulances to clear our highways of carnage. It counts special locks for our doors and the jails for the people who break them. It counts the destruction of our redwoods and the loss of our natural wonder in chaotic sprawl. It counts napalm and it counts nuclear warheads, and armoured cars for police who fight riots in our streets. It counts Whitman's rifle and Speck's knife, and the television programmes, which glorify violence in order to sell toys to our children.
>
> "Yet the gross national product does not allow for the health of our children, the quality of their education, or the joy of their play.
>
> "It does not include the beauty of our poetry or the strength of our marriages; the intelligence of our public debate or the integrity of our public officials.
>
> "It measures neither our wit nor our courage; neither our wisdom nor our learning; neither our compassion nor our devotion to our country; it measures everything, in short, except that which makes life worthwhile..."[2]

War, pollution, and destruction are all measured as positive for GDP. It does not integrate our environmental and social well-being with our financial wealth.

The GDP doesn't register subsistence farming and this has led many countries to move to cash crops. It undervalues a lot of the work women do in the home because they are not paid. Sending children to paid childcare increases GDP, looking after them at home doesn't.

It would be like just measuring the height of your tomato plants with no regard to the amount of fruit, soil health, root depth or the condition of the leaves, and using that measurement to account for the overall productivity of your garden. Increasing GDP has become the goal of governments. This flawed accounting system influences policies and actions. The wrong goal has humanity heading in the wrong direction. We need to move the goal posts to redirect efforts.

The terms 'developed' and 'developing world' are used as a result of GDP measurements. They contain assumptions that need challenging. 'Developed' implies that we have reached our destination, that the developed world is the climax of human society. 'Developing' suggests that they are on the same path and want to reach the same place. I suggest that it is more appropriate to say 'overdeveloped' instead. It is no longer appropriate to think in terms of 'industrialised countries' either, as industry becomes more and more present globally.

The terms 'first world' and 'third world' also imply a hierarchy of value. Any terms suggest boundaries, divisions, hierarchies and differences rather than continuums and connections. But it is useful to have some words to differentiate. I use the term 'the West' to indicate the modern culture set on economic growth and technological advances (I realise this is not totally geographically correct).

The term 'two thirds world' more accurately represents the ratio of the world that still lives with a low GDP. It is also a more accurate ratio of land area, population and biodiversity, I therefore refer to it as the 'majority world'. This term brings to mind the fair shares ethic and illustrates how thinking and approaches need to change.

There are not just inequalities between countries, within a country there are also huge disparities of wealth and access to resources. There are people living in riches alongside those in abject poverty.

GDP is not an accurate way of defining poverty. There are rural areas of the majority world that would be regarded as some of the poorest with under $100 US per person per year. While their financial resources are highly limited they may have a house, livestock, home grown food, some land and a well-bonded family and community structure to support them. There are also extreme poor in the cities of the West who don't have access to any of these things but get more than $100 a year.

Other indicators

In 1972 the king of Bhutan introduced the Global Happiness Product (GHP), rating his country for the happiness of its people. The four main pillars to this are promoting sustainable development, preservation and promotion of cultural values, conservation of the natural environment and the establishment of good governance. Other countries are now adopting this rating.

Ecofootprinting is a method for measuring both individual and whole countries' environmental impact and their use of natural resources. It measures how fast we consume resources and generate waste compared to how fast nature can absorb our waste and generate new resources.[3] Currently humans use the equivalent of one and a half planets globally, or put another way it now takes the Earth one year and six months to regenerate what we use in a year. This is measured by nations and can inform countries about how to manage their natural resources.

The New Economics Foundation started the Happy Planet Index,[4] as a way of combining these two measures alongside life expectancy, to "show the ecological efficiency with which human well-being is delivered around the world". They have used this data to produce a charter of the principles and targets needed to produce a happy sustainable planet. The 10 steps to sustainable well-being that they have laid out are:

- Eradicate extreme poverty and hunger
- Improve healthcare
- Relieve debt
- Shift values
- Support meaningful lives
- Empower people and promote good governance
- Identify environmental limits and design economic policy to work within them
- Design systems for sustainable consumption and production
- Work to tackle climate change
- Measure what counts

This last one is particularly pertinent to our observation of the bigger picture. What can global indexes reveal to us? Which ones provide useful and unbiased information? The many different global indexes can lead us to learn from other cultures.

The world as 100 people

The 100 People Foundation[5] has attempted to create a simple representation of the very complex picture of the planet's population. By keeping all the current statistics the same while shrinking the population size to 100 people, they aim to help us grasp the dynamics in the world more easily. Their vision is 'to cultivate respect, create dialogue, and inspire global citizenship'. With the information gathered they create powerful educational tools and films that enable people to see and engage with the realities of the world's population.

   Their project is a fascinating way to look at the diversity of human experience on the planet, and an approach for understanding our shared humanity as well as our differences. This tool is also useful in evolving our understanding of the problems faced by people around the world. They have created a lens through which questions about global social and environmental issues can be approached. They focus on 10 areas of critical global concern that affect us all: water, food, transportation, health, economy, education, energy, shelter, war and waste. The statistics raise questions such as; is there enough clean water for all of us on the planet? Are there better ways to make it available? How can we shift farming practices and improve agricultural technologies to make sure everyone has enough to eat? What is the full cost of war?

   It is a sobering read when we realise that each of these people actually represents nearly 70 million people across the planet. It reminds us of the urgency within millions of people's lives to improve their conditions and meet their basic needs, and helps us to appreciate what we have and sometimes take for granted. It invites us to take a larger perspective and to be grateful for our place in the world. We can be appreciative of our own privileges and abundances.

Our global village of 100 people would look like this:

50 would be female
50 would be male

20 would be children 0-14 years
66 would be 15–64 years
14 of whom would be 65 and older

There would be:
61 Asians
13 Africans
12 Europeans
9 from Latin America and the Caribbean
5 from North America

As their first language
4 would speak Arabic
4 would speak Russian
7 would speak Spanish
8 would speak Hindi
8 would speak English
17 would speak a Chinese dialect
52 would speak other languages

82 would be able to read and write; 18 would not
44 males and 38 females would be able to read and write
6 males and 12 females would not be able to read and write

38 males would have a primary school education
36 females would have a primary school education
26 people would have no primary school education

75 people would have some supply of food and a place to shelter them from the wind
    and the rain, but 25 would not

1 would be dying of starvation
17 would be undernourished
15 would be overweight

83 would have access to safe drinking water
17 people would have no clean, safe water to drink

53 would live on less than $2 US per week – $100 US a year

47 would be urban dwellers
53 would be rural dwellers

Positive change

It is important for us to be able to observe positive actions. All over the world millions of people and organisations are taking steps towards a more just and environmentally friendly world. Politically there have been big shifts in the last century that would have been previously unthinkable. There have been successes reintroducing and conserving endangered species and protecting habitats.

We can find evidence that positive change is happening if we choose to look for it. Creating a balance of views prevents us getting trapped in thinking that the world is a bad and worsening place. It allows us to feel hope and optimism for a positive and fertile future.

Similarities and differences

There are common human experiences of birth, death, illness, love, food, home and family. Experiences that every person will encounter, although in unique ways.

The groups of race, gender and nationality we belong to influence how we express ourselves, how we respond to what is happening around us, how we perceive the world, and how people perceive and respond to us. Different cultures have different values of the material and spiritual world.

Whether we focus on the differences or the similarities between groups influences how we act and what we can learn. There are both gifts and shadow sides of focusing on similarities or differences, and either can be helpful or unhelpful depending on the circumstances and why we are doing one or the other.

Focusing on the similarities encourages us to give equal voice to everyone. We are able to make sense of the patterns that link us. Throughout this book I have focused on the similarities of the Western human experience to create a picture applicable to most people. The recognition of patterns allows us to think of the parameters and make predictions. We can look at what unites us, rather than what divides us.

The shadow side of the emphasis on similarities is that by treating everyone the same there is no allowance for diversity and exceptions and sweeping generalisations are made. It limits our learning from each other and the expansion of groups. For example, if we focus on how women and men are essentially the same we lose the opportunity to learn skills from each gender.

Focusing on differences has the gift of embracing a wider range of human experiences and thinking. We can find out the needs, characteristics and yields of the different groups we identify, then create more specific solutions rather than generic ones that fit fewer people.

The shadow side of focusing on differences is the creation of group stereotypes and perceived hierarchies. We can get caught up with polarising groups rather than seeing continuums. There is often a fear of 'otherness' that can arise from a fear of losing inherent privileges if we start to allow other people more equal opportunity.

We can also extend this to how we view our human family and other species. Do we look at similarities or differences? Do we think about the 95% of shared

DNA with other primates or the 5% of difference? And does it help us further our understanding and respect, or does it create separation and superiority?

If we can move past surface differences and see our shared humanity, people of different faiths and cultures can come together and work to protect the environment. Instead of using energy and strength to protect the traditions of our faith, we could use it to protect nature. When fighting over small differences they can seem so big, when working together over something big, the differences can seem so small.

Gender gap

Across all nations women and men are treated differently. There is an index of the gender gap in different countries.[6] This index is based on salaries and economic participation, access to jobs, political empowerment, educational attainment and health and well-being. In some countries there is a huge difference, in others this gap is closing considerably. Many of the needs of women are not met globally. Women are still treated poorly worldwide and not given the opportunities to lead and participate in society that men are given. This is illustrated by the higher proportion of men that can read and write and have primary school education in the global village.

It is not just an issue for women though. Men are also oppressed by the same system, as their feminine side is not allowed to grow freely and be expressed. There is a danger that the move to empower women will alienate men. We need the coming together of the genders to bring acceptance and respect, allowing both genders to expand their beliefs about their horizons and skillsets.

Each gender has its own traps and these will be culturally specific. In Britain there is the trap for women of having difficulty managing full time employment because of having to work around school times, and for men to be tied to full time employment and isolated from their families.

We can change the entire future of a country by changing the women's position, because women have direct influence over the next generation. Women need control over their health and fertility and access to resources and education. This shift can start with the younger generation. Sejal Hathi, age 17 is founder and president of Girls Helping Girls. They empower girls to transform their world by mobilising them to engage in cultural exchange, gain a global education, and create and lead social change.[7]

... A girl possesses the key to her community's development and an extraordinary power to effect social change. Girls are the movers and shakers.

SEJAL HATHI

Global problems

We could begin to look at some of the problems in the world with regard to the ethics and how these are compromised.

Earthcare
- Habitat destruction and fragmentation
- Climate change
- Pollution of air, land and waterways

Peoplecare
- Lack of connection and care for each other
- Lack of access to basic needs of food, shelter, water
- Displacement of people after natural disasters and wars

Fair shares
- Unequal distribution of wealth and resources including land ownership
- Inequalities of opportunities for skill development and education
- Not having adequate individual and collective limits on resource use and not leaving enough for other species or future generations

These issues interrelate with each other; every problem could be viewed from the other two ethics. We can delve deeper into each problem by looking at the causes, consequences and solutions contained within the other ethics.

Climate change for example is a problem for both people and the planet. A primary environmental solution is reforestation. Climate change has many consequences for people including fear and uncertainty about the future, displacement of people and disruption of traditional farming practices. When we look within the peoplecare ethic for solutions we see that changing individual and collective patterns can contribute, which starts with education and motivation.

When we use the fair shares ethic as our lens to look at climate change, we discover that it will affect some people more than others; generally the poor and marginalised will feel the effects most and traditional farmers who have built up their knowledge of the seasons for generations will feel the changes sooner. The causes of climate change link with consumption habits, and generally the wealthier consume more energy and material goods and have higher carbon emissions through cars and flying. Solutions that could arise from the fair shares ethic may include taxes for individuals, businesses and countries for their carbon emissions. By asking people to pay for their contribution to the problem, a feedback mechanism is put in place and people would start to reduce their emissions.

Another example is the unequal distribution of land ownership globally. Aside from being a fair shares issue, land is affected as it is managed in a different way if one person owns a thousand acres rather than a thousand people owning one acre each. There are more likely to be monocrops and chemicals used with just one owner. Disconnection from land affects our health, touching the peoplecare ethic.

We could go on to consider personal problems, and see how they relate to global issues and the ethics, such as cigarette smoking. There are huge environmental implications relating to tobacco production. A high amount of pesticides are used on the crop, and wood is needed in the curing of tobacco resulting in deforestation. Brazil alone uses 60

million trees each year in their tobacco production,[8] and they only account for 7% of the global tobacco economy.

With 4.2 million hectares of land used for tobacco cultivation in 2000[9] the fair shares ethic encourages us to ask; is it fair to use land for tobacco production that could be used for food production?

Child labour is frequently used on tobacco farms, where aside from missing out on education, children are exposed to harmful levels of nicotine and pesticides.

Smoking is unethical as well as unhealthy. It says something about our culture that the ethics of smoking are not used to deter people.

All of the global problems could be considered from each ethic, and we could find connections and strands linking them together. Problems need to be addressed from all angles, and no nation can solve these problems alone. There is a complex web of problems that needs a complex web of solutions.

Our personal habits and choices are part of global problems or solutions. 'If you're not part of the solution you are part of the problem.'

ACTIVITY: GLOBAL EQUALITY

What are the limits on global equality?

What's stopping us from living in a more equitable world?

These limits can become building blocks for design.

How can we overcome, reduce or sidestep these limits?

Global systems

Running through our planet are social, economic, political and natural systems that cross national boundaries. Nature has never kept to these borders, and now we live in a time where practically everything from money to art, food and people, travels across the globe.

Water and air are global resources. Trees are the lungs of the Earth providing for us all. We don't have separate climates; climate change is a global problem. There are many social and cultural drivers and influences on environmental problems. These are fundamental resources for life and it should be the highest priority for us to rebalance and stabilise these systems. We could use this mutual global need to work co-operatively and unite us across nations and traditions.

All of the time, thinking, and money could be liberated from military spending and redirected to creating solutions that work for all. How can we wage peace, develop strategies of mass creation and have positive global impacts? How can we enter a new era of peace and co-operation? How can we think and act like a global family? Can we spend money on training negotiators and teaching our children to communicate with each other, discover the needs of other countries and think through long-term solutions?

Wars over water are already looming on the horizon. No war will ever be able to create more water, it will just create more problems. Using existing resources to maintain and stabilise the water cycle would be more appropriate. Tara and Stella Joy of Active Remedy[10] are establishing a project to reforest land in the Himalayas stabilising the global water cycle. If we want to drink fresh water in the cities, the mountain forests are necessary. Having clean and safe drinking water is an invisible privilege that 17 people in our global village do not have.

Water is of course integral to our food growing systems. And permaculture has an important role to play in working towards solutions that can meet people's basic needs, replenish natural systems and work in harmony with nature.

It seems like anything can be traded across the globe; food, medicines, textiles, building materials, as well as illegal trades of drugs, weapons and wild animals. Poverty alleviation can arise through trade when people have access to markets and are paid fairly. Countries in the majority world want fair trade not just aid, so they can break out of a cycle of poverty and stand on their own two feet.

Current trade systems do not generally reward farmers fairly for their time and effort in growing crops. It is usually the middlemen and shops that make most of the profit. This discourages people from staying in or entering farming. Without farmers we will face a global crisis of food shortages.

There are after all just two types of people – farmers, and those dependent on farmers.
CHRIS EVANS

Within the global village of 100 people, there are 17 people undernourished and 15 people overweight. This could indicate that there is enough food on the planet to feed everyone at the moment. What it doesn't tell us is anything about the quality of the food, and it is likely that the food that makes the people overweight is lacking in the nutritional value needed by those undernourished. It also doesn't tell us why people are undernourished: reasons may include crops failing, people being displaced from their land, lacking money to pay for food, or no food being available to buy. What is apparent when we look at this statistic combined with others around wealth and access to clean water is that the system we are currently living in is unfair to a large proportion of the planet.

There are many trades happening globally that are unnecessary. We have crazy situations where countries are importing and exporting the same food. In 2009, 83 million litres of milk was imported into Britain, 446 million litres of milk was exported in the same year.[11] Swapping of food is a sheer waste of transportation. If our resource use was designed more wisely it would give us more time to put other solutions in place. An individual action we might choose is to start with our own shopping habits and not buy anything imported that is produced in our country.

Our perceptions of national boundaries and separation start to break down as we explore the cross-cultural aspects of life. We can see them as the human made, and human maintained, artificial boundaries that they are.

Globally we have abundances of communication, people, ideas, creativity and adaptations to local conditions. Over the coming years we need to cultivate abundances of co-operation, understanding, negotiation and fairness.

ACTIVITY: APPRECIATION OF OUR FOOD

Before eating, take time to appreciate your food. Think of all the farmers from around the world who have cared for the crops and harvested them. Reflect on all the people that have been involved in bringing this food to your plate. Take time to feel the Earth that has held the plants, the sun, and the rain that watered them and the people that have tended them. Give thanks for all these systems.

Regenerative development

Western development

Development is a word thrown about a lot, but often we are not clear what it really means. Development can mean building lots of homes made with concrete or using machines to speed up manufacturing. Development can be seen as just for the majority world, synonymous with aid and food handouts. Development projects build roads but then don't fund or plan their maintenance.

In the majority world, development is centred on meeting basic needs; increasing food security, access to clean water, healthcare and education.

In the West we may feel like we have our basic needs met and yet if our supermarkets were stripped of food imported from other countries there is not enough to go around. In the U.K. we are in a situation of food insecurity as supermarket shelves would run bare within just a few days if the supply chain broke down. In Nepal, one of 'poorest' in the world in terms of GDP, many households will harvest a year's supply of rice, beans and flour with vegetables growing in their gardens.

There are currently many practices that are commonplace in the West that actually inhibit the majority world from meeting their own needs. If we look at food imports, it may seem on the surface that we are providing incomes for bean producers in Kenya for example. However most of this is grown in vast monocultures that are owned by single landowners or companies and the workers themselves receive little payment for their work. Using the land in this way precludes it from growing a diversity of food for local people. Exporting waste and paying rock bottom prices for items that are produced in sweat shops are other examples of ways in which we compromise other countries' progress. Wealth in any country can bring about its own problems as much as poverty. The wealthier have more cars contributing to pollution and which need more roads.

Aid can trap countries in cycles of dependence. When interventions are made from outside, dependency can be fostered. While writing this I heard that the World Food Program was stopping giving rice to people in North Western Nepal. For over a decade they have flown white rice into this area and many farmers have stopped growing their traditional crops. Now they are stopping with just six weeks notice, leaving no time for people to grow more crops.

Incidentally, polished white rice is nutritionally inferior to brown rice and to other traditional crops such as millet and buckwheat. Brown rice is the same rice but with less of the husk taken off, so there could be a more nutritious food with less work, but it would require a big cultural shift as white rice is thought to have a higher status.

Implicit in the global media advertising is 'west is best', 'technology is good'. The downsides of a Western culture are not shown. Surya Adhikari, a farmer in Nepal told me about the blanket opinion he had that all Westerners were wealthy until he opened his farm to overseas volunteers, now he has come to understand that there is a range of wealth in the West, just like in Nepal. What is occurring now across Asia is an overlay of technology over poverty. People who have little money are finding ways to buy mobile phones, this will have further impacts on the home finances.

Regenerative development in the West

In the West we want more and faster, while some people still have none. We want to improve our internet access while 18 of our global village of 100 cannot even read. We hardly value what we do have even though millions of people have hardly anything. We often waste what we do have, our time is wasted on television, our health is wasted on junk food, our money on gambling, and our education on playing around at the back of the class.

Development might have increased the number of tools we have available to us but with all of this complexity we have forgotten to use what we have. We have many different gadgets in the kitchen but we don't know that we can mash potatoes with our hands. It is bringing us satellite navigation systems and eroding our map reading skills.

Kofi Annan, former Secretary General of the United Nations, defined a developed country as "one that allows all its citizens to enjoy a free and healthy life in a safe environment".[12] This is the vision we can aim for.

In order to make the Great Turning to an Earth culture there is as much 'development' needed to take place in the West. Regenerative development would start to repair the damage to our social and natural systems, and use our financial and material capital to regenerate our cultural and living capital. We would develop our family and community connections, move to a more equal society and learn to live with less. We would learn about natural limits and increase our self-responsibility and awareness.

Permaculture development

Meanwhile there are plenty of people in the majority world who could be helped to meet their needs. This is not just about charity; this is about accepting responsibility for everyone as a global family. It recognises that we all need to protect the same environment, and stabilise global systems. Deforestation affects people thousands of miles away.

The emphasis needs to move beyond short-term relief to long-term solutions. The Himalayan Permaculture Centre (HPC)[13] works in some of poorest areas of

Nepal, their approach to development incorporates building up community and self-reliance, rather than making people dependant on external inputs. The aim is to empower rather than disempower. We will look in more detail at the end of this part at their design for a women's health programme and how they are looking to improve well-being in areas where there are no doctors or hospitals.

If you came here to help me, you can go home again. But if you see your survival as part of our struggle for existence, then perhaps we can work together.

ABORIGINAL QUOTE

. . . .

The first step to any development programme is to identify what help is actually needed rather than assuming we know. With regenerative development we need to be aware of the cultural context of the problems we are trying to fix; what the history is and the cultural conditioning that keeps it in place. To fully understand this development workers can't stay on the edge. The more immersed they are in the culture, the more they will be able to find solutions that are culturally appropriate, long lasting and deal with root causes. With proper observation we can find the base limiting factors and design ways to deal with them. Detailed observation will also identify the positives and traditional wisdom to enhance and preserve.

Solutions need to integrate with existing culture and wisdom rather than replace it. Any new technologies introduced that can be maintained, repaired and replicated by the community are preferable. In Nepal, Chris Evans of HPC raised £500 to put a drinking water tap into a village. In the same year politicians fishing for votes spent £17,000 putting cement taps in two villages that have never passed a drop of water, because cement is an external input and difficult to fix. The £500 tap was put in with the villagers help in 1990 using local resources and skills with rocks and carpentry, the only external inputs were the pipe and fittings. It has been running since then, because when something goes wrong they are able to fix it themselves.

The familiar adage of 'give a man a fish and you feed him for the day, teach him how to fish and you feed him for a lifetime' is applicable. Taking this up to the next level would be to teach local people to teach others and gain momentum within their communities, adapting skills for their unique circumstances using their local knowledge.

Designs would look at the whole system and its connections, not just one problem. Trying to deal with problems in isolation can lead us to solutions that have undesirable side effects. The focus on alternatives to petrol has led us to biofuels, which are grown by clearing rainforests or displacing food crops. Sustainable development needs to incorporate all of the ethics, solutions have to be fair and look after the land as well as the people.

Development programmes can pave the way for long-term solutions without dependence, creating and cycling abundances locally. The programmes can jump start these actions rather than being the sole power source, akin to working on the soil and initiating cycles of fertility in the garden. As garden designer we would be helping with the design but not doing all of the gardening work. Micro-finance projects are good examples of this. The more transparent we can be with the design process the easier it is for others to understand, replicate and adapt the design. Once we have started the process we can step out of the way and allow the system to demonstrate its own evolution, making it culturally and environmentally specific. This needs to be balanced with ensuring that forward progress is maintained.

Surya and Saraswati Adhikari from Nepal have observed in their country and other countries the tendency for people to leave the land in the villages and go and work or even beg in the cities. People have access to land but do not use or value it; they get caught up in the perceptions of urban and modern lifestyles. Surya and Saraswati are working to share farming skills and make life in the villages more attractive. Over the last 20 years they have seen how permaculture has been successful in protecting forests, preventing landslides, improving food quality, reducing work loads and increasing overall well-being. They are part of an organic coffee growing co-operative where small-scale farmers come together to get a fair price for their crop. The coffee is grown as part of an integrated food growing system, without the need for external inputs and without encroaching on space for food for themselves.

CHAPTER 14

Learning from others

THIS CHAPTER FOCUSES on the lessons we can learn from other cultures, our ancestors, and extending those lessons into caring for future generations.

Opening ourselves to learning from outside our current culture allows us to see beyond it. As a child we perceived the world in a certain way; as we grow up we see more pieces of the jigsaw, and realise that there are different facets to reality. Looking at the world through the eyes of other cultures, our ancestors or future generations is like peering through different windows for a fresh view. We are able to recognise more than one possible reality. This can open doors to other ways and possibilities and help us to call in the reality that we want.

Learning from other cultures

Why learn from other cultures?

When we are within our own culture we are not necessarily able to distinguish between the conditioning, attitudes, ideas and preconceptions that are our own and our culture's. The inner quadrants of the individual and collective become quite blurred. We can get caught in habitual ways of collective thinking and behaving without even being aware of it. Seeing a Nepali woman gently crack the top of an egg and pour it through the hole showed me that I had learnt to crack an egg in half, and was completely unquestioning of there being another way of doing it.

When we travel we become more acutely aware of national personalities. When we open up our awareness to other cultures, we can see our own culture differently. It is on return that we suddenly see our own culture through new eyes and realise all the ways we have been on automatic pilot with our own behaviours. When we come back from other cultures we might newly notice the amount of material possessions, advertising, use of technology and tools, waste, how we communicate and respond to each other, moods and expressions of feelings. Through learning about other cultures we are able to question our own.

Other cultures can hold part of the solution for our own culture. They can show us alternatives and ways in which we can improve.

Each culture has its own montage of wealth and poverty, ways in which they shine with peoplecare and aspects that are lacking. If we share with other countries based on co-operation rather than competition, we can combine the successes to improve everyone's knowledge and quality of life. We could share what is going well and the challenges in our countries, expressing openness to finding new ways forward.

To Understand
Is to 'Stand Unde'
Which is to 'Look Up to'
Which is a Good Way
To Understand

UNKNOWN
· · · · · · · · · · ·

We are as a global family sharing global resources. When we are open to learning from other cultures it can lead us to greater understanding of each other. From this point of understanding it is easier to negotiate resource use, prevent conflicts and restore peace. We can find an edge of understanding between countries.

Where can we learn from?

There is a continuum of cultures, ranging from ones that are very close to our own to tribal people living in complete harmony and connection with the land. It is more appropriate to think of cultures rather than countries, as mountain people can have more in common with other mountain people across borders than city people in their own country.

We can look at overall patterns; from people to grassroots movements to national policies and values. We can learn as individuals, groups and governments.

We can let go of the idea of a golden age or perfect society. Every culture has its challenges; there are two sides to every story. We can find extremes and polar opposites. Extremes between thinking of the self and thinking of community; having no privacy and lots of sharing and having privacy but no sharing; between the use of shamans and allopathic medicines. In some cultures children contribute greatly to the running of home and farm to the extent that people want large families to help and other cultures where children do nothing and don't even learn basic skills such as washing up. When we look at other cultures we are trying to find balances and keep the positives.

What to learn?

Each country has a distinct set of values that are not necessarily explicitly stated but that implicitly guide actions and create cultural norms of behaviours. These may correspond with one or more of the ethics. For example, Sweden has values of democracy, freedom of speech for all, equality between men and women and an approach to levelling of incomes and decreasing the gap between rich and poor, which all fall within the fair shares ethic.

We could use the outline of the zones of people as a way of thinking about what we could learn from other cultures. From zone 00 what can we learn about how people look after themselves? Each culture has differences in practical and thinking skills, in creativity and resourcefulness. We all have the same bodies but we use them in distinct ways, determining which muscles get developed. In many countries people carry heavy loads on their heads that would be unmanageable if they hadn't been doing this from an early age. The ways we look after our emotional, physical and spiritual health are different. Indians place a strong emphasis on spiritual health that is reflected in their rich architecture and religious celebrations.

Some of the strengths of the West are the freedom and self-dependency of women and empowerment of individuals to make lifestyle decisions for themselves. This can also lead to a weakness for valuing work first, so that if there is no job, people experience a profound lack of purpose. The focus on individuality has also led to a distance between people, who are shy to ask for help, and material possessions are more important than links with other people.

We then move out into the zone of our direct relationships. How are connections with family and friends maintained? Isabel Calabolia, an international volunteer from Spain told me how people there enjoy being with each other, sharing and celebrating life together. There are many links in the community and with the extended family and people have time to help each other. Sadly, though, this is being slowly eroded in Spain as elsewhere.

How people organise themselves in groups and manage meetings is culturally specific. And it is something to be aware of when we have multi cultural groups; even the volume of our voices can determine whether people feel comfortable in the group or not.

Moving out further into society we see that the governance of countries is influenced by their individual and collective goals, which in turn are influenced by the underlying cultural attitudes. For example life expectancy, as well as reflecting the quality of health care systems, also highlights attitudes to exercise, nutrition and well-being and care within the family. Dan Buettner[1] conducted a study to look at the areas of the world with high life expectancy, termed 'blue zones'. He found four categories of lifestyle habits shared by many of the cultures in the 'blue zones'. They moved naturally, had a right outlook on life, ate wisely, and connected with family, friends and community.

Education and healthcare systems vary so widely across the globe that there is much opportunity for learning and sharing best practices. I mentioned briefly Cuba's health system, and there are other countries that integrate complementary treatments into their national care for free.

Different countries have different approaches to food production and connections with their food. A friend, Annika Kuebler talked about how in Germany the slow food and organic movement are quite mainstream and accepted, reflecting a strong green movement and sense of ecology.

In Nepal it is a way of life to share every moment; people sit in front of their houses not inside, and there is a very strong integration of the different generations. This sometimes has extremes where the grandmother is left with the young baby while the mother works in the fields. Maria Svennbeck from Sweden on the other hand, says her country is very segregated with people mixing predominately only with people of their own age.

Moving out again into the global picture, we could look at how different countries relate to the same problem. Waste is a problem for every country, dealt with in different ways. Some people may see waste on the streets of the majority world and think how dirty and inconsiderate it is, but they don't like to see plastics being burnt on the roadsides. However in the West we have more waste but it is pushed away, kept undercover, literally buried under ground or sent to other countries to deal with. Plastic in the majority world has been encouraged by Western development. In the past street food vendors would have used banana leaves as plates and clay cups; now they have been fed the idea that plastic is needed to package food and eat off.

People are brought up to accept things in their country that would not be acceptable in others and, with global communications and increasing knowledge, there is more pressure to change. Even before the internet, ripple effects could be identified globally, for example giving women voting rights. The same could apply to other imbalances. Influences from other cultures can accelerate cultural shifts in behaviours. For example literacy rates have improved in the majority world as they are influenced by the West.

Connecting with nature, belonging to the land and living in harmony are absolutely fundamental to tribal cultures and we have much to lose as a human family as this way of life is more and more threatened. Native American philosophies have continued to guide environmental movements globally.

From an understanding and respect of earthcare, Bolivia is leading the way in protecting nature by law. They have created a Universal Declaration of the Rights of Mother Earth with the help of Polly Higgins,[2] a UK barrister who campaigns for changes in international law to protect the Earth. A Ministry of Mother Earth is to be established and legislation to give nature rights to "life and regeneration; biodiversity and freedom from genetic modification; pure water; clean air; naturally balanced systems; restoration from the effects of human activity; and freedom from contamination."[3] Explicit in the proposal for the law is relationship between people and nature, and the indigenous concept of Vivir Bien (to live well) "Living Well means adopting forms of consumption, behaviour and conduct that are not degrading to nature. It requires an ethical and spiritual relationship with life. Living Well proposes the complete fulfilment of life and collective happiness."[4] There is much we can learn from this forerunning country.

Each culture has a unique path of evolution and development that we can learn from. We can learn how different cultures understand and integrate the past, respond to the present and plan for the future.

There lingers a conceit that while we have been busy inventing the internet or placing men on the moon, the other societies have been intellectually idle. Whether a people's mental potential goes into technical wizardry or unravelling the complex threads of memory inherent in a myth is merely a matter of cultural choice.

WADE DAVIS[5]

How to learn?

We can learn through the internet, books, travel, one-to-one connections, pen pals, twinning of towns and asking questions of people that visit our country.

It is important for us to not just learn about other countries through the television. There would be the danger of this just showing a distorted version, over dramaticising or romanticising the indigenous cultures or the West. Helena Norberg-Hodge wrote in Ancient Futures[6] about the stage dramas they performed in Ladakh to alert people to the challenges of Western development. One of the features of Western development they highlighted is the erosion of community; while people have their material needs met, they have less need to call on their neighbours for help and soon the problems of isolation are felt.

When we analyse global measures such as the Happy Planet Index we can identify trends and patterns of countries that are doing well and ones that are near the bottom. When we start to look at different indexes the picture builds and we might be able to see connections.

Permaculture responses

Permaculture has evolved in unique ways in each country in response to its own strengths, values and challenges.

In Nepal one of the key challenges is overexploitation of resources due to poverty. There is a spiral of erosion; as the forest is cut, human and environmental stress increases. HPC work to reduce the workload by growing firewood and fodder on the edge of farmland and tethering livestock to protect the forest, thereby initiating a spiral of productivity.

In Sweden, there is a very different challenge of creating social connections and a sense of community. Maria Svennbeck who teaches permaculture there, says that as it has a small population it is easier to influence people; they are politically aware and wanting change but not sure what to do. Maria says, "Sweden is trend sensitive and I am working to make permaculture a trend."

The Institute of Permaculture in El Salvador (IPES) has developed an approach of both enhancing the farming practices and reclaiming cultural and religious heritage. Their ethos is one of listening. They make space for people from both sides to talk about their experiences in the civil war. By hearing the trauma of each other, they also see and hear the trauma the land feels under modern agricultural practices. They listen to people before bringing solutions in to communities. When people are heard they can listen to each other and the land. Permaculture courses are run that relate directly to the Mayan calendar and beliefs. They are also working on understanding and promoting the heritage of women.

Permaculture designers can learn and adapt from other cultures, integrating ideas with their own knowledge and weaving global threads of abundance and understanding.

Learning from our ancestors

Why learn from the past?

There is a continuous thread of human lives; our ancestors live on in us both personally and collectively. Identifying with this thread of connections creates a deeper sense of time and responsibility for our present and future generations.

Some people are concerned that a sustainable culture will take us back to the Middle Ages and we will lose the benefits of modern culture. Learning from our ancestors is not about trying to take our society backwards, or idealising the past. It is about taking the best from the past – the designs and ideas – and adapting them to the present to find the relevance for our current and future situations. Permaculture design takes appropriate solutions from any culture or time.

Recognising our heroes and heroines of the past and the continuing ripples of their actions increases our capacity to see the ripples of our actions now. There are current social change movements inspired by past movements, such as the Diggers and the Luddites influencing climate camps, The Land Is Ours,[8] and the current Reclaim the Fields[9] movement. The anti slavery movement boycotted sugar, and this method of resistance is still used now. Gandhi was a key source of inspiration for Nonviolent Communication.

This also applies to those actions that are still having detrimental effects. What could have been done differently? This increases our sense of responsibility to do things differently for future generations. Our ancestors teach us about ourselves and the choices we have in our lives.

Tribal communities ... consider themselves part of a dynamic coherent whole: meaning lies in maintaining this sense of belonging as well as kinship with all forms of life. As a continuation of their ancestors, many tribal peoples are also deeply aware of their place in society, and of the unborn generations: the past and future are always contained in the present.

JOANNA EEDE[7]

What we can learn from the past?

Biologically, human beings have not changed very much over tens of thousands of years. External changes and shifts of thinking from interdependence to individualism have been most influential in the West. Our structures of family and community, technologies, types and pace of work and entertainment are all vastly different from a century or even a generation ago.

Our ancestors lived without many of the resources and technologies that are commonplace nowadays; they could provide us with the knowledge and skills of how to live with less. They overcame many challenges, wars, famines and political struggles, and addressed many inequalities. Looking at how they did this and being able to see the whole picture from initial small actions, to waves of movement and the after-effects allows us to expand our vistas beyond the current era. This enables us to see that the Great Turning has already begun.

Historical hindsight has the benefit of enabling us to see the whole picture, just as we are able to see different phases and transitions through our own lives. We can look back at different eras in history and gain more understanding of the turning points, the edges and the transitions that took place, to identify and deepen our understanding of the turning points of the present.

Our ancestors were generally more in tune with nature and natural rhythms and cycles than we are now. We are now buffered: from eating seasonally by imported food; from working with daylight by electric lighting; from dealing with our waste by large-scale landfill sites. We may well have to realign ourselves with a more natural and seasonal way of life as the costs of fossil fuels increase. The ways of life of our ancestors can provide us with some guidelines.

The Transition movement is focused on the 'great reskilling' where we learn the skills of our ancestors, such as bread making, knitting, weaving, repairing, wood work, coppicing, wild food foraging, and growing our own food.

We could look at what we see around us that has been eroded or lost to see how it used to be, and what we can regain. Care for our elders and traditional wisdom are not what they once were, but they can be restored. Farmers in Nepal can tell from smelling cooked rice whether it was transplanted early, on time or late, as well as the variety. Wool spinners in the UK would know which direction to spin the wool to make it more waterproof. Plant identification for medicines and food was once something we would all learn. Even everyday skills like cooking are being lost with the increase of ready meals.

There are also things from the past that we are pleased to no longer have, and others that we could do with letting go of. The same pattern that we had of our personal beliefs coming from earlier time frames and no longer serving us is also true of collective patterns. Are there collective beliefs and habits that came from a time in history where they were appropriate and are now no longer serving us? Do we have leftover prejudices that could be discarded?

Many people think that if we go back to a way of living from the past, we would compromise our standards of living. The path of abundance invites us to look at the real wealth, to find ways in which we can flourish individually and collectively while using fewer resources.

How can we learn from the past?

Archaeology has provided us with a viewpoint of our prehistory lives. Our biology also gives us clues as to our evolution. Architecture gives us a portrait of a country's history. The secrets of how land was managed in the past are accessible through reading the landscape.[10]

Our more recent history is comprehensible through history books, although they are subject to bias and often retold from the victor's side. Myths, stories, songs, old wives tales and proverbs are all part of our cultural capital, containing wisdom handed down through the generations. Old country sayings such as 'red sky at night shepherd's delight, red sky in the morning, shepherd's warning' pass down insights about nature's rhythms. With a changing climate we can pay attention to these.

Traditionally we learn the wisdom of our ancestors from listening to the stories of our elders, passed from one generation to another. Some Transition initiatives spend time collecting the tales of our elders.

We can look at the present in the context of the past, understanding the habits that have changed and the ones that haven't. Our present is a mirror of the past and an opening into the future.

Caring for future generations

Thinking of unborn generations helps us look beyond our current picture. Future generations represent a continuum from the teenagers and newborns of today to our unborn great grandchildren and beyond, who will become the adults of the tomorrow. Our daughters are born carrying the eggs that might become our grandchildren, already inside of them.

The greatest natural resource that any country can have is its children.

UNKNOWN
....

We can become desensitised to the tragedies and problems of the world now, but when we see them from a different point of view we can reconnect with them in a different way. Future-thinking invites us to comprehend the long-term effects of our decisions and actions. We can imagine the ripples of our actions still being felt in the world, both positively and negatively, individually and collectively.

We are their ancestors. What can we do today that will make them proud of us in the world of tomorrow? How can they feel that we cared for and respected them? How would we like to arrive at a party at the time on the invitation to find that all the food has gone and that we have to do all of the clearing up and look after the people with hangovers?

How can we think about generations a thousand years in the future? The people and cultures of this planet are more interwoven and connected now than they were 100 years ago. In another 50-100 years we may have reached the point of thinking like a global family.

Our children are the next generation and their wisdom needs to be listened to. There are girls and boys, teenagers all over the world who can see that there is trouble looming and urgent need of action. Severn Sukuzi took her message to the Rio Summit in 1992 at the age of 12.

> "I'm only a child and I don't have all the solutions, but I want you to realise, neither do you! You don't know how to bring back an animal now extinct...
>
> "I'm only a child yet I know we are all part of a family, five billion strong, in fact, 30 million species strong and we all share the same air, water and soil – borders and governments will never change that...
>
> "I'm only a child yet I know we are all in this together and should act as one single world towards one single goal...
>
> "I'm only a child yet I know if all the money spent on war was spent on ending poverty and finding environmental answers, what a wonderful place this earth would be!"[11]

We often say if only we had the hindsight to look back on our actions in order to save ourselves mistakes. If we were to sit with our great, great grandchildren what would they tell us that would be useful for us now? When we succeed in the Great Turning and arrive in a sustainable, fair, abundant and peaceful world, the people of that world will have skills and the knowledge to teach us about how to live there. Their stories can give us courage and hope.

Storytelling is part of our cultural capital. Stephanie Bradley spent six months in 2010 walking around England collecting Transition tales. Through the telling of these tales our children can recognise patterns of challenges, resistance, triumphs and benefits. Often the benefits get left out of stories with 'and they all lived happily ever after', but reclaiming the positives for the story motivates us to travel similar paths of bravery. If our children and grandchildren face bleak times in the future these stories can provide resolve to seek out solutions. The stories demonstrate our experiential capital, gardens we planted, and events, community projects and demonstrations we organised.

We can rebuild living capital by planting trees, regenerating soil and cleaning waterways. Centuries ago oak trees were replanted for generations to come to replace those taken for building boats. We can tap into that kind of long-term thinking and plant fruit trees on our streets and our cities to become food forests for future generations.

> *It's 3:23 in the morning*
> *And I'm awake*
> *Because my great great grandchildren*
> *Won't let me sleep*
> *My great great grandchildren*
> *Ask me in dreams*
> *What did you do when the planet was plundered?*
> *What did you do when the earth was unravelling?*
>
> *Surely you did something*
> *When the seasons started failing?*
>
> *As the mammals, reptiles, birds were all dying?*
>
> *Did you fill the streets with protest*
> *When democracy was stolen?*
>
> *What did you do?*
> *Once*
> *You*
> *Knew? ...*
>
> DREW DELLINGER[12]
> ●

ACTIVITY: 30 YEARS HENCE[13]

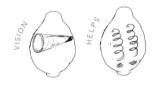

Find a quiet time for this visualisation of a conversation with a child living in a life sustaining Earth culture. This is written by Joanna Macy.

By the power of our imagination, let's move forward in time – 30 years. We've arrived at (name the date and hour 30 years from the present moment). You find yourself in one of your favourite spots. It hasn't changed much, nor have you essentially. You might be pretty long in the tooth by now, but still alive, same gestures, same action of heart and lungs. Don't worry about figuring out how the world has changed. Just know that the major crises that threatened life on Earth have been averted, the weapons have been dismantled, as have the technologies and institutions that polluted and decimated life. Those destructive patterns were so interlocked that the Great Turning to a sustainable society happened faster than anyone expected. By now, that transition seems so logical and inevitable that you take it for granted.

As you sit relaxing in this familiar spot, you see approaching you a child of about eight or nine. She's eager and timid, for she has heard in songs and stories what you and your friends did back then to save the world from disaster. You listen to the questions she wants to ask you. The first is this: "is it true what they say about life back then? Were there really millions and millions of sick and hungry people? And bombs that could blow up whole cities? Could that be so?", *she clearly finds it hard to believe. Listen now, as you answer her...*

Now she asks you a second question. "What was it like for you to live in a world like that? Weren't you sad and scared all the time?" *Hear your own reply...*

The child listens carefully; there is one more thing she wants to ask. "Where did you and your friends find the strength to do what you did? How did you keep on going?" *Hear within yourself how you answer her now...*

The child is ready now to go back to her friends. As she starts to run off, she turns back, looks up at you and says "Thank you".

You watch her go. Now it is time to return to the present. We go back now to that period when there was still so much to be done, though the Great Turning had already begun and may have been further along that we thought.

CHAPTER 15

Connecting
with nature

THIS CHAPTER INVITES awareness of the beings we share the planet with, the soil beneath our feet and the cycles of life. The very essence of permaculture is connection with nature and using nature as our teacher and guide. We need earthcare solutions as much as we need peoplecare solutions. A step towards finding ways of regenerating natural systems is to feel ourselves as part of the Earth.

The Work that Reconnects

Joanna Macy and her colleagues have been developing this work over the last few decades. As the name suggests its purpose is to reconnect us; to ourselves, each other, and the Earth; to the joys and pains of life in this time; to our personal and collective responsibilities; to our ancestors and future generations; and to our power to make a difference and heal the planet. Through opening up and discovering these connections we can start to engage with shared wisdom, our internal skills and resources and feel our potential for transformation.

The disconnection we have allows the harm to continue; when we connect there is opportunity for healing.

It is the work that needs doing to make the inner transition and facilitate the Great Turning. It is 'work' because it doesn't come naturally, we have to focus on it. It comprises four stages. I would encourage you to complete the sequence of four activities given here. Many more activities can be found in the book, *Coming Back to Life*.[1]

Coming from gratitude

Being alive in this world is a miracle in itself. To have before us and within us the skills and resources to participate in the Great Turning is something to be thankful for. Centering our attention firstly on gratitude provides the base for the work to come. This foundation strengthens us to face up to the pain we feel. This phase breaks us away from the moulds of complaining, victim and blaming attitudes that are prevalent in our societies. It opens our heart and allows us to express love.

ACTIVITY: APPRECIATING THE EARTH AND OUR PLACE

Imagine holding this jewel of a planet in your hands. From this distance you can see the swirling global weather patterns, the great expanses of ocean and the contrasting textures and colours of the land. You can feel the perpetual motion.

Peering closer you can see your country; its outline and edges with other countries and the sea. Focus in on the bioregion in which you live. Coming closer still you start to see the movements of people and marvel at the intricacies of animals and plants.

You can see the place you live, the people that surround you and the activities that are happening. Appreciate the amenities you have access to, your friends and family and neighbours. Take a moment or two to feel full gratitude for your place in the world.

Now slowly take your awareness back out to the bioregion, and then the country until you are once more looking at this shining jewel of a planet in your hands. Once again feel the wonder and awe of the beauty and complexity of the Earth.

Honouring our pain

How do we feel the world crying around us, beneath us, within us? We all have feelings associated with the devastation and injustices we are witnessing in the world. Many of us prefer not to face those feelings and are in denial; they can be too painful, too sorrowful. But it takes energy to suppress these emotions.

Caring means to notice the troubles and pains of people and the planet. When we own these feelings inside of us, we are allowing ourselves to hear our inner voice. Anger and pain can be used in positive ways; we can channel these feelings into action for change. We connect with our own personal feelings. All of them are valid; there is no right or wrong.

What we most need to do is to hear within us the sounds of the Earth crying

THICH NHAT HANH

When we unblock the feelings of pain we also unblock the feelings of love and joy we can experience. We can avoid burnout and despair through processing our pain rather than suppressing it.

ACTIVITY: EXPRESSING THE PAIN

When you read about the global problems at the beginning of this part, feelings probably arose, although you may not have paid specific attention to them. Have a look back and then find a way of expressing these feelings symbolically. Painting, drawing or playing with clay or stones may call you. It doesn't need to be a great work of art; this is for you not for anyone else. It may just be an angry scribble that comes.

Seeing with new eyes

We are all connected to each other and to the whole of life. The concept of separation our culture clings to is an illusion. We do not have the capacity to see how we affect the world and the ripples our actions have into the future. Our very presence has an effect; we cannot take ourselves out of the equation. We are in a massive loop of interconnectedness with all parts of the universe. It all matters, it's all important. When we realise this fully we see the world and ourselves differently.

ACTIVITY: HAND MEDITATION

Look at your hands, your palms showing the lines of your life, your fingers with all their sensitivity to touch. Fingernails, painted red or with soil beneath them. The backs of your hands, so familiar to you. Think of all the things you have done today with your hands.

Now think about all the hands around the world and the actions they are doing at this moment in time. Imagine a woman in Uganda holding her child tight in her embrace. A boy in Spain playing with his friends, catching a ball. Think about the hands working in a factory in Taiwan. Hands eating rice in India, picking apricots in Turkey, weeding in America, holding a cup of tea in Scotland. Think of a hunter with his hands on his bow and arrow in the Amazon.

And think about those whose hands hurt at the moment, hands out of action, healing in a plaster cast. And those without hands who have learnt to use their feet or mouths to paint amazing pictures.

A baby's hands reaching out for a toy for the first time. Hands waving goodbye to friends. Hands held in prayer.

We are all as one in our shared humanity.

Going forth

The final stage is to move our anger and our love through into action. To take these energies to empower us into what we can do. When we are in touch with our feelings we can be our authentic selves and we can reconcile our pain with being human and connect with the whole of humanity.

With this stage we find direction for our changes. We can find strength in self-organisation and connect with like-minded people. We can create change together and speak out for injustices.

ACTIVITY: HOPE FOR HUMANITY

What is my positive vision for humanity?

What role can I play in achieving this vision?

Deep ecology

Too often nature can be seen as a background to our human existence. Or even worse, just something to exploit, dominate, or overcome; other species are for food, medicine, working for us, or a nuisance or pest. The underlying assumptions of some major religious views are that humans are the pinnacle of creation and in some way superior and separate from other species. Deep ecology is a term coined by Arne Naess in the 1970s challenging this belief. It is a simple idea that has far reaching implications. There are two main strands: firstly we are part of nature not separate, and secondly, every species has an intrinsic right to exist beyond its use to humans. This affects how we maintain habitats. In contrast, politicians and scientists have been heard to talk about planetary limits to the amount of biodiversity we can 'afford' to lose. I have heard a politician consider how much it would cost for us to replace the work of pollination if bees were to become extinct. The deep ecology view is that we can't afford to lose *any* species.

If we are looking to other species and only valuing them for their worth to us, is this also a mirror of how we look at other people? Do we perceive other people in relation to their usefulness? How can we move to valuing all people and all species for their intrinsic value?

Council of All Beings

To give voice to the brother and sister species that we share the planet with, Joanna Macy and her colleagues devised an activity known as the Council of All Beings. I participated in a Council in summer 2010 and found it a deeply moving experience. Here is our story:

"After settling into the weekend with exercises to reconnect with ourselves and the pain we felt for the world, we moved into preparations for the Council. We began with a silent contemplative walk on the land alone, asking to be shown which species we were to represent. We opened up to owl vision, and practised walking like foxes.

I sat by a stream in a dreamlike, meditative state, listening to its babbling chatter. I was not sure why but the thought of being a salmon came to me, I did wonder if maybe I would be something else but still the answer was to be a salmon. Wandering back through the fields my thoughts settled into the landscape.

My friend's walk led her to follow tracks of the cows escaping from their usual confines and acting as wild animals free to choose their own path. She tuned into the cow's walk out of the fields through some wild and muddy places next to the river not normally walked by humans. She had a glimpse at their experience, not as a farmer's property fenced in, but as a wild animal following its instinct to find food.

When we had found our beings we returned to the barn where there was a hive of silent activity as masks of our beings were made with leaves, sticks, ribbons, card and paint. We proudly wore our masks to process down to the tipi, leaving our human identities behind. Once inside the tipi, the Council began and we spoke of how it was to be alive now and our experiences of the world we live in. There were no humans present, but they were often mentioned as each of our lives were impacted by them.

Cow, snow leopard, river, owl, bee, stream, slug and mole were present alongside my salmon. We spoke of our homes and food sources being lost; of the cruelty and killing; of being caged and poisoned. The cow expressed her sadness and distress of not being given the space she needs, and of having her calves taken from her and slaughtered. But she had an air of forgiveness and hope that humans and cows could relearn to live in harmony as they have done for thousands of years, and optimism for the future of all beings. The mole said that it had never seen a human and was only dimly aware of them; a reminder to us people that perhaps we are not as central as we think, and maybe overestimate our importance. The river spoke of being polluted and the stream of being depleted. The bee said it couldn't breathe because of what the humans are spraying, it talked of working closely with humans and providing for them and yet being taken for granted.

We spoke of our disbelief at human actions; we were not able to understand why they choose to act in this way. Behind the painted masks tears flowed as we experienced the pain of our brother and sister beings.

That evening we brought our masks to the fire to ceremonially burn, releasing their voices and wisdom. Their voices were within us now. Before we said goodbye to them, they shared with us a message of their strengths for us to use on our journeys. We were again reminded that each being holds its own wisdom, and we can learn from each one. There are understandings and insights beyond our human perspectives.

The salmon's message to me was to follow my own path, travel with like-minded beings and work together, accept that sometimes you have to travel up stream and remember to take great leaps.

The mole's message was to look beneath the surface to find deep meaning and sense without our eyes. The mole represented the unseen forces at work all the time. These forces could be destructive, such as unpredictable reactions in ecosystems or could be healing and the Earth may be healing itself in ways that we don't know about. Things could be much better or worse than we humans see.

The bee's lesson was about community; we can achieve so much if we work together, things that would be impossible alone; and that we must do that work in love, to serve the wider community and when our work is done in this way it is a joyous affair – not like work at all. As humans we need community, a hive to be a part of to give us companionship and a sense of purpose in our lives.

It felt like there was value to be had in giving voice to the grief, anger and despair that arose in the Council, and in listening with good intent to the wisdom of the beings present.

We went to bed with the sound of owls hooting and the river bubbling to dream of wild places.

The next day someone phoned saying they had caught a swarm of bees and wanted to bring them to the empty hives on the land where we were staying. After hearing of the troubles of honeybee in the council, it felt like a fitting blessing to have 30,000 bees arrive to end the weekend."

Learning from nature

Why learn from nature?

Permaculture has arisen from the study of nature and the drive to understand its principles at work. Its roots are deeply embedded in the respect and observation of wild places. Its fruits are profound connections with nature, creative approaches to gardening, a move away from chemicals on the land and empowerment of individuals and communities. There is a new branch growing in the permaculture tree where we draw upon this knowledge of natural systems to bring it into our personal and social systems.

When we learn from nature we build respect and tune into bigger processes and time frames. We are nature ourselves and have natural processes occurring within us and between us, so understanding nature helps us to comprehend ourselves better. Following natural patterns and principles can increase our health and real wealth and decrease our stress. Spending time in nature promotes harmony between the planet and us.

If nature is your teacher, your soul will awaken

GOETHE

....

What can we learn?

We can learn how to align ourselves with natural rhythms – daily, seasonally, annually and over much larger timescales. We can think about annual cycles in our own lives: what were we doing when we harvested the blackcurrants last year? We can find the rhythm and pulse to our actions. Within all natural systems are cycles of birth, growth, death and regeneration. Each plant and animal has phases of development. We can tune into the characteristics of the seasons for our own phases of development: times of shedding leaves and letting go, times to grow and times to rest, time for reaching out and times for reaching in.

The life of an oak
Three centuries he grows, and three he stays
Supreme in state, and in three more decays
ANONYMOUS
. . . .

Animals and plants have different paces of life to our own. Some have a lifecycle shorter than our working day, whereas trees are here for hundreds of years, watching life change around them. The trees we plant now could be there for our great, great, great grandchildren. What can we learn from the slow moving snail, or the buzzing bee? We can break away from our human perceptions of time and movement and see beyond to vast wealth and diversity in being.

I stopped on the moors to watch the free-living horses and they came over to my car to use it as a scratching post. Animals are expert perma-culturists, they adapt to what is there, use niches as they appear and any available resources. A jay has just landed by the window to collect an acorn it had buried there, he knows how to *catch and store energy*.

When we look at whole ecosystems we can focus on the connections and inter-dependencies. We can look to individual species and wonder how they relate to the other species around them. What is their part to play in the web of life? How do all of these species function together sustainably? What are the unique gifts each species have that enable them to adapt to their surroundings?

These questions stimulate us to think more deeply about what is going on in the world around us. Nature's rich diversity provides us with bountiful opportunities to expand our thinking beyond our human constraints.

Permaculture originated with looking at the principles of ecology and asking how nature is sustainable. Through bene-ficial connections, energy cycling, producing no waste, diversity and interdependencies ecosystems are resilient with high output and low input. Bringing these principles and patterns into our designs we can emulate nature.

All of nature is of the Great Mystery – the waters, the sky, the rocks, the plants, the grasses, and the animals. They are our true teachers, speaking to us constantly. They speak in the language of mystery, telling humans who we are and our meaning in life, for we are made from them and are one of their voices. You must learn to listen well.
WINDEAGLE AND
RAINBOWHAWK[2]
. . . .

Biomimicry

Biomimicry asks how nature achieves things. We could look to nature and ask questions relating to the three ethics.

For earthcare – how does nature purify rivers, deal with waste and break down oil spills? How does nature restore soil and recolonise barren land?

For peoplecare – how do animals care for their young? How do animals find their own healing plants in the hedgerow? How do they communicate with each other? What behavioural patterns can we find useful in our groups?

For fair shares – how does nature live within limits? How does nature create abundances? How do predator and pest populations maintain a balance over time with each other?

How can we connect with nature?

Connecting with nature is more than just an intellectual process. Being in nature is a whole body and mind experience. As young children we have no concept of nature being different from us, we are just constantly experiencing and learning from the world around us, and our connection to it. This wholeness needs to be maintained or the idea of nature as something separate comes in.

In some cultures children receive a passive but direct education of nature. They learn through their hands the realities of working the land with their parents.

It can be more of an active education in other cultures. A deep spiritual connection with nature is fostered, perhaps with initiation rituals. Stories and myths are used to reinforce and deepen understandings.

In other cultures, particularly in the Western world, there is an absence of any kind of teaching about how to connect with nature. Some children will have the fortune of growing up with access to nature to play in and explore and create their own relationship with. Others sadly miss even this.

Lusi Alderslowe has set up a 'nurture in nature' group in Glasgow, Scotland, where parents and children gather in nature to play. Whatever the weather they meet in city parks or green spaces accessible by bus or train. By being in nature their children have opportunities to meet their needs of organic and free play. They bring no toys with them; the children play with each other and create games in nature. Climbing trees brings them connection and understanding in ways that climbing frames can't. By being out in rain, wind and snow they learn to read weather patterns and feel alive. The group has had the added side effect of encouraging the parents to connect and learn from nature as well. For both parents and children the group meets all nine of Max-Neef's needs for subsistence with eating lunch together; protection with parents present; affection for nature and other people; understanding of nature; participation in a group; leisure and creation by creating toys and games in nature; identity as part of the group and freedom with space to run around.

The simplest way to learn from nature is by just being in nature. By being present and open we can absorb through our pores the essence of natural life, we become aware of our own nature. We can take a step to more active learning with observation exercises, designed to open the curtains to new ways of sensing the world around us. If we have questions in our lives we can take time in nature, allowing answers to emerge from our observations.

In the Council of All Beings each being gave us a message – a metaphor to use in our lives. Metaphors bring in our subconscious and intuitive knowledge of nature's rhythms, cause and effect and cycles of life. The following activity invites nature to share metaphors for our lives.

ACTIVITY: PAST, PRESENT, FUTURE WALK[3]

Take a walk in nature. For the first 10 minutes of the journey think about your past, notice what is stimulated, what is called to mind? Let nature inform you, find the metaphors for your past in nature and the world around. Perhaps you see a bramble thicket that reminds you of a thorny time in your life that bore fruit. The choices you make on the walk are informative. Where does your awareness go, inwards, outwards, up, down, into the detail, or out to the periphery?

Focus on your present life for the next 10 minutes.

The last 10 minutes is time to spend thinking about your future. Again think about what nature is showing you. Are there animals or insects that cross your path? What are the clouds doing?

Gardening

It feels appropriate that we come full circle into the garden, as our permaculture heritage is from there. In the garden we are able to meet the ethics of peoplecare, earthcare and fair shares. It is the place where the ethics, principles and design all fall into place and get woven into our intuition and the wisdom of our hands. It is where we can understand the connection between our own health and planetary well-being. It is the place of optimism, growth and abundance.

The garden is the meeting place for us and other beings. When involved in gardening, farming and woodland management we are actively participating in the conversation with nature. As with all conversations we need to be able to listen and respond appropriately. This active, first hand learning with nature is profound.

Permaculture gardening focuses on integrating useful and edible plants with maintaining and increasing wildlife habitat in a low maintenance way.

Gardening is an integrating activity in itself, stimulating all aspects of personal health. Through exercise, fresh air and wholesome food we improve our physical health. The wonder and satisfaction of growing our own food increases our self-esteem and our emotional health. Planning and designing our garden or window boxes requires some mental agility and flexibility. Connecting with nature and the life cycles of birth and death maintains our spiritual well-being. The food feeds our body and the process of gardening nourishes our soul.

The garden is one of the easiest places to create abundances, and to be witness to the profusion of nature. Gardeners can create surplus to share with neighbours as well as for insects and feathered friends. Many people come to permaculture to improve their gardens or growing spaces and start to change themselves. Other people change their inner landscape leading them into the garden. Inner growth is reflected in outer productivity.

Gardening helps us to be in touch with the realities of life. We are encouraged to think holistically and learn with our hands and senses, not just our head. We can break through the destructive assumptions of separation through our physical contact with the soil.

The ultimate purpose of farming is not the growing of crops, but the cultivation and perfection of human beings.
MASANOBU FUKUOKA[4]
....

Gardening can be inclusive of the whole family and can also be a community activity. The garden can be the classroom, playground, store cupboard, meditation room, gym, office and wilderness.

Top tips

There are many informative books on gardening so I won't go into methods of creating a permaculture garden. I will just share my top tips for enjoying gardening:

- Grow what you want to eat
- Plant useful perennials and fruit bushes
- Use your window sill for seed sprouting and start at your back door
- Guerrilla garden, join a community garden or land share scheme if you don't have a garden
- Treat your gardening as an experiment and be happy to learn from your mistakes
- Enjoy what has happened rather than thinking about what hasn't
- Sow many more seeds then you think you will need; there will always be something to do with the surplus if they all do well
- Think of gardening as play time not work time; activities not jobs
- Spend time with your plants just being
- Marvel at germination, growth and fruiting

Gardening with children

Children are the future. The most effective way of ensuring the future of the planet is by cultivating the next generation of gardeners. From the moment we are born our learning begins. As nature is the greatest teacher it makes sense to fully integrate children into the experience of growing as they themselves grow and develop. Observation of nature leads to a deep understanding and respect, the foundation for restoring harmony with nature.

From a very early age children can develop an interest in gardening that can hold them in good stead for the rest of their lives. The processes learnt in the garden are valuable transferable tools whatever direction their lives take. Gardening can have as profound an effect on children as adults; they can feel empowered by growing their own food and grounded by their connection with the earth. A school garden can serve many of the purposes of education.

Interest is sustained if it's made fun and enjoyable. Yields that they enjoy from the garden are motivating. Correct harvesting can teach them about the use of resources and not being too greedy and taking so much that the plant cannot recover. Having their own garden jobs can help them to learn responsibility and the consequences of their actions. If they look after the plants then they grow and are abundant, if they don't, then the plants wither and die. These lessons can be expanded out into a wider systems view of relationships with the world.

With their sense of wonder in the world, children's observation and questioning skills are often much more heightened than adults' who may take the world and nature for granted. Children are amazing resources with their imagination and creativity. With patient and thoughtful design, their unlimited curiosity and enthusiasm can be harnessed and channelled into happy, productive activity.

Designing for other cultures

When we are designing for other cultures, we are at risk of imposing our own cultural perspective. The most relevant approach is therefore to take a step back and guide them to go through the process themselves.

Opportunities

- We can guide someone else through their thought processes, rather than bringing in our own ideas. This is true whenever we are involving other people, but even more pertinent when you are within another cultural context.
- There is a two way learning process; we can learn about the other culture and they can learn about design.
- This is an opportunity to deepen understanding of the other culture, and then to share our ideas. As Steven Covey would say *seek first to understand then be understood.*[1]
- Designing for other cultures is weighty on observation. We need to take much more time to understand the *helps, limits and patterns.* Often development programmes come in with *helps* and think that money is all that is needed to change a situation. We need to try and understand the whole context.
- We can really practise our listening skills. Who are we listening to, are the women and the children being heard? Are the very poorest and marginalised drawn into the process or are they still excluded?
- We can create the conditions for them to discover for themselves how and what to change.
- We can train people from the other culture to design and facilitate.

How

Naomi Saville works for a Nepalese research organisation helping mothers and infants in Dhanusha district in the plains of Nepal. There are ways in which they work that we can draw upon for designing with other cultures.

Women come together in groups with a trained Female Community Health Volunteer (FCHV) who is part of the government health service. The FCHV is the local person and point of contact between the group and organisation, thereby allowing the groups to evolve without outsiders. This gives the women ownership and makes the groups more replicable. They start with a problem and then through games and discussions find ways of raising awareness and tackling the issue. Over the next six months to one year they implement their plan. With groups that have limited or no literacy, it is important to make the process inclusive and empowering. These groups have taken role plays and card games into their communities. The cards illustrating the problems and solutions have been drawn by a local artist, and with cultural sensitivity. Other activities for low literacy groups could involve theatre, puppets, models, animation and films.

The groups generate a new 'group think' which starts to shift some of the cultural taboos. At one time this led to a march of 800 women against the cultural practice of women being isolated in the cowsheds or outhouse during their first six days after delivering a baby.

The groups follow a participatory action research model of:

Researching or identifying problems → Prioritising problems to be overcome → Designing strategies to overcome prioritised problems → Doing the strategies → Evaluating how well it went and what to do next to improve them → Then moving on to a new problem or issue.

Design Case Study: Women's health programme in Nepal

This design is for a Women's Health Programme (WHP) run by the Himalayan Permaculture Centre (HPC),[2] in Humla a region in North Western Nepal. The design was made in 2011 at the beginning of the programme. Similar programmes have been run previously in the same area. I conducted interviews with Hom Maya Gurung, district co-ordinator and women's health specialist, with Chris Evans translating.

Reflection

What's the current situation of women's health in this area?

This area of Nepal is one of the poorest regions in the country. There is little or no health care, basic hygiene is poor and there is no knowledge of women's health and self-awareness. Women in the area suffer from more types of diseases and more seriously than in other areas.

Vision

What is your vision of what women's health could be?

With HPC's input women can bring improvement to their own health, teach others and become more self-reliant. To have easier, happier lives, be more aware, have less children, better communication with their husbands in running the house/land, more help from their husbands and better techniques for farming. Now in Humla, women say they have no value in living; my vision is that people will think, 'What can I do in my life?'

Limits

What's holding back women's health?

There is big gender differentiation in this area in Nepal and a very patriarchal system. Things are not as open to women as for men – they can't travel so easily. There is pressure to have boys; if they have girls then it is seen as the women's fault and there is pressure to have more children. There are cultural taboos around childbirth and menstruation, relating to diet and hygiene. Men generally own land and control money and women have little access to credit. Women do most of the work around the house, family and farm.

By and large men do not understand about women's health. When men get sick they rest or go and get treatment straight away. When women get sick they get treatment less frequently because they worry about who will do the work.

Once at a women's health camp there was a drunk man accusing the programme of disturbing gender roles. Men are part of the system and part of the cultural patterns in the house and wider community. There have been many cases of reactions from men.

What could limit the programme?

There is only me to do the work, no one else is trained. We have not found anyone as yet that I could train to support my role.

Why would people not want to change?

Not understanding, lack of education, fear from patriarchs, men not wanting to share power, unwillingness of women to rock the boat. There are strong beliefs keeping taboos in place. Even if the taboos are broken, they find negative things that happen to confirm that the taboos need to be kept.

Helps

Why do people want to change?

There is slowly more awareness. Women are now allowed to own land in Nepal. Women also see other people who have made changes and realise that there can be change and the benefits it can bring.

- My skills – training, communication, facilitation, diagnostic and counselling skills. Practical knowledge of uses and preparations of wild and cultivated herbs, for prevention and treatment of women's health problems.
- In HPC – budget, training tools, materials and village groups.
- Externally – friends in other NGOs for advice and training materials.

Patterns

What are the cultural patterns to do with health?

Marriage at a young age, too many children, eating last when all the best food has gone, not getting diagnosed or treatment soon enough, big work loads, carrying heavy loads, smoke in kitchens, poor hygiene, lack of washing facilities and also time to stay clean and taboos particularly around menstruation.

HPC's other work has changed some cultural patterns for the better; now smokeless stoves are commonplace, and people have fresh vegetables to eat in the winter.

Principles

What principles can be applied to the programme?

- *Integrate rather than segregate* – making beneficial connections between family members, family and community, community and community, community and organisations and government. With these connections passing on knowledge, valuing improvements. Involving men and household members.
- *Use and value diversity* – of crops and diet. Different level of teaching for different levels of society. Teaching to the young, middle aged and old.
- *Obtain a yield* – farming techniques where we get more output for less input. Then women get better nutrition and have to do less work. Smokeless stoves reduce the need for firewood and result in cleaner air.

Pause

How can the women of Humla build in the times of rest and quiet?

At the moment women only rest when they are eating and they have one day off a month at the end of menstruation to wash.

In the future perhaps we can have a special training programme where they come and chill out, watch training films, and sing and dance. We need men's participation and agreement for this though, because the women's work has to be done by someone.

Appreciation

How can women appreciate themselves?

During the health training we get them to reflect on their wealth of skills. They find they have many and this builds confidence.

Women have appreciated the general counselling and the rapport that builds up, and the sense of them being supported. Through being listened to they start to build confidence in themselves.

Momentum

How to stop people switching back to bad habits?

Once women have learnt new habits they don't go back to old habits. But the problems they face haven't gone away. They are helped by continued training, follow up activities and the creation of supportive network.

Integration

From this interview the following needs for the design were identified:
1. More female staff
2. Awareness raising for women
3. Awareness raising for men
4. Farming techniques – food security
5. Link WHP with HPC's other work
6. Networking/creating connections – within families as well as between women
7. Preventative measures – hygiene, self diagnosing
8. Treatment
9. Self-esteem and confidence building
10. Education and training
11. Research and understand patterns – why some can change more easily than others, the differences between Humla and other programme areas.
12. Create momentum for women's health

Ideas

We then went on to think of many ways of meeting these needs.

Needs/purpose	Ideas
1. More female staff	More budget; apprenticing/students; teenagers; slowly giving more responsibility to suitable people; opening up to outside people – advertising; volunteers from Humla; exchange with other NGOs.
2. Awareness raising for women	Training and workshops; exchange programmes and exposure trips; film nights; after treatment given responsibility to share and inform other women; health camps.
3. Awareness raising for men	Initial workshop to include men; poster; training HPC staff and board so they can spread the message with HPC's other work; transparency of process; show men the direct and indirect benefits for themselves and household.

4. Farming techniques – food security	All techniques that increase nutrition and/or reduce work: fodder growing; vegetable growing; agroforestry; fruit; stoves; urine collection.
5. WHP link with HPC's other work	HPC staff to share benefits and raise awareness with men and women; specific training on growing and using medicinal herbs.
6. Networking -creating connections	Creating and using the network; connections from the trainings and from the groups; creating microcredit funds.
7. Preventative measures	Teaching them the whys and hows; hygiene; self diagnosing; toilets; improving quality of drinking water and reducing the work to get it; health camps.
8. Treatment	Herbs; prolapse treatment; counselling; health camps.
9. Self-esteem and confidence building	Education and awareness of what is possible; demonstration from others; collecting stories from people/communities that have changed; clinics, counselling and treatment – realising they can get better if treated in right way, place, time; practical literacy; realising their own 'wealth of skills' as part of training; looking at gender roles and who does what, realising women are very skilled; developing income generation – handling money.
10. Education and training	Short and long training; two five day trainings; training materials; short workshops within health camps.
11. Research and understand patterns	Discussion groups; social anthropologist; asking older generations what's changed already; explore feelings around what has changed; change patterns around domestic violence.
12. Create momentum for women's health	Raising awareness; festivals; fun events; keeping it active; demonstration; building on success; how it's taught from one to another within the family and network.

Action

From these ideas the following action points fit with the resources of time, budget and labour for the first year. Hom Maya would design each activity in more detail and look to meet as many of the needs as possible with each activity.

- Training for HPC staff
- Student to shadow and learn from Hom Maya
- Exposure field trip
- Film shows
- Five day health training
- Establishing women's health groups and network
- Collecting stories

The first action is to train HPC male and female staff and board members about the what and why of women's health, the benefits for the whole household and how it relates to the rest of HPC's work. There will then be more people to spread the message and men can talk to the other men in the village groups. This was seen to be the action for *minimum effort and maximum effect.*

PART 6: SENSING OUR FUTURES

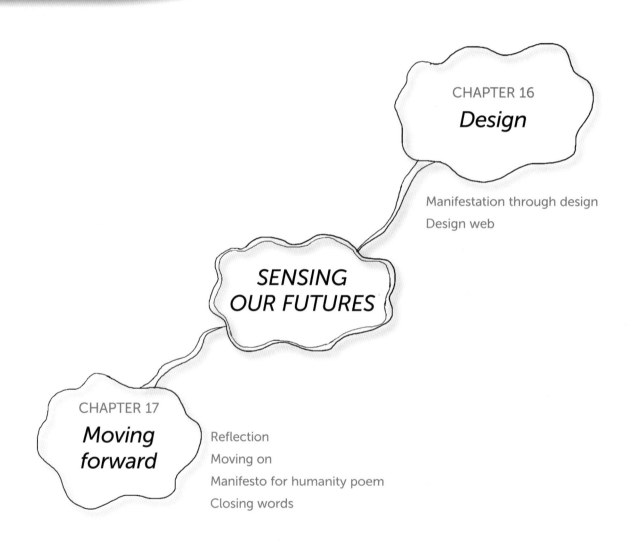

CHAPTER 16
Design

Manifestation through design

Design web

SENSING OUR FUTURES

CHAPTER 17
Moving forward

Reflection

Moving on

Manifesto for humanity poem

Closing words

Design

AFTER HAVING STRETCHED
our thinking and awareness in
many different directions we are
now bringing it back to ourselves. This part looks at how we can make
sense of our future and move towards it. This book is about change and
action, thinking anew and taking responsibility. The design web from
Part 1 (see pp.45-49) provides a support framework during this process
of transformation. We start with looking at how design is a tool for
manifesting our visions. We then look at each anchor point of the design
web in turn and the opportunities it presents with some hints and ideas
on how to apply it and the most common connections between them.

Manifestation through design

Design is a vehicle for manifesting our dreams. Design can help us to know what
we want and to be clear in that vision. When we have clarity of intent, are willing
to invest time and energy and can hold the dream and breathe life into it, then the
vision can manifest into reality.

This is a call to step into the new, into the unknown and to make changes in
your life. This is a place of power and potential. Engaging in the design is exercising
the power of choice, the decision of where to direct our energies and resources. It is
making a commitment and trusting in the decision.

We manifest things all the time: we want a sandwich and we take clear, decisive
steps. We want a forest garden and we do a design, acquire the plants and plant the
trees; we can make it happen. If we want to have a healthy diet, we can vision what it
would look like for ourselves and make the steps necessary for that to happen. When
we are not sure what we want then our dreams can get caught in our everyday lives
and not move anywhere. We can be like hamsters in the wheel, not knowing when
and how to get off.

Nature is the ultimate expert in manifestation. When we want to manifest our
dreams we need to create the right soil conditions for seeds to germinate. There is a
balance between trusting in the process and encouraging things to happen.

To manifest our dreams we need to keep the big vision in mind and do the leg-work. Building a house is done brick by brick, writing a book happens word by word, getting fit happens with regular exercise... Daily reminders and action keep us on track, while the bigger picture lures us forward. Often what are perceived as sudden changes from the outside are the result of thinking, planning and dreaming time.

We need to trust that what we are bringing into reality is for the greater good. The overall aim of permaculture design is to further the three ethics.

We can use permaculture design to take us where we want to go and weave abundance into every aspect of our lives.

Design web

What to design

The first thing to do is to decide what you would like to design. It is useful to give yourself some parameters to the design, even though every system is linked with other systems, otherwise you could end up trying to tackle everything and feeling overwhelmed.

With bigger projects a common problem is the feeling of being unable to complete one design because other related designs are not done and these will impact on the first design. And so people are caught in a catch 22 of inaction and their thinking stalls. Designs do influence each other and we can design a flow of communication between the designs, enabling us to respond to changes and move us beyond paralysis.

Often we are not starting from scratch; there is already a system in place that needs upgrading. Sometimes, rather than just tweaking the system, it is useful to put assumptions and habits to one side and design from first principles.

A good design activity to begin with, is wherever you are losing energy. This could be time, money, emotional energy, or how your house is organised. Most of us subconsciously know where this is. If you are unsure start with keeping a diary for a week of your energy leaks, like Suzi High did for her zone 00 design.

The anchor points

The design web is an active, dynamic and creative process. It is intuitive, holistic, engaging and participatory. New ideas and insights come from just writing things down and thinking in a systematic way. We gain more insights from making connections with what we already know. Ideas float to the surface. The design web creates new pathways for change that might have been there already, just overgrown, like the neural pathways that wiggle each toe separately. Observation is key throughout; we can observe ourselves through the process.

Each anchor point is a system by itself as well as connecting with all the others. The whole design web is connected and information and ideas are flowing around. You can start the design web wherever feels appropriate. All of the activities in the book have built up our experience in designing and have given us different ways

VISION – allow yourself to dream and create goals

PAUSE – incorporate times of rest and rejuvenation

HELPS – identify the things that are going to help

REFLECTION – evaluate progress

LIMITS – identify the things that might block your path or keep it small or slow it down

APPRECIATION – focus on things to be thankful for

Design Web

PATTERNS – identify the helpful and unhelpful patterns

MOMENTUM – how to keep going

IDEAS – gather inspirations

ACTION – make a plan for getting things done

INTEGRATION – bring it all together

PRINCIPLES – look through the lens of each one

of approaching the anchor points. Some of the activities have related to more than one anchor point, demonstrating there are fuzzy edges between them, each one can connect to more than one other, and flow into another. From each one there are different directions we can face. It is like learning a new dance, from each anchor point there are steps we can take into another anchor point, and once you know a few of the basic moves you can adapt it to your own pace and style. Some people may like to spend time slowly delving deeper for insights, others may like to hop about quickly gathering initial thoughts.

We will now look at each anchor point in turn highlighting the opportunities it holds, some hints on how to approach it and a few options for possible next steps.

The expressive phase of the child

 *VISION*

Opportunities

- The *vision* anchor point provides direction; it is at the top of the web, like the North Star.
- This anchor point opens up our imagination and connects us with our dreaming processes.
- This is the time of unboundaried dreaming, to express what abundances we want to create and our ideals; our ideal self, livelihood, family, group and community.
- We can focus on where we want to be and not have to think about how to get there.
- Our vision ignites hope.
- Once voiced we can practice non-attachment to the details of our vision and allow for different things to develop.

How

- Guided visualisations.
- Any art medium – storytelling, collages, painting – is useful to sidestep our automatic limitations and access our dreaming state.
- Give a timescale for the vision: one, five, ten years from now.
- Tell a story of the place you would like to be.

Steps to other anchor points

- Our *vision* leads us to the *helps* – what resources and support we need.
- Our *vision* will give us some of the functions/needs for the *integration* anchor point.
- We can think about what *limits* we have in getting there.

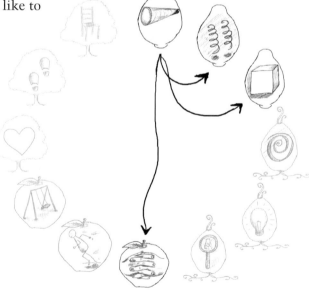

 **HELPS**

Opportunities
- We can overcome our modesty and value what we have. Our internal resources include our skills, knowledge and abilities; our stamina, courage, kindness and joy. Our sense of humour and thoughtfulness can see us through challenging times.
- Within a group of people there are many internal resources. We can honour the experience of others and qualities that they bring.
- Thinking about external resources that we can access opens up our feelings of support.
- Connecting with the reasons why we want change provides incentives.
- Highlighting our motivations shows us where our passions and enthusiasms are. This is where the energy is that we can work and flow with.

How
- Skills audit.
- We can think about the abilities we have in each of the multiple intelligences.
- Identify transferable skills from other areas of life.
- Plant real seeds to represent each of the resources we have and watch them grow.

Steps to other anchor points
- The *helps* we have influence the *action* anchor point and the timescales we are able to give.
- What resources and support do we have to keep up *momentum*?
- We may need to take a *pause* to reassess our motivations.

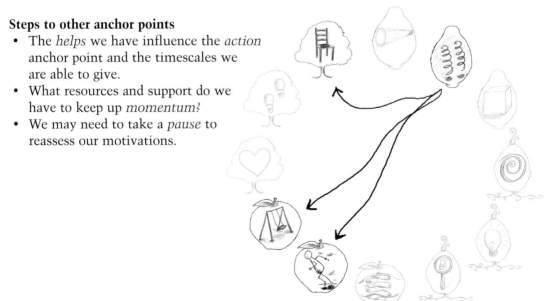

LIMITS

Opportunities

- A chance to recognise energy leaks, concerns, emotional ties, and individual and cultural beliefs.
- Acknowledging these influences allows us to design around them, otherwise they are like hidden wires tripping us up or holding us back.
- We can voice concerns, from the ridiculous and fanciful to the mundane and predictable. Hearing other people's concerns helps to gain perspective and reassurance. Highlighting potential problems allows us to begin putting strategies in place in case they happen.
- The *limits* in our design may be things that are pulling us off route. This gives us a chance to say 'no' because we are saying 'yes' to something else.
- We have the opportunity to revisit this anchor point as the *limits* in our system change over time.

How

- Honesty and awareness are foundations of this anchor point.
- Recognising the edges of our comfort zones and the resistance that there may be to moving out of it.
- Imagine a plant growing – what weeds would you need to take out around it?
- We can use objects to represent the different *limits*.
- Interruption-free space to talk is valuable.

Steps to other anchor points

- We can look to our *helps* and see if there are any resources that could be used to extend our *limits*.
- We could be aware of any *patterns* of thinking, behaving and interacting that are holding us back or patterns we may have around change itself.
- Finding ways to extend our *limits* become functions of the *integration* anchor point.

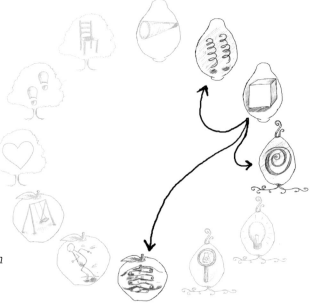

The exploratory phase of the apprentice

PATTERNS

Opportunities
- This anchor point represents an edge in the design between what is and what could be. What old patterns would we like to let go of and what new ones would we like to create in our lives?
- We can identify patterns in our life that are directly influencing the design. Patterns of thinking, behaviour and interaction and spirals of erosion.
- We can take a long view of the patterns at play, encouraging us to solve the problem from a bigger perspective. Instead of just finding solutions to fit the current situation, we seek ones that will endure.
- We can engage in possible solutions and look for sources of inspiration and useful patterns that could be adapted and replicated.
- We can select from all of our life's experience for information and patterns that we can use in this context. The patterns of thinking, behaviour and interaction that led us to our previous success. The patterns of procrastination and arguments that we want to avoid.

How
- We can look at natural processes, cycles and rhythms to find functional patterns that can provide useful metaphors for our design.
- Throughout our lives we use a multitude of tools and methods. Are there some that we use in other areas of our lives that could be of use here? Can we transfer ways of working and thinking into a new situation?
- We can take patterns of scientific research, spiritual wisdom, time management, parenting strategies, organisational structures ... to give us ideas.
- Keeping a biotime diary helps us to tune into our own patterns.

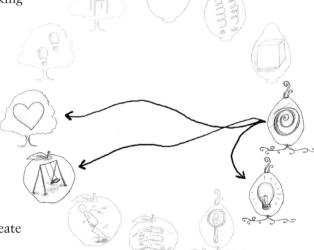

Steps to other anchor points
- This can lead us to *appreciation* of ourselves for the positive *patterns* and previous successes in our lives
- How can we use our *patterns* to create *momentum?*
- What *ideas* do we have from these *patterns?*

IDEAS

Opportunities
- We have the opportunity to let our imagination and creativity flow.
- This anchor point captures the sparks of inspiration, seeds of ideas and glimpses of solutions. They do not need to be fully formed or well thought through.
- We are invited to think beyond the mundane and obvious, to move out of our old habits and discover new things. The ideas can be silly, wacky, and ambitious.
- Every voice can be heard and all ideas captured. Ideas that pop into your head when you are in other stages can be held here.
- A chance to give ideas time to brew, evolve, adapt.

How
- The *ideas* may come through research or from bouncing off other people
- Free yourselves from any screening or analysis of ideas
- Mind mapping
- Use random stimuli around you

Steps to other anchor points
- What *ideas* could you add to your *vision?*
- Can these *ideas* be brought into the design in the *integration* anchor point?
- We could generate *ideas* for different ways of showing *appreciation.*

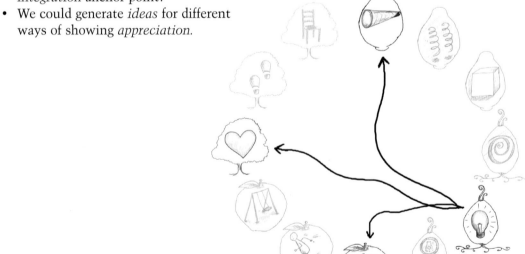

PRINCIPLES

Opportunities
- Using the principles is like throwing in a fishing line; sometimes we will get something useful, sometimes nothing and sometimes something unexpected.
- They can be used to generate more ideas or to analyse existing ideas.
- We can use them to help us with our action plans, or to question our needs.
- The principles will help us to root the ideas we want and discard inappropriate courses of action.
- They can be used to reflect on a problem.

How
- You could choose one principle as an anchor for the design, a reminder to keep the focus.
- Use them as a way of choosing between options.
- Pick one at random and see what it stimulates.
- Use the self-reflection questions for each principle on pages 19-25.

Steps to other anchor points
- The *principles* can generate *ideas* and also be used to check to see if *ideas* fit with them.
- The *principles* can help with choosing priorities in the *action* anchor point. For example *obtain a yield* may encourage us to find actions that will give us quick yields.
- We can use the *principles* to keep us on track and maintain *momentum*.

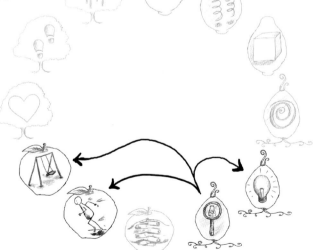

The productive phase of the adult

INTEGRATION

Opportunities
- We are finding ways of how to reach our vision and designing the pathway there.
- We firstly require the functions or the needs – what are we actually trying to achieve with the design? What are the key themes and priorities? Breaking it down into manageable and usable chunks.
- We think about what systems we could put in place that would fulfil these functions.
- We are able to work the other way and think about the ideas we have and what needs they would meet, to help us determine the value of implementing them.
- We can create flows of energy between the systems so they can enhance and support each other. Like a net, the more connections there are the stronger and more stable the whole system is.

How
- The first step is to gather up all the information we have so far, and process it into something usable.
- In this anchor point we move to making decisions.
- Find at least three ways of meeting each of the functions, designing back-ups into our system – *multiple elements for important functions.*
- For each system think of three needs that it can meet – *many yields for each function.*
- Draw a web to make and examine the links and flows between systems. How do the inputs and outputs of one system relate to another?

Steps to other anchor points
- We can visit the *ideas* anchor point for options of how to fulfil the needs.
- We need to move to the *action* anchor point to establish priorities and timescales.
- What on-going maintenance do these systems need to keep *momentum?*

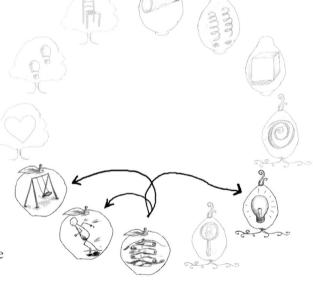

ACTION

Opportunities
- We can gain clarity over what we have to put in and what we are hoping to get out.
- Our inputs include the time needed and any resources such as skills, materials, money and information.
- What are the yields we are expecting to get out of the actions? And what is the timescale for these yields?
- This is a chance to set up a pattern of success by creating achievable action plans. Expressing when things need to happen will soon highlight clashes or overburdens.
- There is a balance to be had between incremental changes and shocking the system into a new equilibrium. Incremental changes are usually more effective in the long-term; however there are circumstances where it is appropriate to make big jumps.

How
- From having done the input and output analysis on each of the systems it is easier to make decisions on what the priorities and commitments are going to be. A useful principle is *minimum effort for maximum effect.* What small things can we do that will have big effects? These are beneficial places to start.
- We might start to identify dependencies, things that we have to do before we can do something else.
- We can use post-it notes on a time-line as a flexible planning tool.
- The key here is to create a plan of action that is achievable, realistic, engaging, adaptable, motivating and easy to follow.

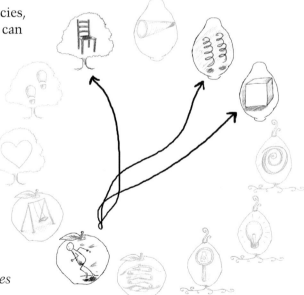

Steps to other anchor points
- The timescales need to be appropriate to the resources available in the *helps* anchor point.
- We need to check our *action* plan is in proportion to the *limits.*
- We can design in times for the *pauses* we need to rejuvenate ourselves.

MOMENTUM

Opportunities
- We are encouraged to keep at something for long enough for it to pay dividends. Trees do not grow overnight, nor does our fitness or healthy relationships. Being patient with the natural processes makes the most of our efforts.
- We are not just carrying out one action hoping for change, we are creating new ways of being and building systems that become part of the fabric of our lives.
- At first when we exercise our muscles can be sore. Likewise starting anything new can be a strain at first and we need strategies for pushing us through the physical or psychological resistance to change.
- As we gain momentum things become easier and our capacities increase. Like a swing we can go higher and higher. We can utilise the momentum for other changes within the design and for future designs.
- Keeping it fun and engaging for everyone builds momentum.

How
- Sometimes we will start something and then realise that we need to take a step sideways or backwards before we can properly start, akin to weeding and preparing the ground before planting.
- Have clear aims, create milestones to navigate with and celebrate progress made.
- The new systems to put in place may require daily, weekly, seasonal, and yearly maintenance. Identifying these up front will ensure that you don't take on more than you can maintain. Make your commitments realistic.
- Sustaining momentum requires keeping to the agreements you make with yourself and others.

Steps to other anchor points
- If we are struggling to keep *momentum* we can return to the *limits*. They can change over time and we can be making good progress and hit new and unexpected limiting factors.
- Is our *momentum* still connected with our *vision* and moving us towards it?
- Are our *pauses* appropriately timed so we keep rather than lose *momentum*?

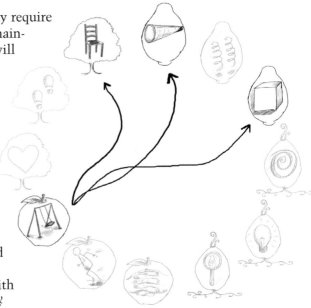

The reflective phase of the elder

APPRECIATION

Opportunities

- It is important to recognise and value the efforts that have been made by everyone involved, and appreciate the support and resources we have used from outside of our system, both human and natural. Taking time to show our gratitude opens up our hearts as well as our minds.
- Appreciation is a need within all of us; meeting this need is motivating and stimulating.
- We can be appreciative of ourselves and others being active in the process; for our thoughts, ideas and honesty; for our visions and dreams and willingness to change; and for our connections and ability to work together. Appreciate the new neurons that have been created and patterns that have shifted.
- This is a time for sharing what we enjoyed and are continuing to enjoy.
- We can celebrate our yields. Perhaps there have been unexpected ripples of our actions and bubbles of joy to share.

How

- Our celebrations can be planned in advance – rewards to look forward to – that bring everyone together with fun and laughter. The celebrations can be used to mark achievements and decisions and remind us of the journey we have embarked upon.
- We can write messages of appreciation to ourselves, family or group members.
- Harvest festivals are a traditional way of sharing our yields and giving thanks. Perhaps we can find a way of adapting this idea to the yields we gain.

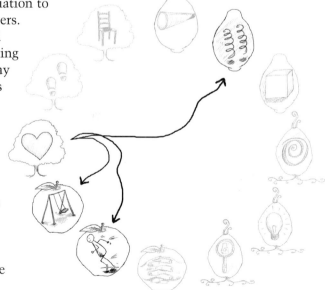

Steps to other anchor points

- Positive emotions and celebrations encourage us to maintain and increase *momentum.*
- This anchor point links with the *helps.* The yields we recognise and value will provide further motivations for change.
- We can show *appreciation* for the *action* we have taken.

REFLECTION

Opportunities
- A chance to listen to the ripples of our actions.
- Focusing on the periphery can give us as much information as paying attention to the centre.
- We can reflect on the emergent qualities of our design. What unexpected things are happening?
- Identify and invite feedback from other sources.
- Evaluate our successes and challenges; what has worked well, what has been challenging and what needs tweaking.

How
- We can create specific times and routes for formal feedback, using methods such as PMI and Six Thinking Hats.
- Keeping a journal allows informal reflections to be recorded.
- Reflect on the process of designing for future designs.
- Create open-ended questions to ask everyone involved.

Steps to other anchor points
- What extra detail can we add to our *vision* as we get closer to it?
- What *patterns* have we noticed?
- We can revisit our *action* anchor point and see if it needs to be updated and if it is realistic.

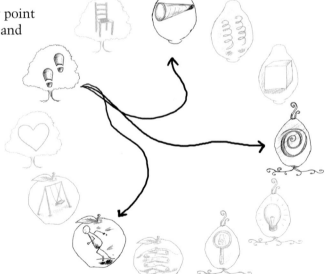

PAUSE

Opportunities
- This anchor point is important to recharge batteries.
- Building in times of rest and rejuvenation is beneficial for self-care and nurturing relationships.
- If you are feeling overwhelmed, low in energy or feel you are getting little out for the effort you are putting in, then it is time to pause.
- Sometimes a break from the process is needed to distance yourself, or a chance to let things cool down if it's getting heated between people.

How
- Here the pause is a conscious break. Time to refresh with a cup of tea, walk, fresh air or game. Healthy energisers to reinvigorate us.
- Times of celebration with group members.
- Times of no structure, times to just be and see what emerges.

Steps to other anchor points
- *Ideas* can bubble up when we have time off.
- During *pauses* we can replenish and access our internal resources and revisit our *helps* anchor point.
- *Pauses* give us space to clarify our *vision.*

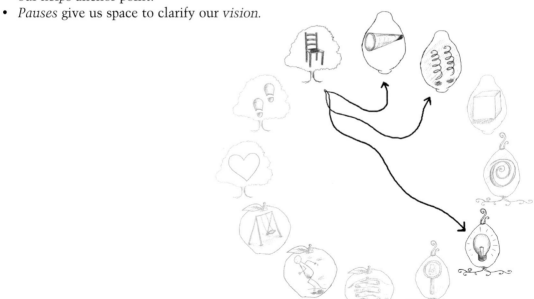

The work on the design web continues. Each stage has growing edges, and we are designing living systems that continue to evolve, requiring us to be responsive to change. Over time some of the information on the anchor points may fall away like petals, making way for the current situation. The design and the system that is being designed are not separate. They are like our thinking and actions, one follows the other and back again.

We can move on to other systems we wish to design. As our effectiveness increases we are more able to engage with others. There are limitless opportunities for design.

Designs can be on the back of an envelope – for a quick focus and shift in direction and pace – or a lifetime's engagement with change and renewal processes, and of course anything in between. Through experience we may move to an intuitive design process woven into our daily lives.

Design is an invitation to experiment, play, enjoy and welcome the stimulation of applying yourself to creating solutions.

CHAPTER 17

Moving forward

THIS FINAL CHAPTER
has activities to reflect on
the book and contemplate
the journey thus far. We move on to prepare ourselves for the coming
adventures.

The end is the beginning of the next part in the story. There is a
'manifesto for humanity' poem, woven from many interviews and
workshops; the direction we want to move in, the vision of hope for
humanity.

Reflection

The book has been your travelling companion for a while. I wonder what life has
thrown your way while you have been reading this and what learning opportunities
you have faced. I look forward to hearing stories and meeting some of you.

This is just part of the journey towards being your full self and moving to a positive
and abundant future. You are now on a pathway to personal, social and planetary
well-being. This is the time to look back on progress, feel a sense of achievement
and make plans for the next stage.

You have been reading this book a word at a time, although perhaps jumping
around chapters. Essentially words are linear; now at the end is the opportunity to
see it holistically, as a complete picture, including the influences and the context
of your journey. There is scope for you to revisit things as the relevancy arises. The
activities bridge the gap between theory and practice and you may want to carry on
with them or go back to ones that you skipped. As you continue to use the book you
will start to see more of the details, connections and applications to your own life.

On one level the principles and ideas are relatively easy to understand; however
practice on the ground can be more challenging. It is the application to our own lives
that provides us with the richest lessons. As our skills and experiences increase so
does our ability to see more complexity.

It is the nature of our human brains to start forgetting what we have learnt if we
don't remind ourselves or use the knowledge. Time spent now, or soon, stops that

energy drain and helps to embody the lessons. Taking time to answer the questions will provide you with insights into your own mind and attitudes. It honours the time you took to read the book to now take time to reflect.

There are plenty of new seeds of ideas, too many to all grow at once, and we need to spend time watering and nurturing those we want to flourish. This process of reflection is like giving the whole garden a good soaking, keeping an eye out for the seeds that are sprouting. Perhaps some will take a while to germinate. We can't know all the effects of our actions; there may well be some unexpected benefits already on their way.

You may be sitting here thinking that you are more confused and overwhelmed than when you started. As your circle of knowledge has increased, so has the edge of what you don't know.

One's mind, once stretched by a new idea, never regains its original dimensions.

OLIVER WENDELL HOLMES

You are able to see more of what you don't know and what needs doing. This has a similar pattern to the competence cycle. Stage one of 'blissful ignorance' is the vast white space of the unknown and we are unaware of what that might contain. Stage two, 'the door opens', is the outside of the fuzzy edge, where we are introduced to something and it comes into our awareness. Stage three, 'awkward know how', is the fuzzy edge where it is almost within our knowledge. Stage four, 'second nature', is our circle of knowledge.

This is an opportunity for you to take time looking within your expanded circle of knowledge, to take comfort in your growth. The following activity stimulates stage five: 'reflective competence', where we are able to see the voyage we have taken.

ACTIVITY: REFLECTIVE COMPETENCE

Firstly look back at your initial entry in your learning journal and your aim and motivations for reading this book.

> *In what ways did I reach my aim? What else do I need to do to get there? What else did I gain along the way?*

Now, looking back at the mindmaps at the beginning of each part, take a few minutes to reflect on the stages of the competence cycle you have been through.

> *What emotions did I go through when reading this part?*
>
> *What was new to me that now feels familiar?*
>
> *What terms come up in conversation, what principles do I see in action?*
>
> *What have I learnt about myself?*
>
> *What would I like to practise to bring it into stage four?*
>
> *What do I want to revisit and carry on researching and learning?*
>
> *What questions am I left with?*
>
> *What could I do differently next time I learn something?*
>
> *What is my pattern of learning?*

Celebration and appreciation

What can you appreciate about yourself over the time you have been reading this? Celebrate any changes you have made. What have you enjoyed about the learning process?

What can you appreciate about your interactions with others over this time? Think of the friends you've talk to, strangers you've observed, people who have confronted you with real life experiences to tackle, people who have nurtured you and ones that have needed support.

Take time to give thanks for the opportunity you have had to read this. Perhaps you have had time on holiday, maybe a friend lent you this book or you borrowed it from a library. Give thanks for the abundance that brought this book to you.

Moving on

The significant thing is what happens next. Can you use permaculture to enhance the quality of your life?

The most effective learning is through doing, thinking and observing for ourselves and allowing the words to percolate into our actions. Bobbi DePorter[1] calls it 'practising into permanence'. Through repetition and trial and error we can come to own this knowledge as our own experience and wisdom. This deepening knowledge of how to look after ourselves, each other and the planet needs to seep into our bones, our muscles, our thoughts and our actions. When it runs through every fibre of our bodies and communities, humanity and the planet will flourish.

This book is a stepping-stone for more exploration of peoplecare and a sustainable Earth culture. We still have to make that journey, each one of us. There are plenty more skills to develop and share, other books to write. Perhaps you will write a book to share your wisdom and inspire others.

*Our Earth is like a small boat Compared with the rest of the cosmos, it is a very small boat, and it is in danger of sinking. We need a person to inspire us with calm confidence, To tell us what to do. Who is that person? The Mahayana Buddhist Sutras tell us that **You** are that person. If you are yourself, if you are at your best, then you are that person. Only with such a person – calm, lucid, aware – will our situation improve. I wish you good luck. Please be yourself. Please be that person.*

THICH NHAT HANH
....

Maddy and Tim Harland of Permanent Publications describe how when they first came across permaculture they discovered how much there is to learn. They went through the observation stage and realised where they didn't have skills, and areas of life they wanted to understand more. Permaculture has given them the humility to acknowledge that they are on a life long learning pathway and slowly gather skills to live in a more constructive and productive way. There are times when it's not possible for them to gain a skill and then they have learned to co-operate with someone who has, building community in the process. Maddy says, "Permaculture has put us in an utterly unexpected place in our lives. I could never have predicted we would be doing what we are doing now. We have to be grateful for this, though it's not always been easy. But when you live life open to a level of creative possibility it can take you to surprising and extraordinary places."

Now we can think about what lies ahead of us. How, what and when do we want to change?

Moving on means going to your edge and looking beyond, deciding what you need to take with you and what to let go of.

This is a time for conscious decision-making, for moulding the changes using designs, using the principles as reminders and the ethics to guide us. We can make active steps towards the ethics, with reducing our consumption, extending our skills, seeing and assessing the consequences of all of our actions, connecting with people and choosing abundance.

Bill Mollison suggests three steps for your own participation in permaculture:

- **Reduce your overall consumption** – of non-renewable resources in particular.

- **Connect with the growing cycle** – even if you do not grow your own, you can buy local, seasonal produce.

- **Align yourself with like-minded people** – mutual support is invaluable.

Anyone can do these and we can start now. With these three steps we become part of a bigger movement that together can make the Great Turning.

ACTIVITY: OPENING THE TIME CAPSULE

Before opening up the time capsule, the envelope that you put away at the beginning of the book, answer the same questions again.

How do I feel about myself?

How do I feel about my connections with other people?

How do I feel about the world?

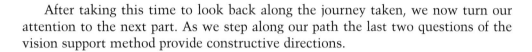

There's no need to try and remember what you wrote before, just write fluidly and spontaneously in the moment. Write for a good 15 minutes, when you come to a close, take a moment to pause, before opening the envelope.

Comparing these make a note of any feelings, thoughts and emotions that emerge.

After taking this time to look back along the journey taken, we now turn our attention to the next part. As we step along our path the last two questions of the vision support method provide constructive directions.

Long term goals and visions

What are your long-term goals and visions?

You can take your vision out in zones: what would you like for yourself, your family, friends, groups, community, society, humanity and the Earth? Think big, think expansively.

What skills would you like to develop? What would you like to know more about? There are many sources of information and inspiration out there; books, courses, internet, other people, website forums, and of course your own self discovery, designing, thinking and experimentation.

Your visions can become real. They can move from dreaming to thinking and planning to doing and into reality and then reflecting and improving.

ACTIVITY: UNBOUNDARIED DREAMING

What are my long-term goals and visions?

Where would I like to be in one year, five years, or twenty years?

What are my wildest ambitions?

Take 10 minutes to answer, either writing in your journal or speaking without interruptions to a friend. Ask them to scribe for you. Remember that you don't need to think about whether these dreams are possible or how they might happen, just open yourself up to the visioning process.

Next achievable steps

What are your next achievable steps?

This is your time for commitment to action. Here is the time to say what you are ready, willing and going to do. Give yourself a timescale for these actions. Timescales can vary from one week to one season. Choose one that suits you, not too long so you forget and not too short that there isn't time to do the actions. You are endeavouring to create a pattern of success, so actions have to be ones that are achievable, and you want to do. Achievable, but not too easy so as to be underselling yourself. The aim is to connect your long-term goals with your everyday reality. Hence your next achievable steps are not just a list of

Shoot for the moon, even if you miss you will land amongst the stars.

LES BROWN

· · · · · · · · · · · ·

things to do, they are steps you are making towards your vision. It may be a small regular commitment to exercise or a step towards restoring peace in your family. It may be the beginnings of a design or further research. Whatever it is, the idea is to stretch and accomplish, thereby bringing your dreams closer to your reality.

ACTIVITY: ONE COMMITMENT AND BLESSING

Think of one medium size thing you are committing to. Make sure you are specific about your action: instead of saying 'I will make our relationship better', give real examples of how.

Think of the qualities you would like to be blessed with to carry out your commitment: peace, understanding, self discipline, stamina, companionship... Open yourself up to these coming to you or from within you.

20 years from now you will be more disappointed by the things you didn't do than by the ones you did do. So throw off the bowlines. Sail away from the safe harbour. Catch the trade winds in your sails. Explore, Dream, Discover.

MARK TWAIN

· · · · · · · · · · · ·

Manifesto for humanity poem

I asked many people for their hope for humanity. What's your highest vision? If we were free from fear and limitations what is the journey for humanity our hearts would like to participate in? On one of my courses we wrote all of our visions on a big roll of paper, taking time to access those imaginings within each one of us. We then read them out one by one and the energy filled the room, as if we were drawing the vision closer; bringing it into this time and place.

This poem has been woven from interviews, workshops and my own dreaming. Read it, share it and bring this vision closer to reality. Let this be the collective voice declaring what we are willing to manifest.

We have slowed down
Woken up
Come into our power,
Our hearts are filled with joy each morning
We exist in a state of wholeness
We see our place in the whole,
We know life is sacred
Every space is sacred
We feel the heartbeats of our fellow beings
The animals and plants our brothers and sisters,
We are thinking and acting like a global family.

We take pride in our Earth home
This shining jewel that breathes beneath us,
Pride in how we leave it for future generations,
Positively impacting on ecosystems,
We have found our hearts, and learn we are connected
To all life
Our spiritual connection woven into the fabric of our lives.
We have a full understanding of love,
We appreciate what it means to be ecological beings
On an ecological planet.
We celebrate an Earth culture.

We know who we truly are and what we are truly capable of
We recognise our own and one another's brilliance
Everyone retains their capacity to smile and laugh
We follow our dreams whatever they may be,
Lives where we enjoy the creativity of being human
Time to be and reflect
We are content
We sing our voices of majesty.

We have learned to negotiate
Communicating our needs and respecting others
We value different ways of working,

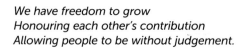

We have freedom to grow
Honouring each other's contribution
Allowing people to be without judgement.

Living together in health and happiness
Greater simplicity of life
With strong social bonds,
Nothing and no one outside of society,
Abundant creative expression
Time for art, music and dancing for all
Farmer poets, gardener philosophers
Communities that share, care and connect.

More wisdom, more integrity
More communication, less fighting
More music, more singing
More dancing, more harmony
More colour, more beauty
More thinking, less rashness
More space for each being to fully become themselves
Weaving abundance into our lives of balance.

Diversity and freedom are the roots of our society
Freedom of thought and action
Our leaders fully representative of all our glorious diversity
Honesty and openness from government and management
Decisions made with consultation and listening
Our leaders are full spectrum conscious and heart based,
A sophisticated approach to social action,
The quietest voices are heard.

Every child has access to education
Following their interests and talents
Learning made easy at their own pace
In their own style,
Meditation and yoga in schools
All taught how to lead,
All taught to reflect
To know why we do things
And the effects of our actions.
Children brought up by the whole community
Everyone is teacher and student
Throughout life
Always growing
Always learning.
Respect, honour and learning from our elders
Conscious parenting supported.
Education brings children to a place of their own wisdom
And sense of being.

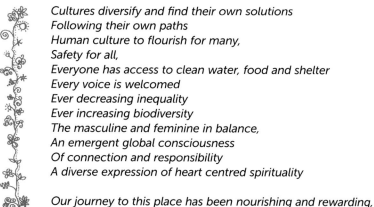

Cultures diversify and find their own solutions
Following their own paths
Human culture to flourish for many,
Safety for all,
Everyone has access to clean water, food and shelter
Every voice is welcomed
Ever decreasing inequality
Ever increasing biodiversity
The masculine and feminine in balance,
An emergent global consciousness
Of connection and responsibility
A diverse expression of heart centred spirituality

Our journey to this place has been nourishing and rewarding,
A smooth energy descent transition,
We regained the value of non-material things
We ended persecution for beliefs
We stopped the violence towards each other, the Earth,
And ourselves
We evolved to a reawakening of spirit.

We are already here at certain times, certain moments,
Certain communities,
A permanent culture around the corner,
Now enough people paying into the consciousness of goodwill and hope
To create the Great Turning
Where war, murder, rape, vandalism, theft
Are shed like a snake's skin
Becoming stories of the past.
We used our knowledge and wisdom
To bring healthy changes to all,
The evolution of happiness
Bringing benefit after benefit.
In times of crisis we were resourceful,
With trust and good connections
We weathered the storms

This is the path of heart
This is the path of abundance
This is your call to action
This is the dream to follow
For our children and grandchildren
For the great forests and deep oceans
For mother Earth and life itself
This is the vision
This is the hope
This is the direction we face
Peace – real peace
Sustained peace

Closing words

We each have our own challenges to face and decisions to make. And our journeys may not be smooth. We have to be kind to ourselves and take the options that are right for us, with no guilt, blame or shame.

Everything is infinitely more complex and interrelated than I have presented here. Change can take time or we can suddenly find ourselves at turning points. Unexpected things can and will happen, which brings me hope. Hope that we will make the journey necessary to create the Great Turning.

Through accessing the deep well of collective wisdom and community spirit we are able to accomplish much in the way of healing. By feeling the rhythm of the Earth beneath our feet we can tune into cycles much greater than ourselves. Through our belonging to the Earth we can find the roots of our shared humanity. From respect friendships, communities, gardens and forests can grow.

We have the opportunity to reconcile the bigger picture with our personal needs. And from this union is a deep sense of connection that motivates us to be our best for the world. We can create a life sustaining Earth culture. We can weave rich tapestries of abundance for ourselves, the planet and future generations.

Begin and the impossible will become possible

Thomas Carlyle

• • • • • • • • • • • • • • • • • •

Principles summary

Principle		Proverbs	How to apply it in peoplecare
	Observe and interact	Beauty is in the eye of the beholder.	Listening to oneself, identifying patterns of behaviour and habits.
	Catch and store energy	Make hay while the sun shines.	Catching the moment, storing positive energy, going with the flow.
	Obtain a yield	You can't work on an empty stomach.	Expanding the concept of yields, meeting short-term needs, and harvesting yields to maintain motivation and momentum.
	Apply self regulation and accept feedback	The sins of our fathers are visited unto the seventh generation.	Being open to feedback, hearing feedback without feeling criticised. Being aware of the consequences of our actions. Giving and receiving appreciation.
	Use renewable services and resources	Let nature take its course.	Finding entertainment and activities that don't involve fossil fuels, creating rather than consuming.
	Produce no waste	Waste not, want not. A stitch in time saves nine.	Preventing our energy from being wasted. Timely maintenance.
	Design from patterns to details	Can't see the wood for the trees.	Looking at the root causes of problems rather than symptoms. Identifying patterns of behaviour, thinking and communication.
	Integrate rather then segregate	Many hands make light work.	Being inclusive, welcoming. Integrating different age groups, or activities. Making connections locally.
	Use edges and value the marginal	Don't think you are on the right track just because it is a well beaten path.	Expanding the edges of our comfort zone. Acknowledging that we can change our habits.
	Use and value diversity	Don't put all your eggs in one basket.	Acknowledging other's strengths and weaknesses. It is healthy to have diversity in our activities, support systems, income, etc.
	Small and slow solutions	Slow and steady wins the race. The bigger they are the harder they fall.	Starting with realistic expectations, keeping change steady and manageable.
	Creatively use and respond to change	Vision is not seeing things as they are but as they will be.	Learning to deal with change and building skills that enable us to adapt to situations.

Glossary

Anchor points
The design web is composed of 12 anchor points, which are different stages in the design process (see pages 45-49 and 260-273).

Biotime diary
A way of collecting and assembling observations regularly over time that allows us to look for patterns (see page 33).

Bioregion
'Life-region' – a part of the earth with similar patterns of plant/animal life, usually dictated by climate and land forms, recognisable by a local community. Examples include a floodplain or a forested slope.

Cash crops
Plants that can be traded as commodities on the international market, rather than plants that are grown to be used locally.

Catch 22
Like the 'Hole-in-my-bucket' song, a catch 22 is a situation where you cannot begin to solve a problem because you have to have solved a different problem first, but that problem cannot be solved until you solve the first one. This 'stuck' phenomenon was first labelled 'Catch 22' in the book of the same name by Joseph Heller.

Climate change
Changes in global climate as a result of human activities, having potentially catastrophic consequences.

Climax trees / climax vegetation
Plants which need a long time, fertile soil and protective shade in order to grow. Contrast with 'pioneer plants', which arrive first in bare soil to help create those conditions.

Competence cycle
Demonstrates our progression in learning through four stages (see pages 78-79).

Crash dieting
Altering one's weight or health by a major rapid one-off change, usually just for a temporary 'improvement'.

Design web
A framework for designing for people (see pages 45-49 and 260-273).

Desire lines
Paths made by the preferred habits of vehicles, humans and other animals, rather than prescriptively laid-out by an architect or town-planner (see page 96).

Eco-footprinting
Way of calculating individual and national environmental impact: consumption of natural resources and creation of pollutants (see page 219).

Energiser
Colloquial term for a game or exercise, within a meeting, workshop or discussion to raise energy, making it easier for people to return with a productive focus (see page 154).

Forest gardens
A method of mimicking nature's forests using edible trees and plants to create a low maintenance, productive garden.

Fossil fuels
Resources that were created during a process that will not be repeated again in a geological timescale. One example is the breakdown of ancient plants into oil and coal, before particular bacteria had evolved that now break them down into new soil. Because of this, such fuels (also gas, peat and brown coal) are finite resources. The Earth also yields fossil minerals, and even fossil water – water held in underground aquifers which cannot be refilled when emptied, because the type of rock loses its absorption-capacity forever if totally depleted once.

Four quadrants
From the integral model by Ken Wilbur, a way of understanding connections between individual and collective thinking and behaviour (see pages 169-170).

Freecycle
An online way of exchanging goods to keep them out of landfill.

Gaia theory
The term chosen by environmental scientist and atmospheric chemist James Lovelock for whole-planet self-regulation. His ideas about the interconnected regulation of sea, earth and atmospheric temperatures and chemical make-up, are now being widely accepted, measured, researched and proven.

The Great Turning
A term used by Joanna Macy to describe the shift in our direction towards a sustainable culture (see pages 9-10).

Gremlin
An internal voice (see pages 62-63).

Guerrilla gardening
The unauthorised planting in public spaces.

Industrial Growth Culture
Our present day culture of industry, technology and pollution (see pages 9-11).

Land fill
The normal method of 'waste disposal' in wealthy industrialised nations, where rubbish is poured into vast holes scraped out of the landscape.

LETS
Local Exchange Trading Systems: a way of sharing skills and resources using a unique local currency.

Majority world
Term typically used to describe countries with low GDPs, traditionally (but impolitely) known as 'developing' or 'under-developed'. Also known as 2/3rds world to reflect their abundance of land area, population and biodiversity (see page 219).

Microfinance
Loans, business plans and other financial services and advice given on a small-scale to small-scale producers and traders – scales of business that could not approach a large bank. Microfinance schemes are sometimes described as 'how banks used to be' with face-to-face client/helper knowledge, and flexible rates and terms. They tend to hold to the principle that the goal of profit need not obliterate an aspiration of service and empowerment.

Mindmaps/Mindmapping
A thinking tool developed by Tony Buzan for visually representing information (see pages 93-94).

Multiple intelligences
A concept from Howard Gardner that maps out a range of abilities and skills to be developed, improved and valued (see pages 80-81).

Mycelium
Mass of sub-soil fungal strands one cell in width that make up the body of a fungus, transporting nutrients and supporting fruiting bodies ('mushrooms' etc.). Are said to be able to communicate nutrient status resulting in exchange of nutrients from nutrient-rich to nutrient-poor areas.

Niche
An environment or place that suits an individual (person/plant/animal etc.) so that they can function to their true potential. Can also apply to roles or jobs that suit you.

NLP
Neuro-Linguistic Programming: tools and methods to change patterns of thinking, speaking and behaviour in order to change outcomes (see page 11).

NVC
Nonviolent Communication: a model and process for personal language and thought, to communicate your needs in a thoughtful and compassionate way, without disrespecting the needs of others (see pages 115-118).

Obsolescence
The characteristic of most 'consumer' products, which means they will wear out or break, so that the consumer will have to buy another one. This property is designed in to objects like cars, biro pens and computer keyboards, even though it would be possible to design and create ones that could be refilled or repaired again and again indefinitely.

Peak oil
Where the discovery of new fossil fuel reserves is less than the current demand.

Peer pressure
The motivation to take up a particular habit increasing because others close to you are doing it. It can be a 'good' habit like recycling, or a 'bad' habit like taking recreational drugs.

Per capita
Per head of the human population.

Permaculture design course (PDC)
Standard training in permaculture design taken over 12-14 days in different formats. Can be preceded by an 'introduction to permaculture' course.

Permaculture diploma
Post PDC, two years of self directed and supported learning in the application of permaculture.

PMI
An evaluation tool from Edward de Bono separating the 'Plus', 'Minus' and 'Interesting' points for any idea/action (see page 94).

Points of intervention and transformation
Specific entry points or times of action that break or halt spirals of erosion and create spirals of abundance (see pages 37-38).

Six thinking hats
A decision making, planning and evaluation tool from Edward de Bono helping us to look at different perspectives (see pages 155-156).

Spirals of erosion
Negative actions leading to more negative actions that create a worsening of the problem (see page 36).

Spirals of abundance
Positive actions leading to more positive actions that lead to improvement in well-being and productivity (see page 37).

SWOC
A process of analysis or evaluation looking at the strengths, weaknesses, opportunities and constraints in turn (see page 196).

Systems theory
This moves us from thinking about 'stuff' and 'what' the universe is made of, to the 'process' and 'how' the universe is made. It encourages us to look at things as wholes and the relationships between them (see pages 25-30).

The West
Indicates modern cultures that have achieved high economic growth with a high use of resources per capita (measured for example by eco foot-printing) (see page 219).

Transition movement/initiatives
A global movement to empower and mobilise communities to respond to the challenges of climate change and peak oil. Transition initiatives are localised actions undertaken by specific communities, e.g. town, village, city (see pages 11 and 195-199).

Zones
In permaculture design, a specific tool about relative placement with the aim of maximising efficient use of time, energy and space (see page 41).

Zone 00
Ourselves, the person at the centre of the design (see page 43).

Notes

Chapter 1 – Setting the Scene

1   *Earth Care Manual*; Patrick Whitefield; Permanent Publications, 2004; p5
2   *Permaculture One*; David Holmgren and Bill Mollison B; Tagari, 1990
3   *The Holistic Life – Sustainability Through Permaculture*; Ian lillington; Axion Publishing, 2007; p26
4   *Food Not Lawns – How To Turn Your Yard Into A Garden And Your Neighbourhood Into a Community*; H.C. Flores; Chelsea Green, 2006; p18
5   *Principles and Pathways Beyond Sustainability*; David Holmgren; Permanent Publications, 2002; pxix
6   *We Are One – a Celebration of Tribal Peoples*; Joanna Ede; Quadrille Publishing Ltd, 2009; p36
7   *Permaculture – A Designer's Manual*; Bill Mollison; Tagari, 1998; p 1
8   Brundtland report 1987, www.un-documents.net/wced-ocf.htm (United Nations)
9   *Coming Back to Life – Practices to Reconnect our Lives, our World*; Joanna Macy; New Society Publishers; 1998
10 Rhythm is Life CD; Rooh Star; 2007; track 13: The Great Turning. www.roohstar.net
11 www.dynamic-equilibrium.co.uk
12 *Beyond you and me – Inspirations and Wisdom for Building Community*; editors Kosha Anja Joubert and Robin Alfred; Permanent Publications, 2007; p58. Available as a free download from www.green-shopping.co.uk/books/ebooks/free-ebooks/beyond-you-me-inspirations-and-wisdom-for-building-community-ebook-edition.html
13 *Gaian Economics – Living Well Within Planetary Limits*; editors Jonathan Dawson, Helena Norberg-Hodge and Ross Jackson; Permanent Publications, 2010; p122. Available as a free download from www.green-shopping.co.uk/books/ebooks/free-ebooks/gaian-economics-ebook-edition.html

Chapter 2 – Nature's lessons

1   www.permaculture.org.uk
2   *Permaculture Principles And Pathways Beyond Sustainability*; David Holmgren; Permanent Publications. 2002; www.holmgren.com.au
3   Original icons created by Richard Telford www.PermaculturePrinciples.com
4   Cited in *Coming Back To Life – Practices To Reconnect Our Lives, Our World*; Joanna Macy and Molly Young Brown; New Society Publishers, 1999; p40
5   *Thinking In Systems*; Donella Meadows; Chelsea Green, 2008; p2
6   *Coming Back To Life – Practices To Reconnect Our Lives, Our World*; Joanna Macy and Molly Young Brown; New Society Publishers, 1999; p41
7   *Thinking In Systems*; Donella Meadows; Chelsea Green, 2008, p79
8   *Permaculture – A Designer's Manual*; Bill Mollison; Tagari, 1998; pix

Chapter 3 – Design

1   *Think! Before It's Too Late*; Edward De Bono; Vermilion, 2009; p 69
2   *Thinking In Systems*; Donella Meadows; Chelsea Green, 2008; p145

Chapter 4 – Our internal landscape

1   *Women And Power – How Far Can We Go?*; Nancy Kline; BBC Books, 1993
2   *You Are Therefore I Am – A Declaration Of Dependence*; Satish Kumar, Green Books, 2002; p89
3   *Meetings with Remarkable Men*; Gurdjieff G.I.; Penguin, 1991
4   *Human Scale Development*; Max-neef; Apex Press, 1991; available as a free download (see booklist)
5   *Nonviolent Communication – A Language Of Life*; Marshall Rosenberg; Puddeledancer Press, 2005
6   www.living-compassion.org
7   *Times Alone – Selected Poems By Antonio Machado*; Antonio Machado, translated by Robert Bly; Wesleyan, 1983
8   Adapted from *Participatory Workshops – A Sourcebook Of 21 Sets Of Ideas And Activities*; Robert Chambers; Earthscan, 2002; p26
9   *Women and Power – How Far Can We Go?*; Nancy Kline; BBC Books, 1993
10 For more guidance on how to channel the benefits of gremlin and put our gremlin to work to access

our inner resources see Directing The Power of Conscious Feelings; Clinton Callaghan; Holm Press, 2010.

11 *The Tibetan Book Of Living And Dying*; Sogyal Rinpoche; HarperOne, 1994; p31
12 *Heart Seeds – A Message from the Ancestors*; Windeagle and Rainbowhawk; Ehama Press, 2003; p40

Chapter 5 – Health and well-being

1 I have used subconscious rather than unconscious as a personal preference rather than any affiliation to a particular school of thought.
2 *We Are The Ones We've Been Waiting For – Light in a Time of Darkness*; Alice Walker; Weidenfeld & Nicolson; 2007
3 From the poem 'A Blessing' by Stephen Philbrick
4 *Frames of Mind – The Theory of Multiple Intelligences*; Howard Gardner; Basic Books 1993
5 Go to www.businessballs.com/howardgardnermultipleintelligences.htm for a detailed questionnaire to assess your multiple intelligences
6 *A Sense Of Wonder*; Rachel Carson; Harper Collins, 1999; p101
7 *We Are One – A Celebration Of Tribal People*; Created and Edited by Joanna Eede; Quadrille Publishing, 2009

Chapter 6 – Being at our best

1 *The Mind Gym – Give Me Time*; Time Warner Books, 2006
2 *The Sound Of Paper – Inspiration And Practical Guidance For Starting The Creative Process*; Julia Cameron; Penguin, 2006
3 *Permaculture – A Designer's Manual*; Bill Mollison; Tagari, 1998
4 *The Mind Map Book – Unlock Your Creativity, Boost Your Memory, Change Your Life*; Tony Buzan; BBC Active 2009
5 *Think! Before It's Too Late*; Edward De Bono; Vermilion, 2009
6 Cited in *Gaian Economics*; editors Jonathan Dawson, Helena Norberg-Hodge and Ross Jackson; Permanent Publications, 2010; p115
7 *Battle For The Trees – Three Months of Responsible Ancestory*; Merrick; Godhaven; 1996; p47
8 Cited in *Permaculture* magazine issue no.68
9 *Find Your Power*; Chris Johnstone; Permanent Publications, 2010
10 Adapted from *Playful Self Discovery*; David Earl; Findhorn Press, 1997

Case Study 1 – Designing for ourselves

1 See www.permaculture.org.uk for details on the permaculture diploma
2 *Permaculture Design – A Step by Step Guide*; Aranya; Permanent Publications, 2012

Chapter 7 – Communication

1 *Nonviolent Communication – A Language Of Life*; Marshall Rosenberg; Puddeledancer Press, 2005
2 *The Nonviolent Communication Companion Workbook – A Practical Guide for Individual, Group or Classroom Study*; Lucy Leu; Puddlerdancer Press, 2003
3 *Women And Power – How Far Can We Go?*; Nancy Kline; BBC Books, 1993
4 *The Earthpath – Grounding Your Spirit In The Rhythms Of Nature*; Starhawk; Harperone, 2004

Chapter 8 – One-to-one relationships

1 Tree of Life Cards; www.treeol.co.uk
2 *How To Talk So Kids Will Listen And Listen So Kids Will Talk*; Adele Faber and Elaine Mazlish; Piccadilly Press, 1999
3 Tree of Life Cards; www.treeol.co.uk

Chapter 9 – Working in groups

1 *Boards That Make A Difference – A New Design For Leadership In Nonprofit And Public Organisations*; John Carver; Jossey Bass, 2006
2 *Participatory Workshops*; Robert Chambers; Earthscan, 2002
3 *Designing Productive Meetings And Events – How To Increase Participation And Enjoyment*; Andy Langford; 1998; available as a free download from: www.designedvisions.com/resources-topmenu-79.html

4 Adapted from *Participatory Workshops – A Sourcebook Of 21 Sets Of Ideas And Activities*; Robert Chambers; Earthscan, 2002; p175
5 see www.seedsforchange.org.uk for more handsignals
6 *Designing Productive Meetings And Events – How To Increase Participation And Enjoyment*; Andy Langford; 1998
7 *Creating A Life Together – Practical Tools To Grow Ecovillages And Intentional Communities*; Diana Leafe Christian; New Society Publishers, 2003
8 *Six Thinking Hats*; Edward de Bono; Penguin, 2000
9 *On Conflict And Consensus – A Handbook For Formal Decision Making*; C.T. Lawrence Butler; Food Not Bombs, 1991
10 Philosophy for communitites www.sapere.org.uk.

Case study 2 – Designing with other people
1 www.permaculture.org.uk
2 *Eat That Frog*; Brian Tracy; Berett-Koehler, 2008
3 Learning and Network Demonstration projects: a scheme whereby projects exemplifying permaculture in Britain can share their learning and inspire new projects. www.permaculture.org.uk/land

Chapter 10 – Where are we?
1 www.positivenews.org.uk
2 www.permaculture.co.uk
3 'Who will feed us?' report at www.ETCgroup.org
4 For a free download of Donella Meadow's chapter on Leverage Points – Places To Intervene In A System from Thinking In Systems see www.sustainer.org/pubs/Leverage_Points.pdf
5 *A Theory Of Everything*; Ken Wilbur; Gateway, 2000

Chapter 11 – Where do we want to be?
1 *The Accelerated Learning Handbook*; Dave Meier; Mcgraw Hill, 2000; pp9-10
2 Philosophy For Communities www.sapere.org.uk
3 library.thinkquest.org/18355/health_care_in_cuba.html
4 www.who.int/countries/cub/en/
5 Based on a diagram by Wolf White
6 www.ageuk.org.uk/get-involved/volunteer/volunteer-in-your-community/integrational-volunteer/

Chapter 12 – How do we get there?
1 *The Seven Habits Of Highly Effective People – Powerful Lessons In Personal Change*; Steven Covey; Simon & Schuster, 1989
2 www.transitionnetwork.org
3 www.response-ability.org.uk
4 'What Do We Mean By Being Green'; Peter Harper and Paul Allen; *Clean Slate*, issue 34, www.cat.org.uk
5 *Primal Leadership – Learning To Lead With Emotional Intelligence*; Daniel Goleman, Richard Boyatzis and Annie Mckee; Harvard Business Press, 2002
6 www.julesheavens.com
7 *Finding Earth, Finding Soul – The Invisible Path To Authentic Leadership*; Tim Macartney; 2007

Case Study 3 – Designing for larger systems
1 *The Transition Handbook – From Oil Dependency To Local Resilience*; Rob Hopkins; Green Books, 2008; p127
2 www.openspaceworld.com
3 www.theworldcafe.org
4 *Ibid.*
5 www.communityrenewal.ca
6 http://greentarbert.wordpress.com/2011/02/08/sustainable-communities-conference-report/

Chapter 13 – The bigger picture

1 The difference between GNP and GDP: GDP measures the economic activity that happens with a country's border. GNP measures the economic activity of the nationality whether it is within the country or abroad. In this discussion either can be used to illustrate the points raised.
2 This quotation is part of Robert F. Kennedy's Address to the University of Kansas, Lawrence, Kansas, March 18, 1968. It exists on youtube.
3 www.footprintnetwork.org
4 www.happyplanetindex.org
5 www.100people.org
6 www.weforum.org/issues/global-gender-gap
7 www.empoweragirl.org
8 Taylor, Peter, 'Smoke Ring: The Politics of Tobacco', Panos Briefing Paper, September 1994, London cited on Wikipedia http://en.wikipedia.org/wiki/Cultivation_of_tobacco
9 *Ibid.*
10 www.activeremedy.org.uk
11 *UK Dairy trade balance* www.bovinetb.info/docs/UK%20Dairy%20Trade%20Balance.pdf
12 http://en.wikipedia.org/wiki/Kofi_Annan
13 www.himalayanpermaculture.com

Chapter 14 – Learning from others

1 www.bluezones.com
2 www.polyhiggins.com
3 Cited in *Positive News*; Sean Dagan Wood; issue 68 Summer 2011
4 *Ibid.*
5 *We Are One – A Celebration Of Tribal People*; created and edited by Joanna Eede; Quadrille Publishing, 2009; p146
6 *Ancient Futures – Learning From Ladakh*; Helena Norberg-Hodge; Rider Books, 1991
7 *We Are One – A Celebration Of Tribal People*; created and edited by Joanna Eede; Quadrille Publishing, 2009 p143
8 The Land Is Ours www.tlio.org.uk
9 Reclaim The Fields www.reclaimthefields.org
10 *The Living Landscape – How To Read And Understand It*; Patrick Whitefield; Permanent Publications, 2009
11 http://www.youtube.com/watch?v=NZvlQwjVOKw The Girl Who Silenced The World
12 www.drewdellinger.org
13 *Coming Back To Life – Practices To Reconnect Our Lives, Our World*; Joanna Macy and Molly Young Brown; New Society Publishers, 1999; p143

Chapter 15 – Connecting with nature

1 *Coming Back To Life – Practices To Reconnect Our Lives, Our World*; Joanna Macy and Molly Young Brown; New Society Publishers, 1999
2 *Heart Seeds – A Message From The Ancestors*; Windeagle and Rainbowhawk; Ehama Press, 2003; p9
3 This activity was created by Jules Heavens
4 *The Road Back To Nature – Regaining The Paradise Lost*; Masanobu Fukuoka Book Venture, 1987

Case study 4 – Designing for other cultures

1 *The Seven Habits Of Highly Effective People*; Steven Covey; Simon & Schuster, 1989
2 www.himalayanpermaculture.com

Chapter 17 – Moving forward

1 *Quantum Learning – Unleasing The Genius In You*; Bobbi DePorter and Mike Hernacki; Dell, 1990

Selected Bibliography

These are just some of the books that have provided inspiration and information.

Part 1

The Basics Of Permaculture Design; Ross Mars; Permanent Publications, 1996

The Earth Care Manual – A Permaculture Handbook For Britain And Other Temperate Climates; Patrick Whitefield; Permanent Publications, 2004

The Earthpath – Grounding Your Spirit In The Rhythms Of Nature; Starhawk; Harperone, 2004

Food Not Lawns – How To Turn Your Yard Into A Garden And Your Neighbourhood Into A Community; H.C. Flores; Chelsea Green, 2006

The Holistic Life – Sustainability Through Permaculture; Ian Lillington; Axion Publishing, 2007

Thinking In Systems; Donella Meadows; Chelsea Green, 2008

Permaculture – A Beginner's Guide; Graham Burnett; 2000

Permaculture – A Designer's Manual; Bill Mollison; Tagari, 1998

Permaculture Principles And Pathways Beyond Sustainability; David Holmgren; Permanent Publications, 2002

Part 2

Clear Your Clutter With Feng Shui; Karen Kingston; Piatkus Books, 2008

Directing The Power Of Conscious Feelings – Living Our Own Truth; Clinton Callahan; Hohm Press, 2010

Find Your Power – A Toolkit For Resilience And Positive Change; Chris Johnstone; Permanent Publications, 2nd edition 2010

Give Me Time; The Mind Gym; Time Warner Books, 2006

Human Scale Development; Macneef; Apex Press, 1991. Available as a free download from: www.max-neef.cl

No More Clutter; Susan Kay; Mobius, 2006

Quantum Learning – Unleash The Genius In You; Bobbi De Porter; Dell, 1992

The Sound Of Paper – Inspiration And Practical Guidance For Starting The Creative Process; Julia Cameron; Penguin, 2006

Think! Before It's Too Late; Edward De Bono; Vermilion, 2009

Wake Your Mind Up; The Mind Gym; Time Warner Books, 2005

Part 3

Beyond You And Me – Inspirations And Wisdom For Building Community; editors Kosha Anja Joubert And Robin Alfred; Permanent Publications, 2007

Creating A Life Together – Practical Tools To Grow Ecovillages And Intentional Communities; Diana Leafe Christian; New Society Publishers, 2003

Creating Harmony – Conflict Resolution In Community; edited by Hildur Jackson; Permanent Publications, 1999

Designing Productive Meetings And Events – How To Increase Participation And Enjoyment; Andy Langford; 1998. Available as a free download from: www.designedvisions.com/resources-topmenu-79.html

How To Talk So Kids Will Listen And Listen So Kids Will Talk; Adele Faber and Elaine Mazlish; Piccadilly Press, 1999

Nonviolent Communication – A Language Of Life; Marshall Rosenberg; Puddeledancer Press, 2005

Participatory Workshops – A Sourcebook Of 21 Sets Of Ideas And Activities; Robert Chambers; Earthscan, 2002

Relationships; The Mind Gym; Sphere, 2009

Secrets Of The People Whisperer; Perry Wood; Rider Books, 2004

Six Thinking Hats; Edward de Bono; Penguin, 2000

The Secret Of Happy Children; Steve Biddulph; Thorsons, 1984

The Seven Habits Of Highly Effective Families; Steven Covey; Simon & Schuster, 1997

Part 4

A Theory Of Everything; Ken Wilbur; Gateway, 2000

Finding Earth, Finding Soul – The Invisible Path To Authentic Leadership; Tim Macartney; 2007

Primal Leadership – Learning To Lead With Emotional Intelligence; Daniel Goleman, Richard Boyatzis and Annie Mckee; Harvard Business Press, 2002

Teach Your Child To Think; Edward De Bono; Viking, 1992

The Accelerated Learning Handbook; Dave Meier; Mcgraw Hill, 2000

The Seven Habits Of Highly Effective People – Powerful Lessons In Personal Change; Steven Covey; Simon & Schuster, 1989

The Transition Handbook – From Oil Dependency To Local Resilience; Rob Hopkins; Green Books, 2008

Women And Power – How Far Can We Go?; Nancy Kline; BBC Books, 1993

Part 5

Ancient Futures – Learning From Ladakh; Helena Norberg–Hodge; Rider Books, 1991

A Sense Of Wonder; Rachel Carson; Harper Collins, 1999

Be The Change – Action And Reflection From People Transforming Our World; Interviews by Trenna Cormack; Love Books, 2007

Beyond A Forest Garden; Robert Hart; Gaia Books, 1996

Coming Back To Life – Practices To Reconnect Our Lives, Our World; Joanna Macy and Molly Young Brown; New Society Publishers, 1999

Heart Seeds – A Message From The Ancestors; Windeagle and Rainbowhawk; Ehama Press, 2003

Gaian Economics – Living Well Within Planetary Limits; editors Jonathan Dawson, Helena Norberg-Hodge and Ross Jackson; Permanent Publications, 2010

Surviving And Thriving On The Land – How To Use Your Time And Energy To Run A Successful Smallholding; Rebecca Laughton; Green Books, 2008

The Great Turning – From Empire To Earth Community; David C. Korten; Berrett-Koehler, 2006

The Road Back To Nature – Regaining The Paradise Lost; Masanobu Fukuoka; Book Venture, 1987 (out of print but available as a free download online)

We Are One – A Celebration Of Tribal People; created and edited by Joanna Eede; Quadrille Publishing, 2009

We Are The Ones We've Been Waiting For – Light In A Time Of Darkness; Alice Walker; Weidenfeld & Nicolson 2007

Widening Circles – A Memoir; Joanna Macy; New Society Publishers, 2000

Wild – an elemental journey; Jay Griffiths, Hamish Hamilton Ltd, 2007

Worlds Apart – An Explorer's Life; Robin Hanbury-Tenison; Arrow Books, 1984

You Are Therefore I Am – A Declaration Of Dependence; Satish Kumar, Green Books, 2002

Looby Macnamara is a partner with

Designed Visions

We are one of the foremost permaculture teaching groups in Britain. We run courses for anyone working towards a holistic sustainable vision for humanity. Our courses are fun, empowering and richly textured with the chance to experience the creation of community with like-minded people.

We offer:

PEOPLE AND PERMACULTURE COURSES

"Thanks for imbuing the whole course with your sense of fun and sharing your knowledge so clearly."

"Looby offers the deep capacity to listen and for new growth. She includes every aspect of learning into the space."

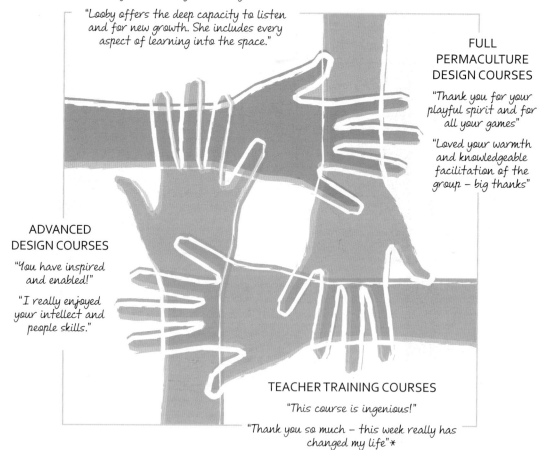

FULL PERMACULTURE DESIGN COURSES

"Thank you for your playful spirit and for all your games"

"Loved your warmth and knowledgeable facilitation of the group – big thanks"

ADVANCED DESIGN COURSES

"You have inspired and enabled!"

"I really enjoyed your intellect and people skills."

TEACHER TRAINING COURSES

"This course is ingenious!"

"Thank you so much – this week really has changed my life" *

This is your opportunity to consider your contribution to the world and take your next step...

www.designedvisions.com

Enjoyed this book?

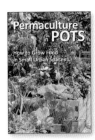   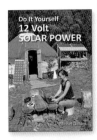 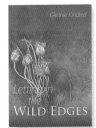

   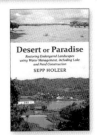 

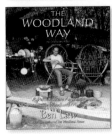   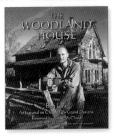

SUBSCRIBE
to *the*
sustainable living magazine

Permaculture magazine offers tried and tested ways of
creating flexible, low cost approaches to sustainable living

BE INSPIRED by practical solutions and ideas

SAVE on our exclusive subscriber offers

FREE home delivery – never miss an issue

HELP US SUPPORT permaculture projects
in places with no access to currency

SUBSCRIBE, CHECK OUR DAILY UPDATES
AND JOIN THE PERMACULTURE ENEWSLETTER TO RECEIVE SPECIAL
OFFERS ON NEW AND EXISTING BOOKS, TOOLS AND PRODUCTS:

www.permaculture.co.uk